About the Editors

Dr Ronaldo Munck is an Argentinian sociologist, currently reader in sociology at the University of Liverpool, who has previously held appointments at the University of Ulster and the University of Durban-Westville in South Africa. He has written extensively in the field of political sociology, especially on labour and development issues, including ten books, among them *Politics and Dependency in the Third World* (Zed Books, 1984) and *Marx@2000: Late Marxist Perspectives* (Macmillan, 1999). He has also recently co-edited major volumes on *Labour Worldwide in the Era of Globalization: Alternative Union Models in the New World Order* (Macmillan, 1998) and *Postmodern Insurgencies: Political Violence, Identity Formation and Peace-making in Comparative Perspective* (Macmillan, 1998). At Liverpool he is director of the Rowntree Project researching social exclusion and empowerment on Merseyside and is coordinator of the inter-university Labour Studies Seminar Series which is funded by the Economic and Social Science Research Council. He is currently researching and writing on globalization, labour flexibility and worker organizations in Latin America.

Dr Denis O'Hearn is both an economist and a sociologist. He was educated at the Universities of New Mexico and Michigan. For several years he taught at the University of Wisconsin, Madison, where he was associate professor of sociology. Currently, he is reader in sociology at Queen's University, Belfast. He is editor of the *Irish Journal of Sociology* and chair of the West Belfast Economic Forum. His recent books include *States, Firms and Raw Materials: A Case from the International Aluminium Industry* (with Bradford Barham and Stephen Bunker) (University of Wisconsin Press, 1995) and *Inside the Celtic Tiger: Irish Economic Change and the Asian Model* (Pluto, 1998).

Critical Development Theory: Contributions to a New Paradigm

Edited by
Ronaldo Munck and Denis O'Hearn

Zed Books

LONDON AND NEW YORK

Critical Development Theory: Contributions to a new paradigm
was first published by Zed Books Ltd, 7 Cynthia Street,
London N1 9JF, UK and Room 400, 175 Fifth Avenue, New
York, NY 10010, USA in 1999.

Distributed exclusively in the USA by St Martin's Press, Inc.,
175 Fifth Avenue, New York, NY 10010, USA.

Cover designed by Andrew Corbett
Set in Monotype Garamond by Ewan Smith
Printed and bound in the United Kingdom by Biddles Ltd,
Guildford and King's Lynn

A catalogue record for this book is available from the British
Library

ISBN 1 85649 637 6 cased
ISBN 1 85649 638 4 limp

Contents

For Vincent Tucker
Cara agus comhchealgaire

About the Contributors

Vincent Tucker was statutory lecturer in sociology at the National University of Ireland in Cork. He was director of the Development Programme and former head of department in Cork, and was an honorary fellow in the Sociology Department of the University of Wisconsin-Madison. He was active in the cooperative movement and in campaigns against environmentally destructive activities by transnational corporations in Ireland and elsewhere. At the time of his death in 1997 he was working on holistic approaches to development, a topic coming out of his work on holistic health. His edited volume *Cultural Perspectives on Development* (London: Frank Cass, 1997) was published posthumously.

Boaventura de Sousa Santos is professor of sociology at the University of Coimbra and professor of sociology and law at the University of Wisconsin-Madison. His areas of interest include political sociology, sociology of law, cultural studies and epistemology. His current research projects are on democracy, counter-hegemonic globalization, and access to justice in Portugal. He is author of *Toward a New Common Sense: Law, Science and Politics in the Paradigmatic Transition* (New York: Routledge, 1995) and (with others) *Os Tribunais nas sociedades contemporaneas* (Porto: Afrontamento, 1996).

Ziauddin Sardar, writer and cultural critic, is visiting professor of science policy, Middlesex University, and consulting editor of *Futures*, the monthly journal of forecasting, planning and policy. Professor Sardar is considered to be an expert on science and development in the Muslim world and a pioneering writer on the future of Islam. He has published over twenty-four books, including *The Future of Muslim Civilization* (1979), *Islamic Futures* (1985), *Barbaric Others* (1993), *Postmodernism and the Other* (1998) and, as editor, *The Touch of Midas: Science and Environment in Islam and the West* (1984), *The Revenge of Athena: Science, Exploitation and the Third World* (1988) and *Cyberfutures: Politics and Economy on the Information Superhighway* (1996).

Jan Nederveen Pieterse is associate professor in sociology at the Institute of Social Studies in The Hague. He has taught in Ghana and the United States and has been visiting professor in Japan and Indonesia. He is co-editor of *Review of International Political Economy* and advisory editor of *European Journal of Social Theory*. His books include *White on Black: Images of Africa and Blacks in Western Popular Culture* (Yale, 1992), *Empire and Emancipation* (Praeger, 1989), which received the 1990 J.C. Ruigrok Award of the Netherlands Society of Sciences, *Development – Deconstructions/Reconstructions* (Sage, in preparation), and several edited volumes.

Diane Perrons is a lecturer in the Department of Geography and Environment and a member of the management committee of the Gender Institute at the London School of Economics and Political Science. Her research is concerned with economic and social cohesion in Europe and focuses on regional and gender dimensions of inequality. She has recently coordinated a cross-national qualitative research project for the European Union on flexible working and the reconciliation of work and family life. She has published articles in *Regional Studies*, *European Urban and Regional Studies* and *Feminist Economics*. Most recently she edited a special issue of *European Urban and Regional Studies* (vol. 5, no. 1, 1998) on gender inequality in Europe. She co-authored *The Arena of Capital* (Macmillan, 1983) with Mick Dunford and *Making Gender Work* (Open University Press, 1995) with Jenny Shaw.

Bob Sutcliffe has taught international and development economics at the universities of Kingston, Massachusetts and Central America (Managua) and now works at the University of the Basque Country in Bilbao. He is co-author (with Francis Green) of *The Profit System* (Penguin, 1987) and has recently edited *El Incendio Frio, ensayos sobre las causas y consecuencias del hambre en el mundo* (Barcelona: Icaria, 1996).

Richard Douthwaite worked as a journalist before studying economics at the University of Essex and the University of the West Indies, Kingston, Jamaica. He was employed by the governments of Jamaica and Montserrat as an economist before moving to Ireland in 1974. There he and his wife set up a manufacturing business and built their own house. When the business was sold in 1985 he returned to journalism and specialized in business, financial and environmental topics related to the West of Ireland. His first book, *The Growth Illusion*, appeared in 1992, and the practical sequel, *Short Circuit*, in 1996. He is now writing an ecological economics textook for Routledge and helping to set up a foundation for the economics of sustainability in Dublin.

Honor Fagan is lecturer in sociology at the National University of Ireland, Maynooth. She previously lectured at the University of Ulster in Ireland, the University of Durban-Westville in South Africa and the University of Leeds in England. Her current research interests lie in a variety of fields including social theory, gender and development, cultural politics, and globalization and culture. She has done field research on early school leavers in Dublin for her book *Cultural Politics and Irish Early School Leavers: Constructing Political Identities* (Bergin and Garvey, 1995) and on women in South African townships. She is currently researching for a book on *Globalization and Culture: Placing Ireland.*

Preface

The new century, like the last, will have to face the problem of development or, rather, underdevelopment. The era of globalization was supposed to offer great opportunities to poor nations and poor people as free-market forces worked their magic. The globally hegemonic neoliberalism sponsored the so-called economic reforms of privatization, deregulation and flexibilization – and these were supposed to usher in an era of unprecedented prosperity for all. All ships would rise with the tide of globalization. The reality, by contrast, has been sombre.

The International Monetary Fund (IMF) has recently admitted that taking the North and the South as broad clusters, 'on average there has been no convergence of per capita income levels between the two groups of countries' (IMF 1997: 72). In fact, the number of low-income countries in the lowest quintile, in terms of global income distribution, has actually risen from 52 in 1965 to 102 in 1995. While the IMF finds these results 'surprising', the United Nations Conference on Trade and Development (UNCTAD) admits bluntly that 'Capital has gained in comparison with labour, and profit shares have risen everywhere' (UNCTAD 1997: 2).

So there has not in fact been a convergence of incomes within or between the nation-states that make up the global system. The rich have got richer and the poor (with a few exceptions) have got relatively poorer. For example, in Latin America average per capita incomes fell from over one third of Northern levels in the late 1970s to around one quarter of Northern levels by the mid-1990s. From the mid-1970s to the mid-1990s the terms of trade of the 'least developed' countries fell by 50 per cent. Nor was the much-vaunted industrialization of some Third World countries much good in so far as terms of trade for their manufactured goods fell by over one third over the same period.

Development theory seeks to account for the uneven pattern of development worldwide and to recommend measures to overcome underdevelopment. Following the Second World War, the modernization perspective, generated in the United States, became the dominant development discourse. Everything would be for the best in the best of all possible worlds if countries and their people followed the US model to the letter. Of course, what this meant in practice was subordination to US imperialism. In response, the dependency approach to under-development emerged in Latin America in the late 1960s committed to a more critical, anti-imperialist vision. In practice it tended to mirror the modernization approach, advocating a national and statist path which was to have diminishing results in most cases. By the late 1980s globalization was making itself felt, and the collapse of state socialism also made the radical alternative seem implausible. In a sense, the impasse in development theory of the 1980s represented a stalemate between the modernization and dependency approaches.

Out of the ashes of dependency theory, however, there arose a series of critical perspectives such as those based on ecology, feminism and countermodernism. The mainstream saw a revival of the old 1950s modernization perspective, dressed in the 1990s garb of globalization and neoliberalism, with a token nod towards issues of gender, ecology, and ethnicity (dressed up as culture).

The editors of this volume both have a background in dependency theory, as applied to Ireland in particular. Munck's study of the Irish economy (Munck 1993) was one of the first to situate its history and current prospects in terms of dependent development. The notion of seeking to apply a Latin American perspective in a part of Europe, albeit a peripheral part, had not hitherto been popular. O'Hearn had even earlier (O'Hearn 1989) placed Ireland within the dependency prob-lematic. Precisely when the dependency approach was losing popularity as a radical panacea it seemed that Ireland might still be the exception that proved the rule (or, as O'Hearn put it, the 'exception to the exceptions'). It was no coincidence that these developments were occurring in Europe's first (and probably last) colony. Ireland was a hybrid society, part European and part Third World. It was in a liminal situation, betwixt and between tradition and modernity. In historical terms it is worth recalling that it was in the context of an engagement with economic and political developments in Ireland that Marx and Engels began to break both with their earlier evolutionist approach to development and with a somewhat paternalist view of anti-colonial struggle. The notion of dependent development can in fact be traced back to Marx and Engels's treatment of Ireland in the nineteenth century.

This volume originated as a response to the death of Vincent Tucker in Ireland in 1997. The editors and contributors all knew Tucker in different ways, but it was not coincidental that they all took a critical approach to development theory. Indeed, most of them enthusiastically agreed to participate in this project because Tucker, through discussion and debate, had influenced them deeply at key points in the development of some of their most innovative work. At the time of his death, Tucker had recently edited a significant collection on cultural perspectives on development (Tucker 1997), but the essay we chose to introduce this volume is an earlier one, 'The Myth of Development'. In this piece, he carries out a wide-ranging view of the critical development perspectives of the 1980s. What he seeks to do is to understand the nature of the crisis facing development both as an intellectual and as a practical project. He is particularly keen to explore and undermine the founding myths and unchallenged assumptions of the development discourse. From the European periphery, but also with considerable experience in Africa, Tucker understands that development is in its essence a Euro-centric concept. He thus explores the various alternatives to the mainstream development theory that were beginning to make their mark in the early 1990s. Tucker's 'The Myth of Development' serves to clear the decks and set the scene for subsequent chapters, which are divided into three sections.

Part One of this volume deals with *Critical Perspectives*, understood not as 'making or involving adverse or censorious comments or judgements' (*Oxford English Dictionary*) but, rather, as decisive, crucial comment on a transitional moment. In Chapter 2 Boaventura de Sousa Santos takes up a central theme from his recent influential text *Toward a New Common Sense* (Santos 1995). He believes that we are living in an era of paradigmatic transition now that modernity has exhausted all its possibilities of renovation. The issue addressed in this chapter is the difficulty of producing a critical theory today. In this transitional period we are still facing modern problems (for example, underdevelopment) for which there are no modern solutions. For Santos, the way forward lies in a postmodern critical theory (or a critical postmodern theory). This would not be the complacent, ultimately conservative, post-modernism of some current theorists but, rather, a disquieting or oppositional postmodernism. This postmodern critical theory would attempt to reconstruct the idea and the practice of emancipatory social transformation.

In Chapter 3, Ziauddin Sardar engages with Tucker's emphasis on development as a Eurocentric concept. Sardar's view on postmodernism (Sardar 1998) is critical, if not hostile: he views it as the new imperialism of Western culture. For Sardar, the real power of the West lies not in its massive economic development and technological advances but, rather, in its power to define. Thus the 'Orient' is a cultural construction of the West with massive political ramifications. Development, for Sardar, represents an ideal instrument for the Eurocentric colonization of time. With one word the West has appropriated and controls the past, the present and the future of the non-West. This colonization of the future, once known as 'Westernization', now goes under the rubric of 'globalization'. Thus, the problem of development is the key problem for knowledge today. It is about finding other ways of knowing and being that are not just mirrors of Europe or the West. Sardar develops several examples of how nations and cultures outside the West have developed their own autonomous knowledges about development.

In Chapter 4, Jan Nederveen Pieterse develops Vincent Tucker's concept of 'critical holism' as a new non-Western approach to development. Nederveen Pieterse has written extensively about the cultural dimensions of empire and emancipation (Nederveen Pieterse 1989). In this chapter he develops a holistic yet critical approach to underdevelopment, arguing that the two terms must be inseparable. Like Sardar, he engages with the critiques of Cartesian science developed in the South. While the source of the concept of 'critical holism' is the field of health it can be broadened out, Nederveen Pieterse argues, to become the new 'Tao' of development. For example, in relation to current debates in globalization this approach would take us beyond prevailing disciplinary methodologies and boundaries. We can thus conceive of a cooperative globalization as against the competitive globalization that now prevails. The Tao of development would impart a new sense of balance across the various dimensions of human existence, and a notion of collective healing which could be applied to economic inequality as much as to political conflict.

Part Two of this volume deals with *Political Economy*, not as a futile return to notions of determination (albeit in the 'last instance') by the economy but in the spirit of Marx's critique of political economy. The subtitle of Chapter 5 by Diane Perrons is, precisely, 'Why Political Economy Still Matters'. In this chapter Perrons develops her earlier work on the critical economic geography of capitalism (Dunford and Perrons 1983). The 'cultural turn' in the social sciences in the 1980s is considered as a challenge to political economy but one that could enrich this perspective, rather than replace it. Thus, a cultural perspective can enhance our understanding of how economic practices are sustained in the daily life of our capitalist and patriarchal societies. It is through the conceptual integration of production and consumption, in their class and gender dimensions, that Perrons particularly contributes to a new understanding of political economy as critique of the dominant order. In terms of a development paradigm this perspective would entail a revived political economy approach drawing on elements of the 'cultural turn' and the overdue recognition by the social sciences of the spatial dimension.

In Chapter 6, Denis O'Hearn broadens out his recent analysis of the so-called tiger economies (O'Hearn 1998) to consider whether their seemingly spectacular growth is sustainable. Often touted as denials of the dependency thesis, the East Asian tigers may prove to be exceptions to the rule after all. This chapter also argues that a political economy of development remains vital today, however much we may learn from more recent perspectives. O'Hearn demonstrates how current strategies for tigerhood are shaky in the era of neoliberal globalization, an argument that is supported by the Asian crisis that began in 1997. He also considers the vexed question of whether the tiger economies can provide the material resources that could enable a more equitable 'social economy' to develop. While showing that growth of production and exports has been largely at the cost of consumption, O'Hearn goes on to consider other radical arguments about economic alternatives. He concludes that one cannot simply 'marginalize' the economy by creating alternative community structures; the issue is about how the 'economy' pervades all aspects of social life.

Bob Sutcliffe, in Chapter 7, carries out a broad survey of theories of imperialism and the new focus on globalization. Sutcliffe participated in some of the significant early 1970s critiques of imperialism (see Owen and Sutcliffe 1972). The apparent disproving of Marxist theories of imperialism in the 1980s due to the rise of the tiger economies is here examined critically. For, if we take a broad view of the world economy, we find that for two hundred years there has been virtually continuous polarization between rich and poor nations. As to globalization, Sutcliffe distinguishes between strong and weak versions of the thesis. He argues that globalization is much less new than is claimed, being to a large extent a re-establishment of the international structure of capitalism that prevailed before the 1880s. Whether globalization is simply imperialism in a new garb is, of course, a hotly debated point. Sutcliffe provides a conceptual map of the theories of development, imperialism and globalization which might help us answer this question.

Part Three turns to *Polemical Perspectives*, not as 'verbal or written attack, especially on a political opponent' (*Oxford English Dictionary*) but, simply, as controversial discussions of important issues. In Chapter 8, Richard Douthwaite addresses the crucial issue of sustainable development taken up in his influential *The Growth Illusion* (Douthwaite 1992). Too often in radical (and, now, mainstream) development theory, the issue of sustainable development is seen as obvious and is accepted without analysis. Douthwaite challenges us to think what sustainable development would mean in practice. He is particularly concerned that a weak sustainability approach is simply not viable. For Douthwaite, the world is in a classic 'Catch-22' situation in which we cannot make the free-market economic system sustainable because it is so unsustainable that if we try it will break down. He shows how ludicrous it is to argue, as some eminent economists do, that growth can be limitless because ideas are limitless. Douthwaite paints a sobering picture of a global economy on autopilot, with no one on the bridge and the individual left totally disempowered.

In Chapter 9, Honor Fagan takes up the cultural dimension of development from the point of view of cultural politics developed in her earlier work (Fagan 1995). We cannot simply 'add culture' to development theory, shake and stir, and expect a radical hybrid to emerge. The cultural dimension came to mean, in the 1980s, an overdue recognition of the voice of the marginalized, the poor and the counter-hegemonic movements. While welcome, this turn is insufficient, argues Fagan. A cultural politics of (post)development would be based on a political understanding that culture produces power, knowledge, and identities in ways that are always contested. So, while Unesco may concern itself with the 'cultural dimension of development' the critical theorists need to go further and consider the struggles over and within the agenda of cultural politics. Fagan's chapter, also, in the central role it accords to a single South African woman (Thembeli) bids us re-consider critically the role of the development researcher. However radical development researchers might be, they are still ultimately part of the development industry.

Finally, in Chapter 10 Ronaldo Munck re-engages with development theory, taken in its modernist, countermodernist and postmodernist guises. Munck moves beyond his earlier work (Munck 1984) to confront the challenge of postmodernism which, if taken seriously, undermines many of the claims of radical, as well as mainstream, social science. Munck argues that the perceived impasse in development theory in the 1980s was largely self-induced by disenchanted Marxists. The counter-modernism of much of the postdevelopment literature is considered critically but is not seen as a viable alternative to the discredited modernist discourses of modernization and Marxism. Finally, Munck explores what a critical postmodernist approach to development might mean, particularly if taken with the feminist critique of malestream. In development theory, knowledge and power are even more closely imbricated than usual, as so much is at stake. Munck ends by (re)considering the political alternatives faced by development theory.

This volume explores many diverse critical approaches to development. The emphasis is certainly on difference and not on developing one unified alternative paradigm to confront the dominant modernization/ globalization paradigm. Thus, there are interesting tensions contained within the volume between, for example, Sardar's critique of Western science and O'Hearn's desire to find ways that semiperipheral and Southern regions can control innovative technologies; between Douthwaite's regional solutions for sustainability and Nederveen Pieterse's call to examine and exploit intersections between the global and the local; or between Santos's celebration of a radical postmodernism and the attempts of Perrons to rehabilitate political economy as a fix for shortcomings of postmodernism. A theme that runs through this volume is that such tensions should be not avoided but, as Nederveen Pieterse argues, instead confronted directly as part of a critically holistic analysis.

In the past, development theory seems to have tried to make up for the fluidity and incomprehensibility of its subject matter by stressing the rigour or novelty of its approach. However, none of the authors here seems to be seeking a new Holy Grail of development. What they have in common is a certain critical realism. Even critical development theories in the past have probably concentrated unduly on seeking the 'missing link' that would allow them, finally, to grasp development. Whether or not the authors subscribe to postmodernism they probably would not wish to construct another master narrative along these lines. The new dominant development paradigm will be global in terms of its unit of analysis and its frame of reference. This paradigm shift will, undoubtedly, be matched by critical social scientists. What the present volume may do, in its diversity and its conflicting internal voices, is contribute towards this new paradigm which we might see as global in aspirations as much as in geographical scope.

Critical development theory has gone through many phases. We had the 'gendering' and 'greening' of development theory. We decided to add a cultural perspective, or we argued for 'bringing the state back in'. At the risk of adding to this litany we should, perhaps, consider bringing politics back in to development theory and practice. A critical postmodern perspective cannot blind us to the enduring confrontation between social exclusion and social inclusion or, to put it broadly, between equality and inequality. Norberto Bobbio (1996) has recently reminded us that we have not really moved 'beyond' left and right, any more than we have reached the 'end of history'. In relation to the pressing realities of underdevelopment in particular, Bobbio has argued that, 'faced with this reality, there is a very clear distinction between the right and the left, for which the ideal of equality has always been the pole star that guides it' (Bobbio 1996: 82). A complacent postmodernism may well lead to political nihilism and despair, seeing a rampant, unchallenged capitalism as 'the only game in town'. A critical development theory would seek to remind us that underdevelopment is the starkest symbol today of the left–right divide.

Ronaldo Munck
Denis O'Hearn

References

Bobbio, Norberto (1996) *Left and Right: The Significance of a Political Distinction*. Cambridge: Polity Press.

Douthwaite, Richard (1992) *The Growth Illusion: How Economic Growth Has Enriched the Few, Impoverished the Many and Endangered the Planet*. Dublin: Lilliput.

Dunford, Michael and Diane Perrons (1983) *The Arena of Capital*. Basingstoke: Macmillan.

Fagan, Honor (1995) *Culture, Politics, and Irish School Dropouts: Constructing Political Identities*. Westport, CT: Bergin and Garvey.

IMF (International Monetary Fund) (1997) *World Economic Outlook. (May) Globalization: Opportunities and Challenges*. Washington, DC: IMF.

Munck, Ronaldo (1984) *Politics and Dependency in the Third World*. London: Zed Books.

— (1993) *The Irish Economy: Results and Prospects*. London: Pluto Press.

Nederveen Pieterse, Jan (1989) *Empire and Emancipation*. New York: Praeger.

O'Hearn, Denis (1989) 'The Irish case of dependency: an exception to the exceptions?' *American Sociological Review*, Vol. 54, No. 4 (August 1989), pp. 578–96. Reprinted in John T. Passe-Smith and Mitchell A. Seligson (eds), *Development and Underdevelopment: The Political Economy of Inequality*. Boulder, CO: Lynne Rienner.

— (1998) *Inside the Celtic Tiger: Irish Economic Change and the Asian Model*. London: Pluto Press.

Owen, Robert and Bob Sutcliffe (eds) (1972) *Studies in the Theory of Imperialism*. London: Longman.

Santos, Boaventura de Sousa (1995) *Toward a New Common Sense: Law, Science, and Politics in the Paradigmatic Transition*. New York: Routledge.

Sardar, Ziauddin (1998) *Postmodernism and the Other: The New Imperialism of Western Culture*. London: Pluto Press.

Tucker, Vincent (ed.) (1997) *Cultural Perspectives on Development*. London: Frank Cass.

UNCTAD (1997) *Trade and Development Report: Globalization, Distribution, and Growth*. New York: United Nations.

CHAPTER I

The Myth of Development: A Critique of a Eurocentric Discourse[1]

Vincent Tucker

Development as a practical and intellectual project has been steeped in optimism. Yet, after more than three decades of development, many areas of the world are worse off today than they were thirty years ago, despite development programmes and aid. Millions of Africans suffer and die from starvation and malnutrition. In the face of such failure, deterioration and destruction, we cannot persist in talking about development as the harbinger of human emancipation. It would seem that the model of development now widely pursued is part of the problem rather than the solution. The sooner we demythologize this ideology the better. It distorts our imagination, limits our vision, blinding us to the alternatives that human ingenuity is capable of imagining and implementing. The myth of development is elevated to the status of natural law, objective reality and evolutionary necessity. In the process all other world views are devalued and dismissed as 'primitive', 'backward', 'irrational' or 'naïve'.

Development is the process whereby other peoples are dominated and their destinies are shaped according to an essentially Western way of conceiving and perceiving the world. The development discourse is part of an imperial process whereby other peoples are appropriated and turned into objects. It is an essential part of the process whereby the 'developed' countries manage, control and even create the Third World economically, politically, sociologically and culturally. It is a process whereby the lives of some peoples, their plans, their hopes, their imaginations, are shaped by others who frequently share neither their lifestyles, nor their hopes nor their values. The real nature of this process is disguised by a discourse that portrays development as a necessary and desirable process, as human destiny itself. The economic, social and political transformations of the Third World are inseparable from the production and reproduction of meanings, symbols and knowledge, that is, cultural reproduction.

Considerable attention has been given to the analysis of the economic mechanisms of underdevelopment and, to a lesser extent, the social and political processes. Dependency theorists have produced important analyses of the ways in which economic processes of development have produced underdevelopment. However, the cultural dimension, the production of cultural meanings and symbols, has not received adequate attention. In development studies, culture has tended to be regarded as something of an epiphenomenon, secondary in importance to the all-important economic and political domains. To date it is the least examined aspect, and this has considerable implications. In this essay I will argue that the failure to critically examine powerful culturally constructed myths is at the root of the current impasse in development thinking and practice. By emphasizing the cultural dimension of the development process I am not replacing one form of reductionism with another. I am neither underestimating the central importance of political economy nor am I proposing culture as a new master paradigm. The purpose of this essay is rather to address a major blind spot in development thinking.

Imagining development

'Development' is not a natural process, although it has been accorded such a status in the mythology of Western beliefs. Regarded as natural it is accepted without question because it bears its own legitimization. It is, rather, a set of practices and beliefs that has been woven into the fabric of Western culture and is specific to it. 'Development' is not a transcultural concept that can claim universal validity (Rist 1990: 12). It is a specifically Western myth and many languages have no equivalent. Such myths or shared beliefs play an important role in mobilizing energies for social reproduction and in legitimizing the actions of the believers.

Shared beliefs and meanings form an essential part of the fabric of society. The myth of development constitutes part of the social imaginary of Western societies. It is for this reason that – despite the transfer of goods, gadgets, capital, technology, hospitals and roads – the economic policies and the socioeconomic accomplishments of the West cannot be replicated in Third World countries. From the material point of view everything is set to go, but the symbolic engine is missing (Rist 1990: 18).

Modernization theorists recognized something of this sort. They were aware of the importance of the cultural dimension of development. However, they approached this problem by reducing other cultures to fossilized stereotypes, inert wholes. Under the rubric of 'traditional society' the worth of these cultures was denied. Traditional societies had no inner dynamism. Modernization theorists were concerned with understanding the culture of other societies so as to manipulate them and adapt them to the exigencies of development. This development was conceived of as economic growth, industrial development and the establishment of complementary social and political institutions designed on the model of the USA. Other cultural formations were viewed primarily as forms of resistance to modernization which had to be overcome.

Modernizers exposed the energizing and legitimizing myths of other societies to the scrutiny of instrumental rationality and discredited them. However, they failed to expose and deconstruct their own myths. In this way myths of progress and development remained potent, providing the motivation and legitimization for transforming other societies in their image. This was not a disembodied encounter between a superior culture and inferior cultures but a contest in which the imperial societies had the means to impose their vision and ideas, violently when necessary.

The myth of development is a central myth of Western society. Once it becomes clear that the practices that we call development depend on shared beliefs rather than on nature or destiny, it becomes possible to challenge them in a way that was not previously possible. In challenging the myth of development it then becomes possible to ask if Third World societies must reproduce themselves according to the Western myth of development or else remain forever in misery and deprivation. Must they develop or perish? Or, put differently, is civilization as we know it compulsory? In addressing these questions we are also led to assess in a different light the actions of those who resist 'development', who refuse what is allegedly good for them.

The central issue here is control over destinies. Will new values simply be imported or imposed in the name of 'development'? Which values must be abandoned and which retained in order to make way for modernization? It is useful to distinguish between two processes of change here. One concerns the production of goods, the mastery over nature, rational organization and technological efficiency. The second concerns the production of structures of power and ideology.

While professing a desire to share technology and abundance with the less developed nations, advanced societies (or sub-systemic units of decision making) struggle to maintain their supremacy in the domains relating to the second set of processes. That is to say, power and ideological mastery are not to be transferred on the same terms and in the same manner as economic progress or scientific knowledge. The crucial problem arises precisely because low-income nations are often thwarted in their pursuit of goals implicit in the first processes by the prevailing structures which govern the second. (Goulet 1977: 15)

It is for this reason that a critical examination of the cultural practices involved in the production of knowledge and meaning, a task that demythologizes the development process by placing it in its historic context, is an essential task if the current impasse in development is to be overcome.

Progress and civilization

The idea of progress with its attendant notions of perfectibility and inevitability gained pre-eminence in the period of the French and English revolutions. Armed with the confidence of having history if not nature on their side, the new economic and political revolutionaries of Britain and France set about changing the world and the way in which it was perceived. With time, their worldview came to be intuitively self-evident and was believed to be universally valid. As such it provided a conceptual and moral basis for colonialism and imperialism.

This was the period of the emergence of the modern economy, of the modern state, and of the concept of universal sovereignty in the form of liberal democracy. It was a period that championed the 'rights of man' but not, it must be said, the rights of all men or the rights of women. It was a period of considerable confidence. Science wedded to instrumental rationality appeared to be capable of conquering nature. It was a period of exploration and experimentation. Like the earlier Europeans who saw their mission as Christianizing those parts of the world that they conquered, the new, modern Europeans saw themselves as missionaries with a universalizing mission. This mission was modernity.

The concept of progress came to be forged in evolutionary terms. In France, progress was seen as being brought about by the application of rationality and science to all domains of society, thus liberating them from ignorance and superstition. Post-Revolutionary French society saw itself as the pinnacle of human societal development. The emergence of industrial capitalism in England, with its new forms of organization of labour and allied concepts of time and efficiency, added a further dimension to modernity. Rationality came to be measured by economic imperatives. The discourse of progress was forged in a context in which other societies were subjected to processes of economic and military domination and even genocide.

These ideas of progress and civilization later came to be enshrined in policy. The General Act of the Berlin Conference (1884–85), at which the imperial nations met to set guidelines for the carving up of Africa, pledged support for missionaries and institutions 'calculated to educate the natives and to teach them to understand and appreciate the benefits of civilization'. In 1919 the League of Nations in Article 22 of its Covenant gave the 'advanced' nations responsibility for those 'peoples not yet able to stand by themselves under the strenuous conditions of the modern world', putting the latter officially under the tutelage of the industrial nations 'as a sacred trust of civilization'. Not only had Europeans a right to conquer and dominate other peoples, they even had a duty to do so.

Discourses of progress and civilization were used to legitimize slavery, genocide, colonialism and all forms of human exploitation. These processes are not a mere aberration from the Enlightenment ideal, they are a central part of it – they are in a real sense the extreme formulation of the Enlightenment vision.

Modernity also had a critical and liberative dimension. This was expressed in a concern for individual human rights and gave rise to critical movements challenging slavery, forced labour and other forms of human domination. These movements led to a critique of the supposedly biologically grounded racist theories of evolution, by which peoples could be placed at different levels of the evolutionary scale on the basis of physical characteristics such as skin colour. These liberative impulses were drawn upon by different groupings to challenge enslavement and later colonialism.

However, these liberative movements replaced biological racism with an equally pernicious form of cultural racism which based its judgements of superiority and inferiority on essentially ethnocentric norms, thereby labelling other cultures as inferior. The Eurocentric concept of rationality was regarded as universal. Democratic ideals tended to fade when confronted with the omnipotence of techno-scientific 'truth' and the 'laws' of the market.

The key question here is the power of one people or one nation to dominate and transform another according to its worldview. The process of domination was economic, political, military and cultural. The cultural dimension is central to any consideration of this process of domination. It is in the sphere of the production of meanings and ideas that we find the cognitive, normative and conative foundations of this process. This cultural discourse provides both the motivating force for and a legitimization of the relationship between those nations that saw themselves as 'advanced', 'civilized', and 'modern' and others whom they labelled 'backward', 'primitive' and 'traditional'. The Other in each case is reduced to an object to be appropriated to the consciousness of the subjects of history and progress. Others were denied a history of their own apart from the history of 'civilization' and 'progress'.

The Enlightenment heritage was thus a double-edged sword. Modernity also harboured its malcontents. They were the Others who, having been written out of history and beyond the pale of progress, now had to convert to the Enlightenment ideals or be pushed aside. The ethnocentrism of the dominant Enlightenment ethos (there were exceptions such as Rousseau) precluded any conception of these peoples as having a progressive role in universal history. But the malcontents continually forced their way on to the stage of history. They forged their own modernity which was a hybridization of European and other traditions. They fashioned counterdiscourses which changed and challenged the modernizers, not only in the colonies but in Europe itself. Liberation, human rights and progress were not the sole prerogative of Europeans.

Here as in later periods the key issue was one of power and self-reliance. Programmes of development in which the recipients are merely objects will always be perceived as alien and will be resisted. Paulo Freire sums up the difference between modernization and authentic development:

> It is essential not to confuse modernisation with development. The former, although it may affect certain groups in the 'satellite society', is almost always induced; and it is the metropolitan society which derives true benefit therefrom. A society which is merely modernised without developing will continue – even if it takes over some minimal delegation of decision making – to depend on the outside country. This is the fate of any dependent society as long as it remains dependent. ... The basic elementary criterion is whether or not a society is a 'being for itself'. If it is not the criterion indicates modernisation rather than development. (Freire 1972: 160)

The question of a people's right to define their own development in the face of outsiders who claim a monopoly of truth and enlightenment will remain the central issue as we consider more recent development discourses.

The genealogy of development thinking

As well as having the capacity for economic, political and military domination, the developed nations also exercise hegemony in the control of the production of knowledge. The production of knowledge is one of the ways in which the West controls and even creates the Third World politically, economically, sociologically and culturally.

Development studies as we know it is a child of the period after the Second World War, when the word 'development' gained its current sense. The words 'development' and 'modernization' were coined by spokespersons for the West to characterize the efforts of others whom they implicitly assumed to be destined to achieve their levels of consumption. This thinking was based on the postulation of an evolutionary scenario in which those left behind in the race for progress could, with the aid of the 'more advanced', catch up and also become modern and developed.

This development thinking, culminating in the UN Development Decades in the 1960s, originated primarily from the USA. President Truman's 1949 Point Four Programme and Kennedy's Alliance for Progress in Latin America and Peace Corps put development at the centre of the political agenda for the first time. The United States was at the height of its power and influence and regarded itself as both the inspiration and the policeman of the world. Anthropologists, sociologists, psychologists and economists all contributed to the modernization project with unquestioning optimism. Progress in its new clothes was not only inevitable, it was obligatory. Adaptation became a key concept. People and groups must adapt.

Modernizing elites and comprador development theorists in 'developing' countries eagerly enrolled in the project. Under the rubric of modernization, Westernization gained the status of a universal goal and destiny. When failure and resistance were encountered they were subsumed under the category of 'tradition', an essentially pejorative term which denoted divergence from the generally accepted norms of reason and progress. The 'reductive universalism' of the modernizers was unshakeable (Berthoud 1990: 26). Orthodox development came to hinge on the certainty of a universal modernity.

While there was considerable diversity among the various theoretical positions deduced from these metatheoretical postulates, the underlying assumptions were so taken for granted that they escaped critical scrutiny. They were rooted in an evolutionary myth, a series of metatheoretical postulates, which reduced history to a series of formal stages honed from the particular experience of European societies and then elevated to the status of universals. This schema became a destiny and a norm by which other societies were judged and moulded.

A Europe-centred development discourse has considerable difficulty in imagining that other ways of organizing the world, other forms of rationality, other ways of life, can possibly provide coherence or satisfaction for their adherents. It tends to colonize and to destroy the imaginary of others. In its failure to confront the historical roots of its own discourse, it reduces other worlds to its own mirror image. It creates a Third World without history, a timeless fossilized relic of Europe's historical imagination (Fabian 1983).

The invention of traditional society

Discourses of progress, development and modernization are constructed on the basis of the false polarities of 'traditional' and 'modern'. These temporal metaphors used to conceptualize otherness and distance in historical time are transposed on to spatial realities and used to designate a normative development trajectory. Societies that deviate from the European techno-economic standards are designated as 'traditional' or 'primitive' despite the fact that they are contemporaneous with those who label them as such. These false and mutually exclusive polarities are united by an evolutionary discourse that postulates them as sequential stages of development. History is reduced to a scale of progress on to which societies are mapped. Development is postulated as a natural process.

'Traditional' society is a myth, however, an invention of the European mind. The discourse of modernization and development is a European monologue conducted with Europeans' own mythic self-image rather than a dialogue with other historically grounded cultures and societies. In the real world there are no traditional societies, only ways of looking at societies as traditional. Yet myths of 'traditional societies' and 'primitive cultures' continue to be perpetuated uncritically by the discourses of development, anthropology and Orientalism.

Much of what is generally conceived of as African 'tradition' is an invention of colonial powers and missionaries, in collaboration with African functionaries and intellectuals. Considerable numbers of African 'traditional' customs, rituals and institutions, including the notion of 'tribes', were 'not so much survivals from a pre-colonial past but rather largely creations by colonial officers and African intellectuals'. What is most characteristic of the colonial period is the 'freezing of political dynamics and the pre-colonial, shifting, fluid imbalance of power' so as to accommodate policies of direct rule (Wim van Binsbergen, quoted in Ranger 1983). Terence Ranger in his excellent essay 'The Invention of Tradition in Africa' concludes:

> ... my point is not so much that 'traditions' changed to accommodate new

circumstances but that at a certain point they had to stop changing; once the 'traditions' relating to community identity and land right were written down in court records and exposed to criteria of the invented customary model, a new and unchanging body of tradition had been created. (Ranger 1983: 251)

The notion of other societies as simple and unchanging by contrast with the complexity and dynamism of Western societies was a convenient fiction which legitimized the right, and even the duty, of 'modern' societies to transform them in their image and likeness. By reducing the vast array of cultures and societies to a single stereotype, modernization theorists ruled out the possibility that these societies had anything of value to offer. They were conceived of mainly as obstacles to modernization and development.

Modernity and its discontents

Neither is modernity a monolithic unity. There are various modernities and not a single one. Modernity is a dynamic historic process, and its components cannot simply be reduced to or deduced from a single causal principle; rather, they have emerged from a particular historical configuration of forces shaped by the historical experience of Europe. Even these 'European' historical forces have their origins in a rarely examined prehistory. This is not to deny that modernity took on its characteristic configuration in the Enlightenment but rather to remind us that the Enlightenment is itself the outcome of a historical configuration which owes much to the Islamic world of scholarship and science. This, in turn, is not simply the mediation to Europe via Islam of 'classical Greek civilization' but, as Martin Bernal has shown in *Black Athena*, a much more complex historical configuration with Afro-Asiatic roots (Bernal 1987). The modern re-creation of the Orient and of Africa and Asia as irrational Others serves to obscure the roots of important aspects of Enlightenment thinking, thus further reinforcing Eurocentrism.

Modernity is not a tightly integrated functional whole. Various components of modernity often diverge or form new configurations. This is especially evident in the European encounter with other societies and cultures. In Latin America, modernity has also led to social disintegration and fragmentation. Industrialization has converged with the erosion of democratic rights. Even the democratization that followed the eclipse of military dictatorships led to a deepening of clientalism, to the privatization of public goods, and to neglect of the poorest sectors.

These encounters have given rise to a variety of modernities.

Modernity is not the monopoly of European or North American societies, although students of modernity have associated it almost exclusively with Europe and North America, for example, Habermas despite his critique of Parsons's evolutionism (Lehmann 1990: 5). As a universalizing process, modernity has affected and been affected by virtually every society on the globe. However, modernity is a discourse that remains largely Europe-centred (although Latin American scholars and Oriental scholars have entered the discourse). This one-sidedness, this tendency towards monologue rather than dialogue, is rooted in the unequal power relations that still characterize the social production of knowledge.

Europe and the United States have at least in recent times achieved some degree of homogeneity, but the experience of modernity is considerably more complex from a Latin American, African or a Middle Eastern point of view. Even a cursory visit to Lagos, Calcutta or any Third World city will suffice to convince one of this fact. Whereas the social, political, economic and cultural dimensions of modernity have tended by and large to converge in Europe and in the United States, in the Third World they have tended to diverge. In these contexts the optimism of an evolution-based social theory cannot be accepted uncritically. If anything analyses must begin from the premise that, in the short term and in the medium term, development is unlikely to take place.

Modernism and the end of history

Perhaps the most extreme statement of the inevitability of universal modernity, in its Western guise, is Francis Fukuyama's claim that we have reached the end of history (Fukuyama 1992). However, rather than experiencing the end of history we are in the presence of a crisis of Western history, a crisis of imagination. It is for this reason that the myth of development is in urgent need of deconstruction; otherwise it will continue to block and subvert other imaginaries. The reason why Fukuyama's rather simplistic thesis has been so attractive is that it articulates the founding myth of the West, the myth of development. It reflects a situation in which street-level common sense and academic theorizing alike share the belief that Europeans and North Americans live in societies that are 'developed' while other peoples are 'underdeveloped'.

The crises we face will not be overcome by negating and subverting other ways of understanding and being:

The prevailing imagery of relationships between developed and under-developed countries assigns the former the role of 'saving' the latter from misery, disease and stagnation, thanks to superior technology. At the deepest level, however, roles may have to be reversed. Perhaps it is 'developed' nations which must be 'saved' from servitude by means of creative options yet to be made in 'underdeveloped' societies as they struggle to 'modernise' in a human mode. (Goulet 1977: 251)

Totalizing theories by their nature colonize and subsume other histories and existence rationalities. These theories are essentially imperial and cannot do justice to the diversity of discourses and cosmologies to be found in different societies.

What Fukuyama proposes is not only the end of history but the end of imagination. This ideology, whether in its more extreme articulations, as above, or in the more nuanced discourses of modernization and development, is a dangerous one. It is dangerous for civilizations that challenge it, such as the Muslim world, but particularly so for indigenous peoples who lack the economic and political clout to support their struggle for a say in the shape of their future. The danger was aptly summed up by a former Sudanese Vice-President: referring to the resistance of the Dinka and Nuer peoples to the Jonglei Canal project which would destroy their nomadic way of life, he declared: 'We will drive them to paradise with a stick if necessary!'

Biologists and ecologists alike recognize the importance of diversity in human and biological evolution.

No single society can reflect all the achievements of which men [sic] are capable in their institutional creation. The basis of cultural diversity as a value, therefore, is simply that the human potential is too rich to be expressed adequately in a single form. Only blind parochialism can make men wish to eliminate this multi-faceted existential wealth from the planet in the name of efficiency or to obey the demands of standardisation. (Goulet 1977: 264)

Diversity and decentredness must be placed at the top of the agenda in reformulating the question of development. The cultural question, the question of the meaning of development, is a central one. For one society to claim universal desirability, while turning its back on others from whom it is convinced it has nothing to learn, is not only cultural elitism but cultural racism.

All this underlines the inadequate treatment of culture, whether in theory or in practice. Development programmes were not sufficiently aware of the importance of culture. In development thinking culture was inadequately theorized, if theorized at all. Economic considerations were paramount, and in this respect dependency theorists were no different from modernization theorists.

The limits of dependency theory

Dependency theory was the first major Third World challenge to Europe-centred academic discourse. It provided a much-needed counter-point to modernization theory. However, it was limited in that it restricted its attention almost exclusively to the economic and, to a lesser extent, the political mechanisms of domination and control. It challenged the ethnocentrism of a political economy derived exclusively from the experience of Europe and the United States and then general-ized to the rest of the world. It provided a trenchant critique of the crusading imperialism of the modernization theorists and provided an alternative vision, which accorded more closely with the experience of Third World countries. But dependency theory failed to address the cultural dimension of domination. This was a crucial omission as cul-tural analysis is central to any understanding of the relations of power and to any strategy of resistance or dependency reversal.

Despite the challenge it posed to the hegemony of the modernization discourse, dependency theory shared some of its basic premises. While criticizing modernization theorists it did not question the desirability of development, still conceived of largely in terms of economic growth, industrialization, and liberal democracy. Together with various other forms of Marxist-influenced development thinking, the dependency theorists implicitly accepted the evolutionary model of progress. The ecological implications of this growth-oriented model of development, and considerations such as the rights of tribal peoples, were not con-cerns in this discourse. Neither were considerations of gender-related differences. The fundamental goal remained the same. Dependency theorists were profoundly modern in their worldview.

While initially providing powerful new insights, dependency theory is now widely believed to have reached an impasse (Booth 1985; Cor-bridge 1990; Sklair 1988; Mouzelis 1988). The debate on the 'impasse' produced considerable refinement of the dependency paradigm and world-systems theory but it failed to address the crucial question of culture. Dependency theorists and their contemporary critics have also singularly failed to address the question of the meaning of development.

In deconstructing the categories used in development discourses it is important to pay greater attention than hitherto to the unequal power relationship that prevails in the production of knowledge. This unequal relationship parallels and reinforces the unequal and dependent relationships in the domains of economy and politics. The production of knowledge about the Third World has taken place in the context of and as an integral part of the unequal relationship between the West and the Third World. In this context one group has the power to articulate and project itself and its worldview on others. The others thus become Others – objects to be studied, described and developed. Overpowered by the hegemonic discourse of the West, Third World societies are stunted in their capacity to articulate their own identities and worldviews. They tend to internalize the perspective of the modernizers and developmentalists, a process that is facilitated by comprador intellectuals in the Third World. This is done not only through control of the media but also through ownership and control of the whole infrastructure of the production of knowledge (Blomström and Hettne 1984: 4).

Europe and North America have the lion's share of universities and institutes and of the access to information and knowledge that goes with them. Major African universities have for some time been unable to maintain subscriptions to key journals. Scholars outside Europe and North America often find it difficult to keep up with and contribute to discussions within their disciplines. The greater availability of research grants from foundations in the West (foundations that tend to support particular worldviews) enables North Americans and Europeans to visit, study and write about Third World societies, whilst Third World students and scholars are generally less able to study the West. When they do study there they are often socialized into the dominant paradigms of Western thinking.

As a result, some cultures and societies find themselves over-determined by Western representations to the point that they can no longer recognize themselves in the discourses that claim to portray them. They are saturated with imposed meanings, ambitions and projects. In this process of identity construction there is little dialogue, little exchange of views, little mutual recognition and respect. Schools of thought such as Orientalism and disciplines such as anthropology speak for the Other, often claiming to know those they study better than they know themselves. This is particularly evident in the way in which Muslim societies and cultures are treated in Western academic and popular discourse (Kabbani 1986; Said 1979, 1981; Sardar and Wyn Davies 1990).

It is for this reason that the deconstruction of the founding Western myths of origin is such an urgent task. While these myths continue to act as metatheoretical premises beyond the reach of critical scrutiny, discussions about the impasse of development theory and development

practice will only scratch the surface. It is only through mutually corrective dialogue – a dialogue made difficult by the above-mentioned
constraints – that the impasse can be overcome. Monologues must be
replaced by dialogues, and these dialogues will necessarily involve
considerable mutual criticism.

Cultures of resistance

At the heart of the problem is the question of unequal power. Some
societies become subjects of their own destinies while reducing weaker
societies to the status of objects. Both imperialist and anti-imperialist
discourses (modernization and dependency discourses) have tended to
reduce the subjects of development to passive objects. While in no way
diminishing the role of powerful global forces which penetrate all parts
of the globe and all aspects of life (and this is the central insight of the
world-systems theorists), we must also recognize that hegemony is never
complete. Whether in visible or invisible forms, resistance is always
present, even in the most repressive of situations. Hegemonic situations
always contain the seed of their own liberation.

Social movement theorists have to some extent redressed the one-
sided emphasis of world-systems theorists on the forces of domination.
In the study of global social movements, such as feminism and environmentalism, they have emphasized the various forms that emancipatory
forces can take. These movements constitute countersystemic forces
operating at a global level. However, social movement theory has
focused mainly on the West. Significant social movements emanating
from the Third World have hitherto received insufficient attention from
social movement theorists. Islamic revivalism is one of the most visible
and significant of these. However, this movement has tended to be
dismissed as an antimodern aberration rather than subjected to serious
analysis. Defined as 'fundamentalist' it is denied contemporaneity, as if
the protagonists are part of some faraway medieval world rather than
citizens of Bradford. Categorized as such Islamic revivalism does not
come under the ambit of a 'new' social movement. The dualistic
thinking that permeates the discourse of modernity again serves to
designate it as 'premodern' and thus outside the ambit of new social
movement theorists.

We must also pay more attention to the invisible and unorganized
forms of resistance as these constitute powerful forces which can nibble
away at projects imposed from outside, undermining them and even
bringing them to a standstill. Here the cultural dimension of resistance
in the life world is significant. Scott (1985) shows how everyday forms

of resistance, which require little or no coordination or planning but rely on implicit understandings and informal networks, can constitute a culture of resistance and can make an utter shambles of policies drawn up by the masters of capital or the state. In the Third World it is rare for peasants to risk outright confrontation with the authorities over taxes, cropping patterns, development policies, or onerous new laws; instead they are likely to nibble away at such policies by non-compliance, foot-dragging, deception. In place of a land invasion, they prefer piecemeal squatting; in place of open mutiny, they prefer desertion; in place of attacks on public or private grain stores, they prefer pilfering (Scott 1985: xxvi). This is not just a struggle in the domain of production but a struggle over meaning and symbols – it is a cultural struggle in the domain of the life world.

Rehabilitating the concept of development

Some scholars have argued that we must abandon the concept of development because of its use in legitimating domination. If we were to follow this logic we would also need to abandon concepts such as socialism, cooperation, and democracy because they have also been abused and manipulated for purposes of domination and exploitation. This would amount to handing over a powerful tool to those who exploit it for their own purposes.

Hitherto development has been something of a unitary field of theory and practice. As such it has been largely reflective of the ethos of the West and has either ignored or domesticated other discourses. Rethinking development in order to redress the problems posed in this essay calls for a plurality of discourses, a plurality of audiences and a plurality of terrains (Said 1985). This is necessary in order to accommodate the diversity of experiences and rationalities. The social scientific discourse of the West is not of itself adequate for this purpose.

All these efforts work out of what might be called a decentred consciousness not less reflective and critical for being decentred, for the most part non- and in some cases antitotalizing and anti-systemic. The result is that instead of seeking common unity by appeals to a centre of sovereign authority, methodological consistency, canonicity and science, they offer the possibility of common grounds of assembly between them. They are, therefore, planes of activity and praxis, rather than one topography commanded by a geographical and historical vision locatable in a known centre of metropolitan power. Second, these activities and praxes are consciously secular, marginal and appositional with reference to the mainstream, generally authoritarian systems against which they now agitate. Third, they are political and

practical inasmuch as they intend – without necessarily succeeding – the
end of dominating, coercive systems of knowledge. (Said 1985: 14)

All this calls for a political and methodological commitment to dis-
mantling systems of domination which are collectively maintained, and
this includes totalizing theoretical systems.

The dominant-system-centred view (which is usually a Eurocentric
or Western-centred perspective) must be replaced by what Gregory
Bateson has called double or multiple descriptions (Bateson 1979: 142).
Such multiple perspectives, which engage each other dialectically in a
process of mutual criticism and mutual correction, are a necessary
acknowledgement of the different contexts of experience, description
and theorizing. Such an approach allows for the possibility of incorporating the experience of other peoples, other perspectives and other
cultures into the development discourse. In practical terms this requires
that Western social scientists engage in dialogue with intellectuals from
other cultural contexts, that they open their worldview to the gaze and
critical scrutiny of the Other.

In addition to the problem of the existing unequal structures of the
production of knowledge, which puts serious obstacles in the way of
any such venture, there is the continual danger of conceiving of the
encounter as consisting of two discrete worlds facing each other rather
than of social worlds that are part of each other yet constituted
differently. This conceptualization can result in forms of reactivism
whereby the West's distortions of the Third World or of the Orient are
countered by distorted images of the West or by nativistic stereotypes.
In such an encounter closed systems, conceptualized as holistic cultures,
face each other as uncompromising totalities. This results in various
fundamentalisms, whether Islamic, Christian, feminist or environmental.

Islam, for example, is constructed in the West as a cultural whole.
Islamic identity is reduced to a selection of essentialist traits portrayed
in the public culture of the West as a monolith. The vast range of
Islamic cultures, political systems, and religious beliefs found in places
as diverse as China, the Philippines, Bangladesh, Saudi Arabia, Palestine,
Iran, Sudan, France, England and the United States is obscured. The
internal debates and dialogues, as well as the syncretization of Islamic
beliefs and practices with a great variety of cultural practices, are ignored
or reduced to a caricature. In order to construct Islam as Other, Western
culture must distance itself from its own past and obscure the degree to
which its own culture is the product of a hybridization with Islam.

What is important to remember here is that discourses do not inhere
in people; rather, we inhabit different discourses which frequently

overlap or are in conflict with each other. The translation, integration, and hybridization our involvement in multiple discourses demands is something each individual must negotiate. But the individual does not negotiate meaning and translate concepts and metaphors from one discourse to another in some internal mental realm of pure ideas. Discourses are not disembodied ideas but the product of social action and interaction. The process of translation and negotiation takes place in a variety of sites in our lives. These sites constitute the contexts of culture creation. The struggle to create meaning takes place in the context of particular historic configurations. Different public cultures selectively emphasize certain ideas and forms of representation while repressing others that are struggling against current hegemony.

In order to come to terms with these processes, development thinking must be underpinned by a conceptualization of culture as a dynamic and conflictual process. The political economy approach that has dominated development theorizing must be complemented by a theory of culture. However, development theory must not simply abandon its political economy approach, and it must also transcend the limitations of text-bound literary theory and the political evasiveness of Eurocentric postmodernism.

Development as dialogue

The process of negotiation and translation take place at a variety of sites where people struggle to have a say, to have their imaginary socially represented. Homi Bhabha elaborates on this useful concept of culture as negotiated reality:

> ... we do negotiate even when we don't know that we are negotiating: we are always negotiating in any situation of political opposition or antagonism. Subversion is negotiation, transgression is negotiation; negotiation is not just some kind of compromise or 'selling out' which people too easily understand it to be. Similarly we need to reformulate what we mean by 'reformism'; all forms of political activity, especially progressive or radical activity, involve reformations and reformulations. ... So I think that political negotiation is a very important issue, and hybridity is precisely about the fact that when a new situation, a new alliance formulates itself, it may demand that you should translate your principles, rethink them, extend them. On the Left there's too much of timid traditionalism – always trying to read a new situation in terms of some pre-given model or paradigm which is a reactionary reflex, a conservative 'mindset'. (Bhabha 1990: 216)

Bhabha's concept of negotiated reality is different from the 'consensual and collusive "liberal" sense of community' (Bhabha 1990: 219). He

argues that both the colonial and the postcolonial experiences force us
to confront the cultural incommensurability and antagonism that are at
the heart of our Western culture as well as being central aspects of the
encounter between Western culture and its Others. For Bhabha the
'founding moment of modernity was the moment of colonialism'
(Bhabha 1990: 218). This tension in the history of the West arises from
the fact that it became a despotic power at the very moment of the
birth of democracy and modernity. This has given rise to unresolved
contradictions. Histories of colonialism and underdevelopment have
emerged as counterhistories to the traditional history of the West
construed as a moral success story and have challenged its claims to
democracy and solidarity.

The myths and narratives of modernism face a crisis precisely because
of the challenge of 'strangers' and 'others' from the imperial domain
who make their appearance in Europe, challenging the dominant
historical narratives and demanding that their perspectives be taken
seriously. Today the material legacy of this 'history of civilization' and
Enlightenment is to be found in the repressed history of postcolonial
peoples, who are now part of the postcolonial metropolis. The great
migrations of enslaved and colonized populations from Africa and Asia
to America and Europe, peoples whose narratives challenge and contradict the narratives of the West, constitute a challenge to the prevailing
myths. Having seen and experienced the other side of the social
imaginary of the West the very presence of these peoples constitutes a
counterpoint to the Western myth of development.

All this points towards a move away from totalizing histories and
universalizing social theories. As Young writes:

> This also implies an interrogation of the imperialism of theory itself. For
> theory, as a form of knowledge and understanding of the spectator, is
> constitutively unable to let the other remain outside itself, outside its repres-
> entation of the panorama which it surveys, in a state of singularity or
> separation. (Young 1990: 14)

Instead Young proposes 'dialogism':

> Dialogism allows for 'radical separation, the strangeness of the interlocutors,
> the revelation of the other to me'. The structure of dialogue, moreover,
> disallows the taking up of any position beyond the interlocutors from which
> they can be integrated into a larger totality. The relation between them,
> therefore, is not oppositional, nor limitrophe, but one of alterity. (Young
> 1990: 15)

In arguing that there is no vantage point beyond the interlocutors we are referring not simply to the context of interpersonal communication but also to the cultural context, one marked by a relationship between unequal imperial and nonimperial powers (Said 1989: 216). When we enter into dialogue the realities of power and the hegemonic Western structures of knowledge production are not simply left behind. It is for this reason that the task of deconstructing Western discourse is so urgent.

A form of relativism that posits the existence of other cosmologies and existence rationalities without *a priori* positing some external normative high ground is an essential premise of dialogism. Likewise deconstruction, with a particular emphasis on the deconstruction of the West, because of its ingrained imperial presuppositions, must also be central to any dialogue if there is to be 'a place for all at the rendezvous of victory' (Aimé Césaire, in James 1984).

The indigenous perspective

The problems of redefining development in a non-Eurocentric fashion, and the problems of how to engage in a dialogue of equals with Others in a world saturated with Western hegemony have only begun to impose themselves on the concerns of Western social science. These problems are nowhere posed more sharply than when we consider the predicament of indigenous peoples. They are not only nonliterate but their cosmologies are cast in metaphors that the West consigns to the realm of myth, superstition and irrationality. These unwilling conscripts of civilization, unlike the Muslim world where the empire has begun to strike back in ways that cannot be ignored, are in a particularly precarious situation. They exist at the periphery of the periphery. They have been consigned to the margins not only of society but also of both social science and the development discourse. Concerned with major issues such as economic growth, industrialization, the state, political conflict, social class and social movements, social theory – and in particular its developmental variety – did not consider such 'marginal' groups as indigenous peoples as being worthy of attention (Stavenhagen 1985: 6). Yet it is from the margins that the most incisive critique of the development project can be constructed.

Indigenous peoples are often characterized as 'natural peoples' in that their way of life and their cosmologies are not premised on a relationship in which the 'human' sphere dominates and exploits the 'natural' sphere. The consequences of exploitative relations are only too evident in the disastrous impact of Western development on the biosphere that sustains human life. A genuine dialogue with indigenous peoples would demand a radical reappraisal of present development practices as well as a fundamental deconstruction of Western social science. This would involve a loosening of the spell of instrumental rationality, a rationality that sees nature as devoid of intrinsic meaning and reduces it to 'stuff' which can be moulded and manipulated as required by the exigencies of development. Deep ecologists such as Bill Devall have come close to the perspective of indigenous peoples in arguing that

> ... both the nihilistic and disenchanted left and the conservative right have failed to understand the need for new images of Nature in post-modern civilization. And both the political left and the political right have failed to understand the need for a new social contract which is concerned not only with social justice of the relations between humans, but the relations between humans and the nonhuman world. (Devall 1990: 27)

I would suggest that such a genuine dialogue with indigenous peoples might be accomplished, not simply by delving deeper into the European past to touch base with earlier and more environment-friendly attitudes and ideas, as is suggested by Klaus Eder (1990), but by engaging in respectful dialogue with contemporary indigenous peoples.

The predicament of indigenous cultures in the face of a universalizing modernism forces us to address the fundamental question of the meaning of development. Development for non-Western peoples often means being consigned to meaninglessness. The annihilation of indigenous cosmologies in the face of a desacralizing instrumental rationality can produce a modernity that has no coherent meaning or conceptual validity for indigenous peoples. All that defines their identity and existence is destroyed. The encounter between Western modernity and indigenous cosmologies is problematic in that the particular concept of secularity deeply ingrained in the normative ideal of Western society leads to an intolerance of societies that it deems religious. Western social science fails to realize that its secularity is in fact a Christian secularity, honed in the context of the particular struggle between Church and society that took place in Europe. As such it is a secularity that places humanity at the centre of the universe. Western cosmologies, whether religious or secular, all place humans at the centre of their world and derive their meaning from logocentred rationality.

Other cosmologies do not place humanity at the centre of their universe. Their relationship to nature is characterized by respect and humility and in this their worldview is closer to that of the deep ecologists. In order to understand and dialogue with these other worldviews we must transcend the dualistic forms of thinking that oppose reason and spirituality, locking them into incompatible mind-sets. Instrumental rationality allows no place for notions of the sacred or of spirituality. Yet these are categories which go beyond utilitarian considerations and have intrinsic or noninstrumental significance (Bhabha 1990: 24). As such the sacred, which is not a religious category in the narrow sense, stands between the West and its Others.

By way of a starting point

This essay has focused mainly on the need to deconstruct the concept of development, exposing its various strands to critical gaze. The task of deconstructing and demythologizing the project of the West is an urgent one. If we are to understand the current crisis in development it is essential that we deconstruct this myth in the same way that we would deconstruct the myths of other societies. As Castoriadis points out, 'the life of the modern world is just as dependent on the imaginary as any archaic or historical culture' (quoted in Tomlinson 1991: 158). The modernization of 'traditional' societies has involved the colonization of the imagination of other societies. The failure to examine critically our own social imaginary has led to a form of mystification that places our myths (by denying that they are myths and instead treating them as science) outside the beam of the critical stare while devaluing those of others. Our myths are taken for granted, seen as natural truths, and used as a standard for measuring the performance of other peoples' social imaginaries. I have argued that this failure is at the root of the so-called crisis in development theory and in development practice.

By turning the concentrated beam of rationality on other cultural imaginations the West has demystified the myths and narratives of these cultural configurations. Western social science has acted as a powerful tool in, to use Weber's phrase, 'the disenchantment of the world'. However the West has failed to deconstruct its own myths. It has failed to examine critically the narrative of its own foundation, a narrative that conceives of itself as a 'universal history' (Young 1990). This history is that of a moral success story. It conceptualizes the West not only as a way of life but as the manifest destiny of all peoples. As such it is a crusading myth and is imbued with notions of moral as well as technical and cultural superiority. The construction of the concept of development and its counterpart, modernity, necessitated the postulation of Others against whom the upward trajectory of development could be measured and assessed. The West consolidated its power and dominant position by constituting subject societies as Others.

The West's cultural imaginary is saturated with the idea of development. Whenever a myth is considered the founding act of one particular society to the exclusion of all others, its role as an ideological tool serving the interests of the dominant is heightened. Myths do not merely perpetuate false consciousness, however; they can also open up new meanings and indicate utopian projects.

A positive hermeneutics offers an opportunity to rescue myths from the ideological abuses of doctrinal prejudice, racist nationalism, class oppression, or totalitarian conformism, and it does so in the name of a universal project of freedom – a project from which no creed, nation, class or individual is excluded. The utopian content of myth differs from the ideological in that it is inclusive rather than exclusive; it opens up human consciousness to a common goal of liberation instead of closing it off in the inherited securities of the status quo (Kearney 1988: 16).

A positive hermeneutics requires that we critically assess the content of each myth, the intentions that animate it and the interests it serves. Where a myth serves the interests of one group or civilization to the detriment of others, its liberative value must be questioned. Liberation cannot be exclusive.

The more difficult task is that of constructing an alternative. The deconstruction of the current hegemonic discourse of development in itself opens up new possibilities. The exclusiveness of the current discourses points to the need for open models that emphasize process and dialogical exchange. To theorize this openness and the interdependent hybridness of human exchange we need to rid ourselves of concepts of culture that are elitist, holistic or relativist. Inadequate conceptualizations of culture as somewhat closed wholes prevent us from seeing the dynamism of cultural exchange and the power relations embedded in it.

Habermas's theory of communicative interaction offers one tool for this task although, as Habermas himself admits, it is a 'Eurocentrically limited view' (see Tomlinson 1991: 146) and has not engaged with the problematic of Third World contexts. Young emphasizes the contribution of deconstruction and postmodernism. He argues that 'postmodernism can best be defined as European culture's awareness that it is no longer the unquestioned and dominant centre of the world' (Young 1990: 19). Young places the origins of postmodernism and post-structuralism not in May 1968, but rather in the moment of the Algerian war of independence, pointing to the fact that Sartre, Althusser, Derrida and Lyotard among others were all either born in Algeria or personally involved with the events of the war (Young 1990: 1). Frantz Fanon has also had an impact here. As a theorist spanning different cultural worlds he provided a powerful cultural critique of both Western cultural imperialism as racism and also the anti-racist racism of the Negritude movement. Fanon forced the European metropolis to think its history together with the history of the colonies it created and exploited. Nederveen Pieterse has argued for the theorizing of emancipation as a counterpoint to the one-sided emphasis on domination and exploitation by radical development theorists. But the task is only beginning. Much work needs to be done to produce theoretical perspectives on development that do justice to the social imaginary of Third World peoples without first reconstructing them in our terms before meeting them.

Such a contribution will also require a shift in epistemological perspectives. It can no longer be a case of simply observing processes that are then described and theorized; rather, it must be a case of looking at ourselves looking. This will entail a new encounter with the other, one in which we are constituted by others as they are constituted by us. This involves a process of dialogue between equals whereby we engage in a process of mutual correction. The practicalities of this process are problematic given the context of unequal structures of production and exchange of knowledge discussed earlier. It will call for greater openness to experimentation in the ways in which we carry out studies and in the ways in which we write about development. We need to identify the arenas where such dialogues are already taking place in order to learn from and improve them.

Some important steps have already been made towards tackling these issues. Kevin Dwyer has been an outspoken advocate of dialogue in anthropology (Dwyer 1991, 1979). His recent book on the human rights debate in the Middle East is one example of how such a problem might be approached. The work of anthropologists George Marcus and Michael Fischer in their influential *Anthropology as Cultural Critique* (1986) and also that of James Clifford in *Writing Culture* (1986) have gone some way towards resolving the question of how to respect difference without resorting to cultural relativism, the classic trap of anthropology. One interesting example of how this might be done is Michael Fischer's and Mehdi Abedi's *Debating Muslims*, a collaborative volume between an Iranian Muslim who studied in the US and a US anthropologist who worked in Iran (Fischer and Abedi 1990). Johannes Fabian has also made important contributions to our understanding of how the Other is represented in Western scholarship and has underlined the problems of dialogism (Fabian 1983). Whatever the approach taken, it must above all require theoretical humility and respect for other rationalities. With such a shift it may then be possible to begin to rehabilitate the concept of development.

Finally, while it is important to emphasize the unequal relations of power in the production of knowledge, and to acknowledge the important role of the development discourse as a central part of the process of domination, it is also important to recognize that attempts to improve or ameliorate the images and perspectives in current circulation will in the long run be unsuccessful if nothing is done to change the economic and political structures of domination. The economic, political and cultural spheres are intimately intertwined. These different spheres do have a degree of autonomy from each other, and it is for this reason that change in the cultural sphere, in the Gramscian sense of a 'war of position', is central to and an important dimension of change in the economic and political spheres. In societies where the political modes of domination and economic structures leave little room for manoeuvre, the cultural sphere of action, the deconstruction and reconstruction of hegemonic discourses, is usually the first and most fruitful domain of action in the struggle against domination and exploitation. However, even if it starts here the struggle cannot stop here: it must extend to action in the political and economic arenas.

Note

1. This is an abridged and slightly edited version of an essay that first appeared as Occasional Paper Series No. 6, Department of Sociology, University College Cork. It is reprinted with the permission of the Tucker family. The editors hope that in abridging Vincent Tucker's original essay they have done a minimum of damage to his arguments.

References

Bateson, Gregory (1979) *Mind and Nature: A Necessary Unity*. New York: E.P. Dutton.

Bernal, Martin (1987) *Black Athena: The Afroasiatic Roots of Classical Civilization*. London: Vintage.

Berthoud, Gerald (1990) 'Modernity and development', *European Journal of Development Research*, Vol. 2., No. 1, pp. 10–21.

Bhabha, Homi (1990) Interview with Homi Bhaba in Jonathan Rutherford (ed.), *Identity, Community, Culture, Difference*. London: Lawrence and Wishart.

Blomström, Magnus and Bjorn Hettne (1984) *Development Theory in Transition: The Dependency Debate and Beyond*. London: Zed Press.

Booth, David (1985) 'Marxism and development sociology: interpreting the impasse', *World Development*, Vol. 13, No. 7, pp. 761–87.

Clifford, James and George E. Marcus (1986) *Writing Culture: The Poetics and Politics of Ethnography*. Berkeley: University of California Press.

Corbridge, Stuart (1990) 'Post-Marxism and development studies: beyond the impasse', *World Development*, Vol. 18, No. 5, pp. 623–39.

Devall, Bill (1990) *Simple in Means Rich in Ends: Practising Deep Ecology*. London: Green Print.

Dwyer, Kevin (1979) 'The dialogue of ethnology', *Dialectic Anthropology*, No. 4 (October), pp. 205–24.

— (1991) *Arab Voices: The Human Rights Debate in the Middle East*. London: Routledge.

Eder, Klaus (1990) 'The cultural code of modernity and the problem of nature: a critique of the naturalistic notion of progress', in J. Alexander and P. Sztompak (eds), *Rethinking Progress*. London: Unwin Hyman.

Fabian, Joannes (1983) *Time and the Other: How Anthropology Makes its Object*. New York: Columbia University Press.

Fanon, Frantz (1961) *The Wretched of the Earth*. New York: Penguin.

Fischer, Michael J. and Abedi, Mehdi (1990) *Debating Muslims: Cultural Dialogues in Postmodernity and Tradition*. Madison: University of Wisconsin Press.

Freire, Paulo (1972) *Pedagogy of the Oppressed*. London: Sheed and Ward.

Fukuyama, Francis (1992) *The End of History and the Last Man*. London: Hamilton.

Goulet, Denis (1977) *The Cruel Choice: A New Concept in the Theory of Development*. New York: Athenium.

Gramsci, Antonio (1988) *A Gramsci Reader*. London: Lawrence and Wishart.

Hall, Stuart (1992) 'The West and the rest: discourse and power,' in Stuart Hall and Bram Gleben (eds), *Formations of Modernity*, London: Polity Press.

James, C.L.R (1984) *At the Rendezvous of Victory*. New York: Allison and Busby.

Kabbani, Rana (1986) *Europe's Myths of Orient*. London: Pandora Press.

Kearney, Richard (1988) 'Myth and the critique of tradition', in Alan D. Falconer (ed.), *Reconciling Memories*. Dublin: Columbia Press.

Lehmann, David (1990) 'Introduction to modernity and popular culture', *European Journal of Development Research*, Vol. 2, No. 1, pp. 1–9.

Marcus, George E. and Michael J. Fischer (1986) *Anthropology as Cultural Critique: An Experimental Moment in the Human Sciences*. Chicago: University of Chicago Press.

Mouzelis, Nicos (1988) 'Sociology of development: reflections on the present crisis,' *Sociology*, Vol. 22, No. 1, pp. 23–44.

Nederveen Pieterse, Jan (1990) *Empire and Emancipation: Power and Liberation on a World Scale*. London: Pluto Press.

— (1991) 'Dilemmas of development discourse: the crisis of developmentalism and the comparative method', *Development and Change*, Vol. 22, pp. 5–29.

Ranger, Terence (1983) 'The invention of tradition in colonial Africa', in E.J. Hobsbawm and T. Ranger (eds), *The Invention of Tradition*. Cambridge: Cambridge University Press.

Rist, Gilbert (1990) '"Development" as part of the modern myth: the Western socio-economic dimension of "development"', *European Journal of Development Alternatives*, Vol. 2, No. 1, pp. 10–21.

Said, Edward (1979) *Orientalism*. New York: Vintage.

— (1981) *Covering Islam: How the Media and the Experts Determine How We See the Rest of the World*. London: Routledge.

— (1985) 'Orientalism reconsidered,' *Race and Class*, Vol. 27, No. 2.

— (1989) 'Representing the colonised: anthropology's interlocutors,' *Critical Inquiry*, Vol. 15 (Winter).

Scott, James (1985) *Forms of Resistance*. New Haven: Yale University Press.

Sklair, Leslie (1988) 'Transcending the impasse: metatheory, theory and empirical research in the sociology of development and underdevelopment', *World Development*, Vol. 16, No. 6, pp. 697–709.

Stavenhagen, Rudolfo (1985) 'The indigenous problematic', *Ifda Dossier*, No. 50 (November/December).

Tomlinson, John (1991) *Cultural Imperialism: A Critical Introduction*. London: Pinter.

Young, Robert (1990) *White Mythologies: Writing History and the West*. London: Routledge.

PART ONE

. . . .

Critical Perspectives

· ·

CHAPTER 2

On Oppositional Postmodernism

Boaventura de Sousa Santos

Perhaps more than ever today, the most important problems faced by each one of the social sciences, far from being specific, are the same as those faced by the social sciences in general. In fact, some of these problems are also faced by the natural and life sciences, and that is what leads me to believe that these problems are the symptoms of a general crisis of the paradigm of modern science. In this chapter I concentrate on a problem that can be formulated by the following question: Why has it become so difficult to construct a critical theory? a question that sociology shares with the remaining social sciences. I shall first formulate the problem and identify the factors that contributed to its particular importance during the 1990s. Next, I shall suggest a few clues for the resolution of this problem. As I do so, what I mean by oppositional postmodernism will be fully outlined.

The problem

The most puzzling problem that the social sciences face today can be formulated like this: if at the close of the century we live in a world where there is so much to be criticized, why has it become so difficult to produce a critical theory? By 'critical theory' I mean the theory that does not reduce 'reality' to what exists. Reality, however conceived it may be, is considered by critical theory as a field of possibilities, the task of critical theory being precisely to define and assess the level of variation that exists beyond what is empirically given. The critical analysis of what exists is based on the assumption that existence does not exhaust the possibilities of existence, and that there are, therefore, alternatives capable of overcoming what is criticizable in what exists. The discomfort, nonconformism or indignation *vis-à-vis* what exists inspires the impulse to theorize its overcoming.

Such situations or conditions as provoke in us discomfort, indignation, and nonconformism do not seem to be lacking in the world today. Suffice it to recall how the great promises of modernity remain unfulfilled or how their fulfilment has turned out to have perverse effects. The promise of equality is a case in point. The advanced capitalist countries, amounting to 21 per cent of the world's population, control 78 per cent of the world production of goods and services and consume 75 per cent of all the energy produced. Textile or electronics workers in the Third World earn twenty times less than workers in Europe and North America doing the same jobs with the same productivity. Since the debt crisis emerged in the early eighties, Third World countries in debt have been contributing to the wealth of the developed countries in liquid terms, by paying them each year an average of $30 billion more than what they get as new loans. During the same period, available food in Third World countries decreased by about 30 per cent. However, the area of soya bean production in Brazil alone would suffice to feed 40 million people if corn and beans were cultivated there instead. More people died of hunger in the twentieth century than in any of the preceding centuries. The gap between rich and poor countries has not stopped widening.

The promise of liberty too is unfulfilled. Violations of human rights in countries living formally in peace and democracy reach overwhelming proportions. Fifteen million children work in bondage in India alone (they are the bonded child labourers); police and prison violence is inordinate in Brazil and Venezuela; racial conflicts in the UK increased almost threefold between 1989 and 1996. Sexual violence against women, child prostitution, street kids, thousands of victims of anti-personnel land mines, discrimination against drug addicts, HIV-positives and homosexuals, trials of citizens by faceless judges in Colombia and Peru, ethnic cleansing and religious chauvinism – such are some of the manifestations of the Diaspora of liberty, such are some of the events through which liberty has been negated or denied.

With respect to the promise of perpetual peace that Kant formulated so eloquently, while in the eighteenth century 4.4 million people died in 68 wars, in the twentieth century 99 million people died in 237 wars. Between the eighteenth and the twentieth century the world population increased 3.6 times, whereas war casualties increased 22.4 times. After the fall of the Berlin Wall and the end of the Cold War, the peace that many thought at long last possible became a cruel mirage in view of the increase of conflicts among states and inside states.

The promise of domination over nature was fulfilled in a perverse way in the destruction of nature and the ecological crisis. Two examples will suffice. During the past fifty years the world has lost about one third of its forests. In spite of the fact that the tropical forest provides 42 per cent of plant biomass and oxygen, 600,000 acres of Mexican forests are destroyed every year. Nowadays, multinational corporations hold the right to fell trees in 12 million acres of the Amazon forest. Desertification and water scarcity are the problems that will most affect Third World countries in the first decade of the twenty-first century. One-fifth of humankind no longer have access to water fit for drinking.

This brief enumeration of the problems that cause us discomfort or indignation should suffice to make us not only question ourselves critically about the nature and moral quality of our society but also search for alternatives theoretically grounded on the answers we give to such questions. Such questioning and searching were always the basis of modern critical theory. Max Horkheimer has defined modern critical theory better than anyone else. Modern critical theory is, above all, a theory epistemologically grounded on the need to overcome the bourgeois dualism between the individual scientist as autonomous producer of knowledge and the totality of the social activity surrounding him. Horkheimer says: 'Reason cannot become transparent to itself as long as men act as members of an organism that lacks reason' (Horkheimer 1972: 208). The irrationality of modern society lies in the fact that society is the product of a particular will, that of capitalism, and not of a general will, 'a united and self-conscious will' (Horkheimer 1972: 208). Hence, critical theory cannot accept such concepts as 'goodness', 'usefulness', 'appropriateness', 'productivity' or 'value' as they are understood by the existing social order, and refuses to conceive of them as nonscientific presuppositions about which nothing can be done. '[T]he critical acceptance of the categories which rule social life contains simultaneously their condemnation' (Horkheimer 1972: 208). This why the identification of critical thought with its society is always full of tensions.

Modern critical theory draws from historical analysis the goals of human activity, particularly the idea of a reasonable social organization capable of fulfilling the needs of the community as a whole. Such goals, though immanent to human work, 'are not correctly grasped by individuals or by the common mind' (Horkheimer 1972: 213). The struggle for such goals is intrinsic to the theory, and hence 'the first consequence of the theory which urges a transformation of society as a whole is only an intensification of the struggle with which the theory is connected' (Horkheimer 1972: 219).

Marx's influence on Horkheimer's conception of modern critical theory is obvious. Indeed, Marxism has been the fundamental supporting basis of critical sociology in the twentieth century. However, critical sociology also has sources in eighteenth-century romanticism, nineteenth-century utopianism, and twentieth-century American pragmatism. It developed along multiple theoretical orientations, such as structuralism, existentialism, psychoanalysis, phenomenology, its most prominent analytical icons being perhaps class, conflict, elite, alienation, domination, exploitation, imperialism, racism, sexism, dependency, world system, liberation theology.

That all these concepts and their theoretical configurations are still today part and parcel of the work of sociologists and social scientists might allow us to think that it is still today as easy or as possible as before to produce critical social theory. But I believe this is not the case. In the first place, many of these concepts no longer have the centrality they used to have, or they have been so much re-elaborated and nuanced in themselves that they have lost much of their critical power. Second, conventional sociology, both in its positivist and its antipositivist guises, managed to make acceptable, as remedy for the crisis of sociology, the critique of critical sociology. In the case of positivist sociology, this critique is based on the idea that the methodological rigour and social usefulness of sociology presuppose that it should concentrate on the analysis of what exists and not on alternatives to what exists; in the case of antipositivist sociology, the critique is based on the idea that social scientists cannot impose their normative preferences because they lack the privileged viewpoint that would allow them to do so.

As a consequence, the question that has always been the starting point for critical theory – Which side are you on? – became for some illegitimate, for others irrelevant, for others still an unanswerable question. Some, believing that they do not have to take sides, have stopped worrying about the question and criticize those who still do; others, perhaps the youngest generation of social scientists, would like to answer the question and take sides, but see sometimes with anguish the seemingly increasing difficulty in identifying alternative positions in relation to which it would be imperative to take sides. They are also the ones most affected by the problem that is my starting point here: why, if there is so much to criticize, perhaps more than ever before, is it so difficult to construct a critical theory?

Possible causes

In what follows I will identify some of the factors that, to my mind, are the cause of the difficulty in constructing a critical theory. Following Horkheimer's position quoted above, modern critical theory conceives of society as a totality, thereby proposing a total alternative to the existing society. Marxist theory is the clearest example. But the concept of society as a totality is a social construction like any other. It is distinguished from rival constructions only by its grounding pre-suppositions: a form of knowledge that is itself total (or absolute) as a condition to grasp totality in a credible way; a single principle of social transformation and a collective agent, likewise a single one, capable of accomplishing it; a well-defined institutional political context allowing for the formulation of struggles deemed credible in the light of the goals they propose. The critique of these presuppositions has been done and I am not going to repeat it here. All I want is to understand the place we ended up in with that critique.

Totalizing knowledge is the knowledge of order over chaos. What in this respect distinguishes functionalist sociology from Marxist sociology is the fact that the former aims at the order of social regulation whereas the latter aims at the order of social emancipation. At the end of the twentieth century, we face disorder – both of social regulation and of emancipation. Our place is in societies that are authoritarian and liber-tarian at the same time.

The last great attempt at producing a modern critical theory was that of Foucault, who addressed precisely the totalizing knowledge of modernity, modern science. Contrary to current opinion, Foucault is, to my mind, a modern, not a postmodern, critic. He represents, paradoxically, both the climax and the collapse of modern critical theory. By pushing to its ultimate consequences the disciplinary power of the panoptic built by modern science, Foucault demonstrates that, in this 'regime of truth', there is no emancipatory way out, since resistance itself becomes a disciplinary power, hence a consented, because internal-ized, oppression.

Foucault's great merit was to show the opacities and silences pro-duced by modern science, thus giving credibility to the search for alternative 'regimes of truth', for other ways of knowing that have been marginalized, suppressed, and discredited by modern science. Our place today is a multicultural place, a place that is constantly engaged in a hermeneutics of suspicion against presumed universalisms or totalities. Multiculturalism has, however, flourished in cultural studies, transdisciplinary configurations that converge the different social sciences as well as literary studies, and where critical knowledge – feminist, antisexist, antiracist, postcolonial knowledge – is steadily being produced.[1]

The single principle of social transformation underlying modern critical theory is based on the inevitability of a socialist future generated by the constant development of the productive forces and the class struggles that signify it. Unlike what happened in previous transitions, a majority, the working class, not a minority, will be the protagonist in overcoming capitalist society. As I said, modern critical sociology has interpreted this principle with great freedom and added sometimes profound revisions. In this respect, modern critical theory shares with conventional sociology two important points. On the one hand, the conception of the historical agent corresponds perfectly to the duality of structure and agency underlying all sociology. On the other, both sociological traditions had the same conception of the relations between nature and society, and both saw in industrialization the midwife of development.

No wonder, then, that in this respect the crisis of modern critical theory becomes largely confused with the crisis of sociology in general. Our position can be summarized thus. First, there is no single principle of social transformation; even those who continue to believe in a socialist future see it as a possible future in competition with other and alternative futures. There are no historical agents nor is there a single form of domination. The faces of domination and oppression are multiple, and many of them, such as patriarchal domination, have been irresponsibly neglected by modern critical theory. Not by chance for the last couple of decades feminist sociology has produced the best critical theory. If the faces of domination are multiple, so must be resistance to it as well as the agents of resistance. In the absence of a single principle, it is not possible to gather all resistance and all agents under the aegis of one common grand theory. More than a common theory, we need a theory of translation capable of making the different struggles mutually intelligible and allowing for the collective actors to talk about the oppressions they resist and the aspirations that mobilize them. Second, industrialization is not the motor of progress nor the midwife of development. On the one hand, industrialization presupposes a retrograde conception of nature in that it misses the relationship between the degradation of nature and the degradation of the society supported by nature. On the other hand, for two thirds of humankind industrialization has brought no development. If by development is meant the growth of GNP and of the wealth of less developed countries so that they can come closer to developed countries, it is easy to show that such a goal is a mirage, for, as I mentioned above, the inequality between rich and poor countries has not ceased to increase. If by development is meant the growth of GNP to grant the populations a better way of life, it is today simple to demonstrate that the welfare of populations does not depend so much on amount as on distribution of wealth. Since the failure or the mirage of development appears today more and more obvious, perhaps rather than looking for models of alternative development the time has come to create alternatives to development. Even the phrase 'the Third World' is increasingly meaningless, and not only because 'the Second World' is no longer there.

In this respect, the crisis of modern critical theory has some disturbing consequences. For a long time, scientific alternatives were unequivocally political alternatives as well, and they were identified by distinct analytical icons that made it easy to distinguish the political fields and their contradictions. The crisis of modern critical theory brought about the crisis of the iconic distinction. The same icons began to be shared by political fields whose opposition was previously well demarcated or, alternatively, hybrid icons were created which eclectically included elements from different fields. Thus, the icon of the opposition capitalism/socialism was in turn replaced by the icon of industrial society, postindustrial society, and at last informational society. The opposition between imperialism and modernization was gradually replaced by the intrinsically hybrid concept of globalization. The opposition revolution/democracy was in almost drastic fashion replaced by the concepts of structural adjustment, and Washington consensus, as well as by the hybrid concepts of participation and sustainable development. By way of this semantic policy the fields stopped having a name and a badge, thus stopping largely to be distinct. Herein lies the difficulty of those who, though willing to take sides, find it hard to identify the fields among which sides must be taken.

The correlative of the difficulty in identifying the fields is the enemy's or adversary's lack of definition or determination, a syndrome that is only reinforced by the discovery of the multiplicity of the above-mentioned oppressions, resistances, and agents. When at the beginning of the nineteenth century the Luddites were breaking the machines that were robbing them of their jobs, it might have been easy to show them that the enemy was not the machines but whoever had the power to buy and use them. Nowadays, the opacity of the enemy or adversary seems to be much greater. Behind the nearest enemy there seems to be always another one. Besides, whoever is behind may also be before. At any rate, virtual space may well be the metaphor for this indeterminacy: the screen before may likewise be behind.

In sum, the difficulties today in constructing a critical theory may be formulated like this. Because they were not fulfilled, the promises of modernity have become problems for which there seems to be no solution. In the meantime, the conditions that brought about the crisis of modern critical theory have not yet become the conditions to overcome the crisis. Hence the complexity of our transitional position, which can be summed up thus: we are facing modern problems for which there are no modern solutions. According to one stance, which might be called 'reassuring postmodernity', the fact that there are no modern solutions indicates that probably there are no modern problems either nor, before them, any promises of modernity. What exists is therefore to be accepted and celebrated. According to another stance, which I designate as 'disquieting or oppositional postmodernity', the disjunction between the modernity of the problems and the post-modernity of the possible solutions must be entirely assumed and turned into a starting point in order to face the challenges of con-structing a postmodern critical theory. The latter is my stance and I cannot but sum it up here in very broad terms.

Towards a postmodern critical theory

One of the failures of modern critical theory was not to have recognized that the reason that criticizes cannot be the same reason that thinks, constructs, and legitimizes that which is criticizable. There is no knowledge in general as there is no ignorance in general. What we ignore is always ignorance of a certain way of knowing; conversely, what we know is always knowledge *vis-à-vis* a certain form of ignorance. Every act of knowing is a trajectory from a point A that we designate as ignorance to a point B that we designate as knowledge.

Within the project of modernity we can distinguish two forms of knowledge: knowledge-as-regulation, whose point of ignorance is called chaos and whose point of knowledge is called order, and knowledge-as-emancipation, whose point of ignorance is called colonialism and whose point of knowledge is called solidarity.[2] Though both forms of know-ledge are inscribed in the matrix of Eurocentric modernity, the truth is that knowledge-as-regulation ended up overriding knowledge-as-emancipation. This was a result of the way in which modern science became hegemonic and was thus institutionalized. By neglecting the epistemological critique of modern science, modern critical theory, though claiming to be a form of knowledge-as-emancipation, rapidly became a form of knowledge-as-regulation.

On the contrary, in a postmodern critical theory, all critical know-ledge must begin by a critique of knowledge itself. In the current phase of paradigmatic transition, postmodern critical theory is constructed on the basis of a marginalized and discredited epistemological tradition of modernity, what I call knowledge-as-emancipation. In this form of knowledge, ignorance is colonialism, colonialism being the conception of the other as object, hence not recognizing the other as subject. According to this form of knowledge, to know is to recognize the other as subject of knowledge, to progress by bringing the other up from the status of object to that of subject. Such is the way of knowing as recognition that I designate as solidarity.

We are so used to conceiving of knowledge as a principle of order over things and people that we find it difficult to imagine a form of knowledge that might work as a principle of solidarity. However, such difficulty is a challenge that must be faced. Knowing what happened to the alternatives proposed by modern critical theory, we cannot rest content with merely thinking alternatives. We need an alternative thinking of alternatives.

What I mean by knowledge-as-emancipation may become clearer if, resorting to a kind of thought experiment, we go back to the origins of modern science. At the origin of modern science, in the seventeenth century, the coexistence of regulation and emancipation at the core of the enterprise of knowledge advancement is transparent. The new knowledge of nature – that is, to overcome the threatening chaos of unmastered natural processes by bringing them under a principle of order sound enough to dominate them – has no purpose other than to liberate human beings from the fetters of whatever has been previously considered to be natural: God, tradition, customs, community, ranks. Liberal society is emerging as a society of individuals, free and equal, and equally endowed with freedom of choice. The emancipatory character of this new societal paradigm lies in this extremely broad principle of recognition of the other as an equal, such reciprocal recognition being nothing else but the modern principle of solidarity. As modern science advances in its regulation of nature it also promotes the emancipation of humankind. But this virtuous circle is fraught with tensions and contradictions. To begin with, what counts as nature and what counts as humankind was itself problematic and the object of debate. Seen from our perspective today, nature at that early moment is a much broader concept, including sections of what we would call today 'humankind': slaves, indigenous peoples, women, children. These groups were not included in the circle of reciprocity because they were considered to be nature, or closer to nature than humankind in its presumed proper sense. To know them was to regulate them, to bring their chaotic and irrational behaviour under a principle of order.

Moreover, the liberal society that was then emerging was also a market society, a capitalist society. In this society the powers of individuals are premised upon access to enough land or capital to work on, access, that is, to means of labour. If the means of labour are concentrated in the hands of a few, he who has no access to them has to pay a price to get it. As Macpherson says:

[I]f he can get some access but cannot get it for nothing, then his powers are reduced by the amount of them that he has to hand over to get the necessary access. This is exactly the situation most men are in, and necessarily so, in the capitalist market society. They must, in the nature of the system, permit a net transfer of part of their powers to those who own the means of labor. (Macpherson 1982: 43)

This net transfer of power as a structural feature of the liberal capitalist society became a source of conflict. It posed a problem of order – to the extent that conflicts caused chaos – as much as it posed a problem of solidarity, to the extent that large sections of populations were deprived of effective reciprocity and hence of real recognition as being free and equal. However, when in the nineteenth century the social sciences started their process of institutionalization the issue of order was privileged to the detriment of the issue of solidarity. The workers became 'dangerous classes', prone to outbursts of irrational behaviour. Knowledge of nature provided the model for the knowledge of society, and so knowledge in general became knowledge-as-regulation.

My plea for the reinvention of knowledge-as-emancipation implies a revisitation of the principle of solidarity as well as of the principle of order. As regards the principle of solidarity, I conceive of it as both the guiding principle and the always incomplete product of knowledge and normative action. Knowledge becomes a question of ethics, meaning that, since there is no universal ethics, there is no universal knowledge. There are knowledges – different ways of knowing. Both alternatives of knowledge and alternatives of action must be searched for, either where they have been most obviously suppressed or where they have managed to survive, in however marginalized or discredited a form. In either case, they have to be searched for in the South, the South being my metaphor for human suffering under global capitalism (Santos 1995: 506). The social scientist is neither to be dissolved in the activist nor to keep his identity without reference to the activist.

As regards the principle of order, knowledge-as-emancipation excels in a hermeneutics of suspicion vis-à-vis order, and reassesses chaos, rather than as a form of ignorance, as a form of knowledge. This reassessment is guided by the need to reduce the discrepancy between the capacity to act and the capacity to predict, engendered by modern science while knowledge-as-regulation. 'Chaos invites us to a praxis that insists on immediate effects, and warns against distant effects, a style of action that privileges a transparent, localized connection between action and its consequences. That is, chaos invites us to a prudent knowledge' (Santos 1995: 26). The adoption of knowledge-as-emancipation has three implications for the social sciences in general and for sociology in particular.

The first one can be formulated as follows: from monoculturalism towards multiculturalism. Since solidarity is a form of knowledge that is acquired by means of the recognition of the other, the other can only be known as a producer of knowledge. Hence, all knowledge-as-emancipation is necessarily multicultural. The construction of multi-cultural knowledge faces two difficulties: silence and difference. The global dominion of modern science as knowledge-as-regulation brought about the destruction of many forms of knowledge, particularly those that were peculiar to peoples subjected to Western colonialism. Such destruction provoked silences that rendered unpronounceable the needs and aspirations of the peoples or social groups whose forms of know-ledge were subjected to destruction. Let us not forget that under the guise of universal values authorized by reason, the reason of a race, sex, and social class was in fact imposed. Thus, the question is: how is it possible to engage in a multicultural dialogue when some cultures were reduced to silence and their forms of seeing and knowing the world have become unpronounceable? In other words, how is it possible to make silence speak without having it necessarily speak the hegemonic language that would have it speak? These questions constitute a great challenge for a multicultural dialogue. The unpronounceable silences and needs are graspable only by means of a sociology of absences capable of advancing through a comparison between the available hegemonic and counterhegemonic discourses as well as through the analysis of the hierarchies among them and the empty spaces such hierarchies create. Silence is, therefore, a construction that asserts itself as the symptom of a blockade, a potentiality that cannot be developed.

The second difficulty facing multicultural knowledge is difference. There is knowledge, hence solidarity, only in differences. Now, difference without intelligibility leads to incommensurability and, lastly, to indiffer-ence. Hence the need for a theory of translation as an integral part of postmodern critical theory. It is through translation and what I call diatopical hermeneutics (Santos 1995: 340) that a need, an aspiration, a practice in a given culture can be made comprehensible and intelligible for another culture. Knowledge-as-emancipation does not aim at a grand theory, rather at a theory of translation that may become the epistemo-logical basis of emancipatory practices, all of them finite and incomplete and therefore sustainable only so long as they become networked. Multiculturalism is one of those hybrid concepts I mentioned above.

There are regulatory as well as emancipatory conceptions of multi-culturalism. It is up to postmodern critical theory to specify the conditions of either type of conception, a task that is beyond the scope of these comments.

The second challenge of knowledge-as-emancipation can be formulated in the following way: from heroic expertise to edifying knowledge. Modern science, and hence modern critical theory as well, resides in the assumption that knowledge is valid regardless of the conditions that made it possible. Consequently, its application is likewise independent of all the conditions that are not indispensable to guaranteeing the technical operationality of its application. Such operationality is constructed by means of a process that I designate as trans-scaling and which consists in producing and hiding an imbalance of scale between the technical action and the technical consequences. By this imbalance the large scale (detailed map) of action is juxtaposed to the small scale (undetailed map) of consequences. Trans-scaling is crucial in this paradigm of knowledge. Since modern science has developed a great capacity for action but not a correspondent capacity for prediction, the consequences of a scientific action tend to be less scientific than the scientific action itself.

This imbalance together with the trans-scaling that hides it is what makes possible the technical heroism of the scientist. Once decontextualized, all knowledge is potentially absolute. The kind of professionalization prevailing today is the outcome of such decontextualization. Even though the situation seems to be changing, it is still quite easy today to produce or apply knowledge while escaping the consequences thereof. The personal tragedy of knowledge can only now be observed in the biographies of the great creators of modern science at the end of the nineteenth and beginning of the twentieth century.

Postmodern critical theory starts from the presupposition that knowledge is always contextualized by the conditions that make it possible and that it only progresses so long as it changes such conditions in a progressive way. Thus, knowledge-as-emancipation is earned by assuming the consequences of its impact. And that is why it is a prudent, finite knowledge that keeps the scale of actions as much as possible on a level with the scale of consequences.

The professionalization of knowledge is necessary, but only in so far as the shared and deprofessionalized application of knowledge is made possible. At the basis to this mutual responsibilization there lies an ethical commitment. In this regard we live today in a paradoxical society. The discursive affirmation of values is all the more necessary to the extent that dominant social practices render impossible the realization of such values. We live in a society dominated by what Saint Thomas Aquinas called 'habitus principiorum', the habit to proclaim principles so as not to be compelled to abide by them. It should, therefore, come as no surprise that postmodern theory relativizes values and hence strongly partakes of deconstruction, as prominently in Derrida. But oppositional postmodernism cannot stop at deconstruction, for deconstruction pushed to its limits deconstructs the very possibility of resistance and alternatives. From this derives the third challenge of knowledge-as-emancipation to the social sciences in general and to sociology in particular.

These challenges can be formulated thus: from conformist action to rebellious action. Modern critical theory, just like conventional sociology, has focused on the dichotomy structure / agency and constructed upon it its theoretical and analytical framework. I do not question the usefulness of the dichotomy but note that in time it became more a debate on order than a debate on solidarity. That is to say, it was absorbed by the epistemological field of knowledge-as-regulation.

From the point of view of postmodern critical theory we must focus on another duality: the duality of conformist and rebellious action.[3] Both in the realm of production and in the realm of consumption capitalist society appears increasingly as a fragmentary, plural and multiple society, whose borders seem to be there only to be trespassed. The relative replacement of the provision of goods and services by the market of goods and services creates fields of choice that are easily confused with exercises of autonomy and liberation of desires. All this occurs within the narrow limits of selecting choices and having the means to make them effective. However, such limits are easily constructed symbolically as real opportunities, be they loyalty to choices or credit consumption. Under such conditions, conformist action easily passes for rebellious action. By the same token, the rebellious action appears to be so easy that it readily turns into a form of alternative conformism.

It is in this context that postmodern critical theory attempts to reconstruct the idea and the practice of emancipatory social transformation. The most important task of postmodern theory is to inquire into the specific forms of socialization, education, and work that promote rebellious or, on the contrary, conformist subjectivities.

The three challenges of knowledge-as-emancipation that I have identified have significant implications for the future of sociology or, if you like, for the sociology of the future. How such challenges will be faced and the impact they will have in the current practice of the social sciences, remain to be seen. But they are unavoidable issues. Indeed, if we want alternatives, we must also want the society where such alternatives are possible.

Conclusion

I grant that it is not difficult to see in oppositional postmodernism more of a modernist than a postmodernist stance. This is partly because the dominant version of postmodern theory has been much more of a celebratory rather than an oppositional kind. This fact alone might explain why such a serious scholar as Terry Eagleton engaged in a rash and superficial critique of postmodernism (Eagleton 1996). Since celebratory postmodernism reduces the idea of social transformation to the notion of accelerated repetition and refuses to distinguish between emancipatory or progressive and regulatory or conservative versions of hybridity, it has been easy for modernist critics to claim for modern critical theory the monopoly of the idea of a better society and normative action. Oppositional postmodernism, on the other hand, radically disputes these monopolies. The idea of a better society is central to it but, contrary to modern critical theory, it conceives of socialism as a radical democratic aspiration, one among other possible futures, neither inevitable nor ever to be fully accomplished. It also claims a normativity which both posits sides and establishes criteria to choose among them. However, contrary to modern critical theory, oppositional postmodernism conceives of such normativity as being constructed from the bottom up and in a participatory and multicultural fashion. Given the crisis of modern critical theory, in spite of Habermas's brilliant *tour de force*, it is my contention that the antagonism between oppositional and celebratory postmodernism is much more pregnant of political and theoretical consequences than the antagonism between modernism and postmodernism. Unfortunately, the former antagonism has been obfuscated by the latter due to the awkwardly convergent discourse of reconstructed modernists and hyperdeconstructed postmodernists.

Notes

1. Elsewhere, I have specified the conditions of an emancipatory, progressive conception of multiculturalism in the field of human rights (Santos 1997: 13).
2. I develop this distinction in great detail elsewhere (Santos 1995: 7–55).
3. The outline of a theory of history centred around this duality can be read in Santos 1998.

References

Eagleton, Terry (1996) *The Illusions of Postmodernism*. Oxford: Blackwell.

Horkheimer, Max (1972) *Critical Theory: Selected Essays*. New York: Herder and Herder.

Macpherson, C.B. (1982) *The Real World of Democracy*. New York: Oxford University Press. Originally published in 1966.

Santos, Boaventura de Sousa (1995) *Toward a New Common Sense: Law, Science and Politics in the Paradigmatic Transition*. New York: Routledge.

— (1997) 'Toward a multicultural conception of human rights', *Zeitschrift für Rechtssoziologie*, 18: 1–15. Also available as Working Paper Series on Political Economy of Legal Change, No. 2, Global Studies Program, University of Wisconsin-Madison (December 1996).

— (1998) 'The fall of the *Angelus Novus*: beyond the modern game of roots and options', *Current Sociology*, Vol. 46, No. 2 (April 1998), pp. 81–118.

CHAPTER 3

Development and the Locations of Eurocentrism

Ziauddin Sardar

The West

The real power of the West is not located in its economic muscle and technological might. Rather, it resides in its power to define. The West defines what is, for example, freedom, progress and civil behaviour; law, tradition and community; reason, mathematics and science; what is real and what it means to be human. The non-Western civilizations have simply to accept these definitions or be defined out of existence. To understand Eurocentrism we thus have to deconstruct the definitional power of the West. Eurocentrism is located wherever there is the defining influence of Europe, or more appropriately, the generic form of Europe – 'the West'. Wherever there is the West, there is Europe, and Eurocentrism is not usually that far behind. So, where is the West?

As a civilization, the West is, of course, everywhere: the Western civilization is not located in a geographical space but in these days of globalization it envelops the globe with its desires, images, politics, and consumer and cultural products. As a worldview, the West is the dominant outlook of the planet. Thus, Eurocentrism is not simply *out there* – in the West. It is also *in here* – in the non-West. As a concept and a worldview, the West has colonized the intellectuals in non-European societies. Eurocentrism is thus just as rampant and deep in non-Western societies as in Europe and the USA: intellectuals, academics, writers, thinkers, novelists, politicians and decision-makers in Asia, Africa and Latin America use the West, almost instinctively, as the standard for judgements and as the yardstick for measuring the social and political progress of their own societies. The non-West thus promotes Euro-centrism, both wittingly and unwittingly, and colludes in its own victimization as well as in maintaining the global system of inequality.

But Eurocentrism is 'in here' in another way. And it is related to my second question: when was the West? As a conceptual and instrumental category, the West is located in the history of colonization, from Columbus's 'discovery' of the 'New World' to the present day. Rampant Eurocentrism is easily recognizable in colonial constructions of the 'lazy native', the licentious and barbaric Muslim, the shifty, effeminate and untrustworthy Hindu and other representations of the non-West in Orientalist fiction, travel literature and scholarly explorations. But the time dimension of the West extends from colonialism to modernity, modernity to postmodernism and to the future. Modernity's construction of tradition as an impediment to advancement, of the non-West as 'developing societies' and 'Third World', and of instrumental rationality as justification for progress are just as Eurocentric as the plainly racist categorization of colonialism. This variety of Eurocentrism, like its colonial counterpart, is now also widely recognized. What is not appreciated, however, is the Eurocentric nature of postmodernism. This is largely due to the fact that postmodernism emerged as a reaction against modernity and self-avowedly tried to shape itself in pluralistic terms. But the basic premises of postmodernism are just as Eurocentric as modernity, if not even more so. For example, postmodernism's overriding concern with the demolition of grand narratives such as Religion, Tradition and History are detrimental to the very existence of the non-West for it is these very narratives that make the non-West what it is: not West. The insistence that everything is meaningless and that nothing can give meaning and direction to our lives is a distinctively Western view that finds no echo whatsoever in non-Western cultures, societies and civilizations. Moreover, postmodernism's obsession with irony, ridicule and cynicism becomes an instrument for further marginalizing and hence writing off the non-West. A discourse that seeks to give representation to the Other, to give a voice to the voiceless, paradoxically seeks to absorb the non-West in 'bourgeoisie liberalism' and the secular history of the West. it is not just that postmodernism continues the Eurocentric journey of modernity and colonialism: we get higher, more sophisticated forms of Eurocentrism as we move towards the future.[1]

The time dimension of the West is thus not limited to the past and the present: the West is also the future. The West was not just in history; it is remade in the present and reconstructed in the future. At each stage, it is internalized more and more and becomes an integral part of the global consciousness. As such, the future has been colonized by the West.[2] Eurocentrism is thus located not just in the past and the present; we need to appreciate that it is also located in the future.

The future is defined in the image of the West. There is an in-built

Western momentum that is taking us towards a single, determined future. In this Eurocentric vision of the future, technology is projected as an autonomous and desirable force: as the advertisement for a brand of toothpaste declares, we are heading towards 'a brighter, whiter future'. Its desirable products generate more desire; its second-order side effects require more technology to solve them. There is thus a perpetual feedback loop. One need not be a technological determinist to appreciate the fact that this self-perpetuating momentum has locked us in a linear, one-dimensional trajectory that has actually foreclosed the future for the non-West. An illusion of accelerated movement is produced to create an illusion of inevitability and to shroud the Eurocentric dimension of the exercise. Conventionally, the colonization of the future was known as 'Westernization'. Now it goes under the rubric of 'globalization'. It may be naïve to equate the former with the latter, but the end product is the same: the process that is transforming the world into the proverbial 'global village', rapidly shrinking distances, compressing space and time, is also shaping the world in the image of a single culture and civilization.

In postmodern fashion, the notion of development collapses the notion of time and space inherent in the Western power of definition. All developing societies are caught in a time warp where they can never really 'catch up' with the West. The present of the non-West is the past of the West – sometimes the distant, preindustrial revolution past of the developed world. The future of the developing countries is the present of the West. When the non-West reaches the point of arrival where it becomes 'developed', it has already become the past of the West. Thus the developing world cannot even live in the transcendent present, or as Vinay Lal puts it, 'thrive in the being-in-itself, since its present was already transcended somewhere else: even the much-emulated fakir, saint, and yogi of the East will have his or her renewed birth in the developed West'. The non-West thus has no real future 'since its future is already known to Europe and America':

> ... indeed, the developed world lives the future of the developing world, and lives it better just as it knows that world, having had the advantage of experiential wisdom, better than do the natives. As the lodestar shines in the West, the Orient must orient itself towards the Occident: it must forget that it is the Orient. (Lal 1997)

The mechanics of development are thus the ideal instrument for the Eurocentric colonization of time. With a single definitional category, the West can, and indeed has, written off the past, present and the future of the non-West.

Eurocentrism

What holds the past, present and the future of the non-West in the grip of Eurocentrism? It is the categories of thought that have their origins in colonialism, modernity and postmodernism which have been internalized by Western as well as by non-Western thinkers, scholars and writers. Many categories of Western thought, from political concepts to analytical tools, stem from European colonial cultural milieus and are therefore intrinsically Eurocentric. Consider, for example, the colonial notion of 'civilization'. The idea of civilization, as Michael Adas (1989) shows so brilliantly in his *Machines as the Measure of Men*, was intrinsically linked to technology during the colonial age. The advent of the 'industrial revolution' led to the rapid spread of machines throughout Europe. As machines invaded more and more aspects of life in Europe, they also became the instruments for expressing its social and political culture. Europeans came to believe that because of their machines their culture was unique and their civilization superior to all others; or the machines proved that they were right. Other civilizations were thus measured according to the level of their technology, or how they related to and relied on machines. Machines came to be seen as essential to civilization; indeed, machines were civilizers. A culture without machines was thus naturally uncivilized. Non-Western cultures were thus ranked in order of their technological capabilities. This idea not only survived in modernity, it became a fundamental component of modernization. In order to modernize and become fully civilized, non-Western cultures had to embrace Western technology.

A similar Eurocentrism exists in the modern idea of nation-state. Modernist political theory has seen the nation-state as the only desirable and legitimate form of political organization. A people without a nation-state are thus a people without a home. The persecution of Jews in Europe was a product of this notion: as a stateless people the perpetual 'homelessness' of the Jews was a major problem for Europe. Without a nation-state, the Jews were not a legitimate community and could not participate in the universal aspirations of man to fight for King and Country. The Jews become a real people only when they acquired a nation-state. The gypsies present Europe with a similar problem. As a travelling people, they have no home, no nation-state to call their own. They are thus despised and seen as a sinister enemy.

The Eurocentric idea of nation-state has played havoc with non-Western societies. Islam, for example, is an intrinsically universal creed and worldview. It seeks to break all barriers of race, tribe and language and insists on the equality of all before God. It recognizes no geographical boundaries. Virtually all of the Sunnah, the life of the Prophet Muhammad, was a struggle for eradicating such barriers and establishing a community based on equality and justice. Islam and nationalism are thus an antithesis. When the universalist idea of Islam is confined to the geographical boundaries of the state, two contradictory ideas come together to create a pathological anomaly. The notion of 'Islamic state' is the creation of those who have internalized the modernist, Western idea of the nation-state. This is the genesis of Islamic fundamentalism. In Islamic fundamentalism, the state is fundamental to the vision of Islam. Islam is thus equated with a state, the state thus appropriates the power of religion, and an absolutist authoritarianism follows (Manzoor 1991). As such, Islamic fundamentalism is purely a product of modernity; it has no counterpart in Islamic history.

As a reaction to this misuse of religion, postmodernism posits 'liberal secularism' as its theory of salvation. In this category of Eurocentric thought, secularism is seen as the only guarantor of pluralism and freedom. Quite apart from the fact that this transforms 'liberal secularism' into a grand narrative, thus undermining the basis of postmodernism, the notion of 'liberal secularism' undermines the non-Western concepts of freedom and denies the pluralistic history of the non-West. In non-Western cultures, the notions of freedom incorporate the idea of freedom from basic needs such as hunger and housing, and subordination of freedom for higher goals such as community and tradition. The postmodern liberal perspective sees this egalitarian approach of non-Western cultures as denying the basic characteristics of freedom – the way freedom has been defined by the West. We can see that in both classical and modern definitions of freedom, people with needs are excluded. In his famous *Essay on Liberty*, John Stuart Mill excluded 'the backward nations', women and children from the rights to liberty; and John Rawls (1971), in his celebrated *Theory of Justice*, acknowledges that societies where the basic needs of the individuals are not fulfilled do not fit into his framework of liberty. Western ideas of freedom thus filter the vast majority of humankind out of any notion of freedom. Liberalism also has a serious problem with the notion of 'community', for belonging to a community consciously demands some discipline and sacrifice. Indeed, no community can exist if every individual goes his or her own way and defines his or her own morality. Postmodern liberalism thus promotes the cultural anarchy of individualism against the non-Western aspirations for community and tradition. Moreover, the argument that religious worldviews cannot sustain plurality is parallel to the colonial suggestion that Other cultures are not civilized. The Islamic heritage of communal concerns and social consciousness, for example, allowed independent non-Muslim cultures to flourish in Islamic Spain and pluralism to bloom, in more recent times, in Bosnia and today in Malaysia. In contrast, Western individualism and liberal secularism have led to the destruction of numerous native cultures – Tasmanian Aboriginal and Native American tribes to give just two examples – as well as to anti-Semitism and other forms of racism in recent years. Indeed, liberal secularism is unable to deal easily with any kind of collective identity except those defined by geography. It is not surprising, then, that postmodern liberalism is happy only when the non-Western cultures ditch their traditions and sacred notions and subscribe fully to the creed of secularism.

All these Eurocentric categories – liberal secularism, freedom, nation-state and civilization – play an intrinsic role in development. For the idea of development to have any meaning, there must be an evaluative scale. Development must propose that there are nations that have embraced Western technology enough to be developed; there are other nations on a slightly lower scale of civilization that are developing; and there are still other nations that, steeped in religion and tradition, reject all forms of liberalism and secularism and thus doggedly remain underdeveloped (a testament to the Oriental laziness and barbarism so inherent in the Other). Numerous attempts have been made to do away with this evaluative scale but to no effect, for they are integral to the whole notion of development. We can use the terms 'First World' and 'Third World' (the Second World now being eclipsed), or describe the developed nations as 'post-industrial societies', or as nations in the throes of 'advanced capitalism' or an 'information revolution' and the non-West as merely 'industrializing', but we cannot expunge the Euro-centric notion out of development. Development continues to mean what it has always meant: a standard by which the West measures the non-West.

The disciplines

If Eurocentrism is intrinsic in the way we think and conceptualize, it is also inherent in the way we organize knowledge. Virtually all the disciplines of social sciences, from economics to anthropology, emerged when Europe was formulating its worldview, and virtually all are geared to serving the needs and requirements of Western society and promoting its outlook. Eurocentrism is entrenched in the way these disciplines are structured, the concepts and categories they use for analysis, and the way progress is defined within the disciplines (Joseph *et al.* 1990). Of course, disciplines have evolved and changed with time.

But just as modernity represents a more sophisticated form of Euro-centrism than colonialism, and postmodernism refines it even further, so the evolution of disciplines has made them more and not less Eurocentric. But whereas in the colonial shape of these disciplines Eurocentrism was overt and obvious, in their modernist and postmodern incarnations Eurocentrism is more deeply embedded and therefore not so easily discerned.

There is nothing that says social and physical reality is laid out as defined by the disciplinary structure of the Western knowledge system. The idea that reality is compartmentalized as 'physics' and 'sociology', 'religion' and 'politics', 'law' and 'ethics' is not based on some universal axiom; rather, it is a product of the worldview of the West. When the West wanted to reduce physical reality into smaller and smaller parts, remove each part from its context, and then study it as an artificial construction, it called the process 'physics'. When it desired to study its own society, it called it 'sociology'. When it wanted to study other societies, it dubbed the study 'anthropology'. Each discipline had a different function. The object of physics was to conquer nature, the purpose of sociology was to understand Western societies, the business of anthropology was to control and manage Other cultures. But the overall narrative was the same: to perpetuate the worldview of the West. This narrative still informs all disciplines. Thus Eurocentrism is embedded in the very structure of knowledge and the construction of individual disciplines. Just because these disciplines are accepted and practised throughout the world does not mean that they are universally valid. As I have written elsewhere:

> ... burgers and coke are eaten and drunk throughout the world but one would hardly classify them as a universally embraced and acceptable food: what the presence of burgers and coke in every city and town in the world demonstrates is not their universality but the power and dominance of the culture that has produced them. Disciplines too are like burgers and coke: they are made not in heaven nor do they exist out there in some 'reality' but are socially constructed and develop and grow within specific worldviews and cultural milieus. Neither nature nor human activities are divided into watertight compartments marked 'sociology', 'political science' or 'eco-nomics'. All those disciplines ... are culturally specific: they are all products of a particular culture and a particular way of looking at the world and are hierarchically subordinate to that culture and worldview. They do not have autonomous existence of their own but have meaning largely in the world-view of their origins and evolution. (Sardar 1996)

It is not surprising that many modern disciplines have no real mean-ing in non-Western cultures. What, for example, would anthropology mean from the perspective of Australian Aborigine scholars? Should they do anthropology to manage and control themselves? Or should they do anthropology to promote their exoticism? Or should they do anthropology on Western societies? Clearly, in an Australian Aborigine perspective, anthropology is an absurd entity; indeed, it has no right to exist from any non-Western perspective. It is interesting to note that there is no non-Western counterpart of anthropology: a discipline that studies the Occident. To give another example: in Islam, the discipline of law *per se* does not exist as law; ethics and morality are one and the same thing and are collectively described as 'the Shariah'. Now the word *shariah* is frequently mistranslated as 'Islamic law' so that it could be reduced to a Western discipline. In fact, *shariah* means a way to a watering hole: it represents the moral and ethical quest of a Muslim society, a quest that requires them to follow certain Qur'anic laws and frame new ones according to their absolute reference frame. But under the Shariah, law is always subordinate to ethics and morality so it makes no sense for Muslim civilization to have a discipline called 'law'. Moreover, one would search in vain for a category called 'ethics' within the Muslim civilization as it does not exist as a separate entity: to study ethics is to study the Shariah.

The structure of modern knowledge, and its divisions into various disciplines, is a direct reflection of the Western worldview. How this worldview perceived reality and what it considered to be its civilizational problems came to be crystallized as disciplines. Orientalism, to give an example, evolved because Western civilization perceived Islam as a 'problem'. Islam presented three problems to Western Christianity. Why was there a need for a new Arabian prophet when God's own son had died on the Cross to bring salvation and redeem humanity? Why was classical Islam intellectually so much more advanced than Christian Europe? What military challenge did Islam pose to Christendom? These problems became the foundations of the intellectual discipline that came to be known as Orientalism; to this day, all Orientalist studies of Islam reflect these concerns (with secularism taking the place of Christianity). Economics was based on the reality of eighteenth-century England, incorporating both the religious as well as the philosophical beliefs of the period. These beliefs were based on a 'whatever is, is right' worldview. Adam Smith, for example, made the religious and philosophical optimism of Europe the basis for his economic theories. He assumed that market forces operated unhindered, evaporating all discord from the society. The invisible hand of the market transformed all baneful forces into common good. Islam, on the other hand, did not consider the market to be totally benign and beneficial. Indeed, Islam insisted on checking market forces by outlawing all forms of usury and introducing into the economic framework specific moral institutions such as *hisbah* (whose function was to ensure that hoarding, monopoly and other activities against the public interest – *istislah* – were checked).

As a discipline, development too has been shaped by the cultural forces of the West. It evolved because the West saw the non-West as a problem. How could the newly independent non-Western countries be made to look like a pale imitation of the West? How could the non-West be made into a viable market for the goods and technologies of the West? How could the non-West, after centuries of colonialism, be dragged into modernity? A fundamental tenet of classical development economics was the notion of modernization. Modernization was defined as the process by which a society comes to be characterized by a belief in the rational and scientific control of man's physical and social environment and the application of technology to that end. Despite the fact that the overwhelming majority of the population of the newly independent countries was based in rural areas, urbanization was seen as one of the main indicators of modernization. In a noted study of the late fifties, Daniel Lerner (1958) used urbanization as an 'index of development' to construct a matrix containing data on urbanization, along with literacy, voting and media participation and then used it to calculate the modernization rate of the Middle East countries. The higher the level of urbanization, the more 'modern' the society. Moreover, agriculture was seen as a rather unimportant activity for the new states; it was argued that the only route to modernization was through industrialization. Lerner's analysis led him and many others to conclude that the traditional society was dead. In the time-honoured fashion of Eurocentrism, tradition was demonized and seen as an impediment to modernization and development. Non-Western countries were encouraged to ditch their traditional lifestyles, beliefs and value systems in favour of modern norms and values. This analysis, and the policies based on it, led to massive migrations from the rural areas and destroyed the agricultural bases of most non-Western states. The little industry that was established in the 'developing countries' faced immense production problems. The machinery, the spare parts, the skilled staff and sometimes even the raw materials had to be imported. Unemployment rose rapidly. Wealth became concentrated in fewer and fewer hands, and most non-Western nations plunged into deeper poverty (Nandy 1988; Trainer 1989; Wilkinson 1973).

Of course, development has gone through many transformations since the fifties. In the sixties, development became associated with social concerns and was meant to be comprehensive. In the seventies the cultural dimension of development came to be considered as important as economic growth; emphasis was also placed on self-reliance. It was argued that nations and people should have the capacity for autonomous decision-making and implementation in all aspects of the development process. In the eighties, environment and ecological sustainability became the main themes of development. The development process, it was suggested, should take the finiteness of resources and the fragility of the global system into consideration. In the eighties and nineties, globalization came into vogue. 'Liberalization' and 'open markets' became the driving force of development. But at each stage, the reshaping of development economics reflected the agenda of the West. And its main thrust, that the non-West should reflect the growth patterns of the West, remained intact. Indeed, the underlying dynamic had to remain intact if the discipline was to maintain its integrity. Thus no matter how development is redefined, how it is hedged and confined with new ideas and notions, its essential characteristics remain the same. As a discipline, development is intrinsically Eurocentric. It can only lead to further subjugation of the non-West.

Science and technology

The ideology of science and technology is the most formidable of all forces that keep development entrenched and ensure that Eurocentrism continues unabated. It is a rationality of domination. The intention of such seventeenth-century thinkers as Descartes and Bacon, the fathers of modern science, was to investigate external nature while leaving to religion the task of specifying the rules of social conduct. But through Comte and others, scientific method became absolutized as the basis for social reconstruction in a 'positive' manner. By basing social reconstruction on scientifically certain grounds, they raised science and technology to the level of an absolute utopia, the perfect fusion of unlimited power and good to which all willingly submit, hence reconciling cultural and social conflicts. Although science and technology remain limited by real interests and structures of power, they claim to be one over-arching power. They thus take on the classical form of ideology, being an inversion of reality. Scientific and technocratic consciousness maintains the status quo and legitimizes the present structures within nations and between nations (Sardar 1988; Mendelssohn 1976; Sangwan 1991; Harding 1993). It does not project a future time when men's hopes will be fulfilled. Rather, it tells us that the future is already here in essentials, if not in full maturity. That future comes, then, as incremental addition of the products of science and technology rather than as a structural transformation. It is the end of transcendental hope. The only course open is development along the well-trodden and true path of the industrialized countries.

Recent work in the sociology of knowledge and history and philosophy of science has exposed the ideological and cultural bias of science (Fuller 1997; Rose 1994; Knorr-Cetina 1981; Latour and Woolgar 1979). Here, I am concerned only to show how deeply Eurocentrism is embedded in what is seen to be objective and universally valid.

Let us begin with a consideration of mathematics. Given that mathematics is seen as the most objective, neutral and universal of all disciplines, it is difficult to comprehend its Eurocentric dimensions – indeed, even to concede it could be value-laden and biased towards any culture. But, as George Gheverghese Joseph has shown so brilliantly, 'in reality, not only has mathematics in the Western tradition been a vehicle for hierarchical values but also, in the case of British education, mathematics has compounded the Eurocentric biases of the "Western" approach with those congenial to the imperial experience' (Joseph 1995, 1990). As in the case of other branches of knowledge, colonialism first suppressed and made invisible non-Western forms of mathematics and then constructed the fable that mathematics was in fact a European invention that it brought to the colonized Other as a civilizing gift. The colonial education system reinforced the idea that it was quite unthinkable for a non-Western culture or civilization to produce any form of mathematical knowledge. This despite the fact that the West borrowed all it knew about mathematics from Islam and India.

The West defined mathematics, just as it defined other forms of knowledge, in a specifically Eurocentric way. This definition ensured that certain non-Western notions of mathematics could not be included in mathematics as it came to be seen the West. Mathematics was reformulated as a deductive, aprioristic system, that proceeded from axiomatic foundations and revealed the underlying reality of the physical universe. In non-Western worldviews, mathematics is a purely human invention. Like music or literature, it is a product of human mind. We invent it, we use it, but we do not discover it. It has a practical and social function. The West, however, elevated mathematics into Platonic reality: it really exists, there is a pi in the sky, laws of physics are laid down in heaven in mathematical formulae and mathematics simply discover them. This approach elevates mathematics pretty close to God in traditional theology. Mathematics is part of the world, but it also transcends it. It must exist before and after the universe. Most scientists and mathematicians operate as if Platonism is true, regardless of whether they believe that it is. In contrast:

The Indian or Chinese concept of mathematics is very different. Its aim is not to build an imposing edifice on a few self-evident axioms, but to validate a result by any method, including visual demonstrations. Some of the most impressive works in Indian and Chinese mathematics (the summations of complex mathematical series, the use of the Pascal triangle in solutions of higher-order numerical equations, and the derivations of infinite series and 'proofs' of the so-called Pythagorean theorem) involve the use of visual demonstrations that are not formulated with reference to any formal deductive system. Furthermore, the Indian view concerning the nature of mathematical objects, like numbers, is based on a framework developed by Indian logicians (and linguists), and differs significantly at the foundational level from the set-theory universe of modern mathematics. Prime among [the differences] are an idealist rejection of any practical, material(ist) basis for mathematics – from which stems the tendency to view mathematics as a value-free pursuit, detached from any social and political concerns – and an elitist perspective that sees mathematical work as the exclusive province of a pure, high-minded, nearly priestly caste removed from mundane preoccupations and operating in a superior intellectual sphere. (Joseph 1995)

So even something that is supposed to be totally pure and uncontaminated by ethnocentricity (after all, what could be more pure than a simple equation?) turns out to be deeply entrenched in Eurocentrism. Mathematical traditions of the non-Western cultures – all the way from Egypt and Mesopotamia to India, China and Islam (algebra, after all, came about only as a by-product of attempts to distribute family wealth according to certain laws of inheritance) – have often been dismissed as empirical exercises undertaken for utilitarian goals!

Now, consider the Second Law of Thermodynamics, one of the foundations of modern physics. Non-Western scholars have shown that the Second Law, by postulating that the entropy of a system can only increase and favouring high energies, has a Eurocentric core. The efficiency criterion derived from the Second Law stipulates that the loss of energy in a conversion becomes smaller as the temperature at which the conversion takes place is increased. Thus, higher temperatures are of high value and systems that operate at low temperatures are inefficient. Thus resources such as petroleum and coal that can generate high temperature are more valued than low-temperature energy systems. Low-temperature systems are by definition declared inefficient and there is an inherent bias towards the allocation of resources to big industries. The monsoon, for example, which transfers vast amounts of energy from one end of India to another at ambient temperatures, enabling certain forms of agriculture to function, is thus declared inefficient. Nuclear energy by contrast is very efficient. As the late C.V. Seshadri pointed out, both nature and non-Western persons prove to be losers when the thermodynamic definition of efficiency becomes the criterion for development (Seshadri 1982). Refined sugar is more efficient and important than *gur*, produced from unrefined sugar cane, despite the fact that *gur* is far healthier than white sugar. Claude Alvares (1992) provides a host of other examples to demonstrate the inherent Eurocentrism of physical sciences.

Science is Eurocentric in a number of other ways. The objectification of nature and the consequent duality between 'man' and 'nature', for example, is a wholly Western enterprise. In all non-Western worldviews, nature is an integral part of 'man'. Similarly, the divorce of values from all concerns of scientific enterprise is purely a Western construct. The new postmodern sciences of chaos and complexity have now shown that the Second Law is not the whole story. Entropy does not always increase in a system; self-organization can lead to order and a decrease in entropy. Moreover, nature cannot be separated from 'man'; it is integral to our existence. We need to understand the whole in order to understand a part. Complexity can be generated from simplicity. But there is nothing really new in the insights of the 'new' sciences of chaos and complexity, their postmodernism notwithstanding. These are the things that the non-West has not only believed but also acted upon. They are intrinsic in most non-Western worldviews: indeed, indigenous non-Western societies have always seen themselves and their place in the cosmos in these terms.

One of the key insights of chaos theory is that of sensitive dependence: minute differences in the initial conditions of two otherwise completely similar systems can lead them into totally divergent paths. Much of the alternative development literature, from the critiques of the Latin American schools of dependencies to the Indian criticism of modernization to the Muslim scholarship on Westernization, has argued that sensitive dependence on initial conditions would not allow the Western model of development to work in their region! Over and over again the critique of non-Western experience has urged that the complex initial conditions of non-Western civilizations and environments have been insufficiently understood, that valued elements in the non-Western holistic context have not been taken into account, and thus the grandly devised deterministic development programmes could not achieve their projected ends (Sardar 1977; Solomon *et al.* 1994). Twenty years on, chaos theory encapsulates the same criticism in mathematics and eye-catching computer graphics. One could say that the arrival of chaos theory substantiates that critique as authoritative just as it confirms the non-Western position on nature, the lack of division between the doer and the done-to, and the interconnection between all things.

But to acknowledge this would in itself be an act of Eurocentrism. The non-West needs to be acknowledged and appreciated on its own terms and not because fashionable mathematics has confirmed the validity of its basic notions and axioms.

Non-Western concepts

All non-Western scientists, as well as all those located in Western social science disciplines, including those working on chaos and complexity in so far as they seek to appropriate non-Western concepts and categories to refuel the trajectory of Western science, wherever they live and whatever their creed or colour, are actually working for the benefit of Western civilization. One may eschew Eurocentrism, but one does Eurocentrism, knowingly or unknowingly, simply by working within an established disciplinary field of inquiry in the natural or social sciences.

Resistance to Eurocentrism, and hence development, can only come from non-Western concepts and categories. The non-Western cultures and civilizations have to reconstruct themselves, almost brick by brick, in accordance with their own worldviews and according to their own norms and values. This means that the non-West has to create a whole new body of knowledge, rediscover its lost and suppressed intellectual heritage, and shape a host of new disciplines. To some extent this is already beginning to happen as we see, for example, in the Muslim discourse of Islamization of knowledge, the reshaping of disciplines such as mathematics and psychology in India, and the resurgence of indigenous categories of analysis in Chinese thought.[3] What would this mean in terms of the idea of development?

It is hardly surprising that the non-West has no exact counterpart to the notion of development. In Islamic economics, which after three decades of research has evolved into a fully fledged discipline, the notion of growth is promoted by the concept of *tazkiyah*. The literal meaning of *tazkiyah* is 'purification'; the patterns of growth it promotes are similar to those we find in eco-systems. A tree, for example, conforms well to the dictates of *tazkiyah*. Muslim societies see themselves as trees, and see various societal activities – scientific, technological, economic, educational, managerial, organizational – as so many branches of a single tree, which grows and sends forth leaves and fruits in conformity with the nature of the tree itself. However, branches of a tree do not continue to grow indefinitely; thus a particular activity of the society cannot be pursued beyond a certain limit or at the expense of other activities. If a branch of a tree grew indefinitely it would certainly end up destroying the whole tree. Similarly, indefinite techno-logical growth would eventually destroy the society which is the basis of its nourishment. If organizations continued to grow they would develop inertia which would suffocate them. And so on. If a society cannot meet its basic needs, it must pursue economic growth vigorously just as a sapling needs to grow to become a tree. But once a sustainable stage is reached, further economic growth can lead to self-destruction. Brakes must now be applied.

Growth through *tazkiyah* demands that preservation of moral and environmental integrity, cultural strength and the practice of such vital Islamic concepts as *ijma* (consensus of the people), *shura* (cooperation for the good) and *istislah* (public interest) must be the cornerstones of science, technology and economic policy. The practice of *tazkiyah* on a national level dictates that growth policies must have four basic components: self-reliance, self-sufficiency, social justice and cultural authenticity. It is not possible for a society to *purify* its wealth unless it is equitably distributed within the various segments of society. Neither it is possible for a society to operationalize one of the main instruments of *tazkiyah*, *mahasbah* (criticism and self-criticism), if it is economically or technologically dependent on outside powers. Similarly, the whole practice of *tazkiyah* makes no sense unless a society is true to its cultural and traditional roots.

Thus in the framework of Islamic economics, growth through *tazkiyah* aims to create an infrastructure to meet the basic needs of a society. However, once such an infrastructure is created, *tazkiyah* is then concerned with maintaining a dynamic equilibrium between the infrastructure and the society. Essentially, the creation of a suitable infra-structure to meet the dictates of *tazkiyah* can be resolved into four basic components:

1. Sustaining the society in dynamic equilibrium: pursuing policies of conservation, fuller utilization of resources, recycling of waste, controlling and avoiding pollution, and providing facilities and regula-tions for health and safety.
2. Support systems: providing social, cultural, educational and informa-tional support systems that are adequate for the achievement of the goals of *tazkiyah*, generate a community feeling and a sense of dignity and protect and stimulate cultural creativity and responsibility.
3. The political environment: growth through *tazkiyah* aims at creating political stability, increasing the quantity and quality of participation in decision making and the degree of accountability of political office-bearers, improving the efficiency of administration of public

programmes, and improving the planning and allocations of social capital and resources.

4. The economic environment: growth through *tazkiyah* is based on technological activity that can be easily controlled and provides employment and does not present an environmental and cultural threat. It aims at equality in the distribution of resources; optimum use of natural and human resources; adequacy in the quantity and quality of goods and services without undue waste, including ad-ministration and working conditions and the distribution system; improvements in the level and quality of accountability of the economic system to the community; and political authority for its planning, efficiency, administration and allocation of resources.

In Chinese thought, an analogous concept is *kongsi*. It indicates the notion of partnership, societal concerns and economic growth. Literally it means 'government by a general public' or in modern parlance 'participatory democracy'. The word *kongsi* itself is derived from the Hokkien dialect, in which it reads as *kung-sze*. *Kongsi* has deep roots in Chinese history and tradition and can be seen in its mature form as early as the twelfth century. In 1455, the idea became the focus of a rebellion led by Teng Mao-Chi, who established *kongsi* as a new way of life based on the equality of partnership. Subsequently, Chinese sea merchants frequently established self-governing communities on the basis of *kongsi*. However, in Orientalist scholarship *kongsi* came to signify Chinese 'secret' societies. This was mainly due to the fact that as the prime Chinese concept of autonomous rule, *kongsi* was an instrument for resisting colonial rule – all Chinese social and political organizations during colonialism were 'secret' or underground. But recent scholarship has thoroughly debunked the relationship between *kongsi* and 'secret' societies.

The importance of *kongsi* in the flowering of Chinese industry, commerce and navigation and the economic flourishing of overseas communities cannot be overestimated. When Chinese communities began to be established in Southeast Asia in the eighteenth century, *kongsi* was used by the mining communities to establish themselves and ensure the economic growth of the community. This particular ex-ample, frequently cited in literature, associated *kongsi* largely with mining. But *kongsi* is a much more general notion of partnership or brotherhood. Its prime function is to form an open government based on partnership and brotherhood to protect economic gains and resist outside powers and aggressors. In a *kongsi* partnership, no individual can have a monopoly of wealth or hold a private fortune, and the economic gains are shared out equally among its members. As every member is a brother and partner of the other (this includes women as well), everyone has equal rights and participates equally in the governance. Administrators are open to scrutiny and criticism and are freely elected or dismissed in the general meeting in the *kongsi*-house. In *kongsi*, politics and economics are not two distinct disciplines but a single part of an overall reality.

Eurocentrism tempts us to equate *kongsi* government, particularly its representative function, public accessibility, and elections, with the Western concept of democracy. As Wang Tai Peng notes:

> ... the Westerners who saw *kongsi* through the distorting lens of Western concepts found it to be something of a republic. Similarly those Chinese scholars using the same lens have also found republican elements in *kongsi*. Such an approach to the history of *kongsi* is evidently Eurocentric. *Kongsi*, no doubt, bears some resemblance to Western democracy and republicanism, but this resemblance lies only in government by elected representatives. Beyond that, an equation of *kongsi* government with Western democracy would be completely misleading. *Kongsi* government was essentially a synthesis of extended partnership and sworn-brotherhood, which was uniquely Chinese. No Western democracy, however open and direct, was or is such a system. (Wang Tai Peng 1994: 4–5)

Both the Islamic concept of *tazkiyah* and the Chinese concept of *kongsi* not only open up totally different universes of discourses but could provide a basis for the emergence of new, distinctively non-Western disciplines. They provide a good indication of what could easily replace the increasingly superfluous Eurocentric notion of development.

Conclusion

The problem of Eurocentrism, and hence the problem of development, is thus the problem of knowledge. It is a problem of discovering Other ways of knowing, being and doing. It is a problem of how to be human in ways Other than those of Europe. It is also a problem of how the West could liberate its true self from its colonial history and moorings.

Notes

1. For a detailed analysis of the relationship between postmodernism, modernity and colonialism see Sardar 1998.
2. See *Seminar*, December 1997, the whole issue of which is devoted to 'Contesting Futures'.

3. For a discussion of the Islamization of knowledge and other new thought in Islam see Sardar 1985 and 1989; on India see Krishna 1987 and Sinha 1985.

References

Adas, Michael (1989) *Machines as the Measure of Men: Science, Technology and Ideologies of Western Dominance*. Ithaca: Cornell University Press.

Alvares, Claude (1992) *Science, Development and Violence*. New Delhi: Oxford University Press.

Fuller, Steve (1997) *Science*. Milton Keynes: Open University Press.

Harding, Sandar (ed.) (1993) *The Racial Economy of Science*. Bloomington: Indiana University Press.

Joseph, George Gheverghese (1990) *The Crest of the Peacock: Non-European Roots of Mathematics*. London: Penguin.

— (1995) 'Eurocentrism and mathematics', in Silvia Frederici, *Enduring Western Civilization*. Westport, CT: Praeger.

Joseph, George Gheverghese, Vasu Reddy and Mary Searle-Chatterjee (1990) 'Eurocentrism in social sciences', *Race and Class*, Vol. 31, No. 4.

Knorr-Cetina, Karin (1981) *The Manufacture of Knowledge*. Oxford: Pergamon.

Krishna, Daya (ed.) (1987) *India's Intellectual Tradition: Attempts at Conceptual Reconstruction*. Delhi: Motilal Banarsidass.

Lal, Vinay (1997) 'Future histories and epistemologies of India', *Futures*, Vol. 29, No. 10.

Latour, Bruno and Steve Woolgar (1979) *Laboratory Life*. Princeton: Princeton University Press.

Lerner, Daniel (1958) *Passing of the Traditional Society*. New York: Free Press.

Manzoor, S. Parvez (1991) 'The future of Muslim politics: a critique of the fundamentalist theory of the Islamic state', *Futures*, Vol. 23, No. 3, pp. 289–301.

Mendelssohn, Kurt (1976) *Science and Western Domination*. London: Thames and Hudson.

Nandy, Ashis (ed.) (1988) *Science, Hegemony and Violence: A Requiem for Modernity*. Oxford: Oxford University Press.

Rawls, John (1971) *A Theory of Justice*. Cambridge, MA: Harvard University Press.

Rose, Hilary (1994) *Love, Power and Knowledge*. Cambridge: Polity Press.

Sangwan, Saatpal (1991) *Science, Technology and Colonization*. Delhi: Anamika.

Sardar, Ziauddin (1977) *Science, Technology and Development in the Muslim World*. London: Croom Helm.

— (1985) *Islamic Futures*. London: Mansell.

— (ed.) (1988) *The Revenge of Athena: Science, Exploitation and the Third World*. London: Mansell.

— (ed.) (1989) *An Early Crescent: The Future of Knowledge and Environment in Islam*. London: Mansell.

— (1996) 'Beyond development: an Islamic perspective', *European Journal of Development Research*, Vol. 8, No. 2, pp. 36–55.

— (1998) *Postmodernism and the Other: The New Imperialism of Western Culture*. London: Pluto Press.

Seshadri, C.V. (1982) *Development and Thermodynamics*. Bombay: MCRC.

Sinha, J. (1985) *Indian Psychology*. Delhi.

Solomon, Jean-Jacques *et al.* (1994) *The Uncertain Quest: Science, Technology and Development*. Tokyo: United Nations University Press.

Trainer, Ted (1989) *Developed to Death*. London: Green Print.

Wang Tai Peng (1994) *The Origins of Chinese Kongsi*. Selangor: Pelanduk.

Wilkinson, Richard (1973) *Poverty and Progress*. London: Methuen.

. . . .

CHAPTER 4

Critical Holism and the Tao of Development

Jan Nederveen Pieterse[1]

Remedying remedies

Development processes take place across dimensions – physical, ecological, social, emotional, mental, political, historical, moral and semantics. Given the partial nature of development theories – reflecting disciplinary territories, policy interventions and political and institutional interests – the development field is carved up in many ways. How then can we arrive at a comprehensive approach? One could identify development as 'a totality of fragments', and capitalism as 'difference within a structured totality' (Pred and Watts 1992: 11). But that does not tell us very much since the notion of 'fragments' implies some kind of pre-existing wholeness. Responding to this dilemma is the context of this chapter.

This treatment is inspired by Vincent Tucker's work on critical holism, which combines the sociology of health with critical development studies. In criticizing the role of transnational pharmaceutical industries and their commercialization of health, he arrives at a new combination of concerns: holism and critical thinking, or 'holism with attitude'. This derives from an anthropological sensitivity to cultural dimensions of development (Tucker 1996b), a personal engagement with healing (which included following a holistic health course and taking a degree in holistic massage), and interests ranging from music to psychotherapy.

Tucker's starting point is modern medicine, or the biomedical approach – 'a pill for every ill', a magical fix for all ailments, and the idea that 'health = doctors + drugs' (Tucker 1996a: 37, 30, 17) – a hegemonic system sustained and propagated by medical professionals and pharmaceutical industries. His interest is not just the politics of dependence in the South and in Ireland, but the possibilities for dependency reversal (Tucker 1996c) and, likewise, alternatives to conventional medicine. In this respect, his approach differs from treatments of modern medicine that are primarily critical (for example, Nandy 1995; Kothari and Mehta 1988). He contrasts modern medicine with an emerging 'new holistic health paradigm' (Tucker 1997: 32) at several levels. 'The emergence of the holistic paradigm will require not only a change in the practice of medicine and health care, but also in the knowledge system and the model of science on which it is based. It will also require changes in the institutional fabric of health care' (Tucker 1997: 32). At the same time he is concerned with addressing 'weaknesses in holistic thinking and practice by incorporating into the model perspectives from more critical traditions of public health' (Tucker 1996a: 1). For instance, Fritjof Capra's work, 'like most approaches to holism, is less well developed when it comes to incorporating social, economic and cultural systems into the model' (Tucker 1997: 42). Hence, Tucker distinguishes between

> two versions or tendencies in holistic thinking. One focuses primarily on the individual organism. Most holistic health practice belongs to this tendency. It differs from biomedicine in that in its diagnostic techniques and therapies it takes into account a broader range of systems, which include the biological, the energetic, the psychic, the interpersonal and the spiritual. While it is more cognisant of the social and environmental factors which impact on the health of the individual, and takes these into account in its diagnosis, it does not provide ways of analysing or intervening in these macro systems. The second version of holism derives from the more sociological approach of Engels and Virchow. ... It also derives from the public health tradition. It encompasses economic and political systems as well as biological and environmental systems and is based on the notion that health and illness are not simply biological phenomena but are socially produced. This more sociologically informed holism has been further developed by Marxist political economy and radical development theory. (Tucker 1997: 42)

He then initiates a further move. While the sociological tradition 'adds a critical edge often missing in holistic health practice', 'it has little to contribute to our understanding of the personal and interpersonal dimensions of illness and wellbeing'. Finally, 'The critical combination of these two perspectives, which forms the basis of an expanded and more critical notion of holism, can provide a comprehensive alternative to the biomedical model' (Tucker 1997: 43).

Vincent Tucker's synthesis involves multiple movements: from biomedical reductionism to holism, from individual holism to sociological holism, from sociology and political economy to holism in personal, interpersonal and spiritual dimensions. The components of critical holism are spelled out in several places: 'a critical synthesis of holistic medicine, political economy, development theory, environmentalism and feminism', 'a theoretical synthesis of holistic theory, Marxist political economy and culture critique' (1996b: 3); 'critical holism encompasses social, economic, political and environmental systems including world systems' (1996b: 41). In health practice what this implies is:

> A holistic perspective on health promotion, while not excluding biomedical interventions, may include public health practices, environmental campaigns, political action, educational activities and complementary forms of medicine. It will include not only changes in personal life style, but also collective action to challenge organisations and institutions ... which act in ways detrimental to public health. (Tucker 1997: 45)

This is a high-wire synthesis. While it is developed in relation to health, it addresses gaps in our knowledge that are of general relevance. Its triple movement, providing remedies and remedying not only the original deficiencies but the shortcomings of the remedies as well, is welcome in development studies and social sciences generally. It involves a developed sense of balance. Thus, we all know the limitations of modern medicine. We may acknowledge the merits of holism, while its weakness is also evident: no critical edge, no political economy. The reverse applies to political economy: materialist savvy and sociological finesse, but no emotional or spiritual depth. If in a combined movement all these are brought together, balancing the limitations of each with the strengths of others, we have a bridge of uncommon strength and sophistication. This has been Vincent Tucker's contribution. In passing, Tucker notes that his critical holism paradigm 'also provides a basis for elaborating a general theory of human development' (Tucker 1996a: 1), so it is worth probing what would be the general ramifications of this synthesis.

Critical holism is an uncommon synthesis. Criticism and holism refer to different modes of cognition. This makes it a welcome synthesis: without a critical edge, holism easily becomes totalizing, romantic, soggy. Without holism, criticism easily turns flat, sour. If we recode these sensibilities, perhaps the synthesis becomes easier. 'Criticism' has several strands: the exercise of analytical faculties; a repudiation, in the Enlightenment tradition, of 'faith' and dogmatism; and a commitment to class struggle in Marxism, to emancipatory knowledge in critical theory, to equity and social justice in dependency theory. Key elements of criticism, then, are analysis, anti-dogmatism, and social justice. How does this tally with holism as a concern for the whole, the totality? If we take criticism in its affirmative sense it means acknowledging dimensions that have been *left out*. Through criticism an *inclusive* knowledge is to be achieved, representing elements that are outside or not acknowledged in the status quo. Accordingly, criticism is also an attempt at healing in the sense of restoring wholeness by acknowledging and rendering visible that which has been left out. In a broad sense, then, both criticism and holism refer to modes of healing: from the point of view of completeness in a societal sense by way of emancipation and justice, and from the point of view of wholeness in a multidimensional sense.

Conventional therapies implicitly refer to 'wholeness' by responding to deficiencies: through 'additives' or supplements, food or vitamin deficiencies can be remedied, only here wholeness is confined to the physical sphere, which permits medicalization and 'fixing'. Modern medicine recognizes psychological dimensions of health, as in psychosomatic illness, only these are compartmentalized away in domains such as psychology, psychiatry, neurology. The difference between holistic and conventional therapies is that the former acknowledge emotional, psychological, spiritual (at times also moral and social) levels of being as dimensions of health and well-being, and seek to integrate them into the healing process.

Wholeness, holism

Once the whole is divided, the parts need new names.
(Lao Tsu 1973: 29)

According to the *Bloomsbury Dictionary of Word Origins*, 'Whole is at the centre of a tightly knit family of English words descended from prehistoric Germanic *khailaz* "undamaged".' In Germanic languages, there is a connection between health, healing, holiness and wholeness. A similar connection exists in other language groups, as in Latin *salvus* 'healthy', *salus* 'bliss, health', Irish *slan* 'healthy, whole', Greek *holos* 'whole', old Indian *sarva* 'undamaged, whole'. 'Saviour' (Dutch *heiland*) means 'healer' and connects to the Greek *soter* (de Vries 1963: 257, 96). The Dutch *genezen* (healing, healed) refers to Gothic *ganisan* 'saved, healthy, holy', which may be connected to Greek *neomai* 'I come back, come home', giving the meaning of 'coming home safely'.

Health, then, refers to a state of wholeness, and healing restores a person to wholeness. Viewed in this light, 'holistic healing' is a tautology since health already basically means wholeness and healing means 'making whole'. This tautology makes sense only in distinction to conventional medicine. Holism, in this light, is an attempt at *recovery* of interconnections lost in the course of analysis.

The *Random House Dictionary* defines 'holism' as 'the theory that whole entities, as fundamental and determining components of reality, have an existence other than as the mere sum of their parts'. According to Craig (1992: 4–5), Jan Christiaan Smuts popularized the word in his 1926 book *Holism and Evolution*, in which he 'advocated the exploration of matter, life, and mind in relation to each other, rather than as isolable realms of existence'. Since then, *holistic* has been used in the humanities, social sciences and the sciences to refer to approaches that privilege the study of a whole system over analysis of its parts. Smuts uses wholeness and holism interchangeably in his book, which was influenced by the Cambridge Platonists, Bergson's vitalism and ideas of evolution from Darwin to de Vries (van Meurs 1997). For him, holism is 'the ultimate activity which prompts and pulsates through all other activities in the universe' (Smuts, quoted in van Meurs 1997: 115).

Apparently, however, there is slippage between wholeness and holism. While wholeness is evocative and descriptive, holism has a programmatic element. Holism involves systems thinking, which is part of the analysis recovery syndrome. Once the analytical mode has generated distinctions and separations, systems thinking is an attempt to piece together again what has been taken apart. The attributes of *system,* however, are unlike the properties of *wholeness*. Holism is a step forward in relation to the Enlightenment habit of taking everything apart, but it is short of wholeness. Humpty Dumpty put together again is not the same Humpty Dumpty. *Esprit de système* is not the spirit of wholeness. More precisely, there are different notions of *system*. It derives from the Greek *syn-histanai*, 'to place together', so to understand things systematically means to put them in a context and to establish the nature of their relationship. This relationship may be thought of as calculable and machinelike, as in mechanistic notions of system; or as approximate network relations, as in general systems theory (Capra 1996: 27f.). In social science the notion of system ranges from structural functionalism *à la* Parsons, to world-systems theory, and to the complex multidimensional systems approach of Niklas Luhmann.

One problem of systems approaches is that they imply a closure of the field; they achieve understanding (and manipulability) by enframing the field, and even reflexivity may not remedy this. It makes sense then to distinguish between *wholeness* and *holism* as perspectives with related but separate lineages. Wholeness refers to an original comprehensive field; holism is the systemic or scientific recombination of fragments in a new totality. From a historical point of view, wholeness resonates with Neolithic and older sensibilities while holism brings to mind the technology and mind-set of the industrial era. While there are continuities between wholeness and holism, 'the differences between modern holistic thinkers and earlier ones are [not] easily reconcilable' (Dunn 1986: 3). Both are relevant angles, each with their range of applicability.

As a theme, wholeness functions like a kaleidoscope of sensibilities. Among lineages of holism Vincent Tucker mentions ecological thinking in biology which spread to social science, and related currents of Gestalt psychology, psychotherapy and Buddhist thought (Tucker 1997: 41). Wholeness is thematized in several ways in social sciences. Marxism represents a commitment to the 'whole' within a materialist ontology. Harrod's plea for 'a re-search for a lost completeness' refers to a return to critical political economy, in other words to the Marxian whole (Harrod 1997: 108). Gestalt psychology led Ruth Benedict (1935) to a view on cultures as wholes or 'configurations' organized around core meanings. Parsons's social systems approach has been mentioned already. In the social sphere, wholeness is often associated with romanticism and nostalgia, as in the idealization of 'tradition', communitarianism and the idealization of 'community'. In politics, it can involve homogenizing projects of 'totality', as in some types of utopian politics, or nostalgia for a lost political 'unity'. In this light, a dose of difference can be quite a relief. A different and concrete angle on wholeness is the social exclusion approach (for example, Bhalla and Lapeyre 1997). This sensibility matches the 'preferential option for the poor' in liberation theology. For the architect Robert Venturi, part of postmodern sensibilities is 'the obligation toward the difficult whole' (quoted in McHale 1992: 3).

Modernity and its contradictions

The question of modern medicine is a subset of the larger problem of modernity and its contradictions – in particular, the contradiction between the 'two cultures' of science and art. The core of scientific culture is often traced back to Descartes and his project of 'certain knowledge' on the basis of mathematics as a universal scientific method. The mathematical mind abstracts, generalizes, dichotomizes and is given to formalism (Davis and Hersh 1986; compare Passmore 1978).[2] Critiques of Cartesianism go back a long way, among others to the Neapolitan philosopher Giambattista Vico: 'Mathematics is created in the self-alienation of the human spirit. The spirit cannot discover itself in mathematics. The human spirit lives in human institutions' (quoted in Davis and Hersh 1986: x). This general current of dissent is as old as 'the other West of William Blake and Paracelsus' (Nandy 1995: 60). A different twist to this kind of dispute is the argument between Habermas and Lyotard on the virtues of the Enlightenment and the debate on postmodernism.

There is something jarring about the way the tension within modernity is usually conceptualized and represented on either side. Viewing the relationship between scientific and humanistic cultures in terms of a dichotomy itself follows a Cartesian paradigm that is clearly a superficial representation from the outset. In addition it involves a one-sided representation of the Enlightenment, which is a much more complex historical field than is granted in conventional views.[3] Viewing this relationship as a continuum of views which meet and diverge on multiple levels is more adequate. This is worth keeping in mind when considering the long-standing attempts to bridge these worlds and reintegrate the sciences and humanities.

In 1957, Siu attempted such a reintegration in his *The Tao of Science*, long before Capra's *The Tao of Physics*. Generally elements of this fusion include:

- Ecology. Ecological knowledge as part of a general systems approach (Bateson 1973) and deep ecology (as in Arne Naess).
- History of science. Joseph Needham's work on the history of Chinese science and technology and its influence on Western science is part of a wider body of work documenting the historical connections between 'Western knowledge and Eastern wisdom'. The Enlightenment includes figures such as Leibniz and Goethe who bridged Western and Eastern sensibilities. On a conceptual level, Kuhn's work on scientific revolutions (Kuhn 1962) debunked the self-representation of progress in science, and through the notion of paradigm shifts introduced a meta level of critical analysis of scientific procedures and gatekeeping.
- Physics. Subatomic physics has generated a stream of findings that upset Descartes's certain knowledge, including Heisenberg's uncertainty principle. In the 1920s Alfred North Whitehead developed an inclusive notion of reality beyond dualisms such as those of mind and matter: 'In a certain sense, everything is everywhere at all times. For every location involves an aspect of itself in every other location' (quoted in Siu 1957: 157). In quantum physics this has been taken further in David Bohm's work on the implicate order (1980). Several of these reorientations have been grouped together under the heading of the 'holographic paradigm' (Wilber 1982a), building on Dennis Gabor's work on holography.
- New science. This includes developments such as catastrophe theory, chaos theory, complexity theory, fuzzy logic, the theory of emergence, self-organizing systems (Prigogine), and new trends in biology and mind–brain research (Karl Pribram).

Some of these reorientations turn on the fusion of 'Western knowledge and Eastern wisdom'. But what is the status of this fusion? The new science is not such a marginal concern if we think of developments such as chaos theory (Gleick 1988), which has found wide application in business (Peters 1988) and social science (Eve *et al.* 1997; Anderla *et al.* 1997). Several accounts suggest that on the other side of science are findings that intimate an interconnectedness of being similar to what has been intuited in mysticism – a complementarity between 'moon-shine physics' and ground-floor mysticism.[4] In this view, the splitting process carried all the way through, to the subatomic quantums and quarks, arrives at the ultimate unity of all being, or the universe as a 'sea of quarks' (Adachi 1995). At these deeper strata, contradictions such as those between the sciences and the humanities unravel. They turn out to be 'regional contradictions', dualisms that make sense within a certain limited context, but do not hold in the larger field. It is true, of course, that the world of everyday action is not a world of quantums or quarks; yet on the level of the foundational claims of science and epistemology it does matter that the Cartesian and Newtonian premises pertain within a narrow range only. This argument cuts two ways. By this wide-angle logic, while all human faculties and expressions may contain a 'territorial drive' and an urge towards functional autonomy, all are part of the whole and none can be denied their potential to contribute to wholeness. In other words, 'both reductionism and holism are necessary' (Capra in Weber 1982: 241). New science does not replace but supplements Newtonian science.

> Typically, the new paradigm demonstrates that knowledge gained under the old paradigm is true *under specific boundary conditions*. Thus, the rules of motion put forth by Newton are not demolished by Einsteinian physics, but are shown to be a special case of a larger, more inclusive physics. ... Chaos and complexity do not 'overthrow' former conceptions and scientific knowledge, but merely supplement them. (Eve 1997: 275)

Development and high modernism

The contradictions of modernity are of profound relevance to development studies. Considering that development is applied modernity, all the contradictions of modernity are reproduced within development as dramatically unresolved tensions. Development theory is torn between paradigms – mainstream, alternative and post-development (Nederveen Pieterse 1998) – between internal and external critiques. What, then, is the relevance of these disputes over modernity for attempts to reconceptualize development studies? The most fundamental question is the meaning of development, which in turn boils down to the question 'What is evolution?'

Development thinking goes back to nineteenth-century political economy but modern development thinking is no more than fifty years old. In relation to the complexities of social life, development as applied social science has been an arena of ideological posturing or pragmatic reformism, either way involving brutal simplifications and crude interventions. At times, in relation to the collective body, development interventions seem like performing surgery with a chainsaw. Still, in some conditions surgery with heavy equipment beats no surgery at all.

Development knowledge is fragmented by discipline-centrism. Each discipline compartmentalizes development 'to suit its own areas of specialization, research methods, and theoretical frameworks' (Brohman 1995: 303). Within this division of labour there has been a definite hierarchy.

> Development in its halcyon days was mainly economic development. Other disciplines entered the area apologetically or stealthily – as the supplementary knowledge of social structures facilitating or hindering economic growth, as insights into the psychological factors motivating or discouraging economic growth, as information about the political factors influencing economic decisions. (Nandy 1995: 146)

Meanwhile divergent theories are often applied in different policy spheres and economic sectors at the same time, making really-existing development a patchwork of zigzag premises and policies.

Neoclassical development economics, steeped in mathematics, is a formidable instance of applied Cartesianism. Partly, this is a rendezvous with intellectual and managerial power to classify, administer and change the world. The theoretical and methodological characteristics of neoclassical economics – assumptions of universal applicability, measurability, objectivity, formal modelling – make it a powerful instrument. Reductionism and disciplinary fragmentation have made expert regimes and technocratic interventions possible, and generously contributed to development policy failures. According to a former president of the American Economic Association:

> When you dig deep down, economists are scared to death of being sociologists. The one great thing [they] have going for [them] is the premise that individuals act rationally in trying to satisfy their preferences. This is an incredibly powerful tool because you can model it. (Charles Schultze in Brohman 1995: 302)

Conventional development is a politics of measurement, a matter of 'fixing' within limited spheres, achieving desired change by manipulating indicators and modifying numerical relationships, such as the ratio of external debt to GDP, or debt to exports. The gap between economic development and social and cultural development, or the hard and soft dimensions of development, is reproduced in the institutional division between the Bretton Woods institutions and UN agencies, in which the former hold the purse strings. Indeed, this mathematical universe is inhabited in many different ways for the sake of macroeconomic and financial management, by the International Monetary Fund (IMF) and Bank of International Settlements; for economic growth in combination with sustainable development and poverty alleviation, by the World Bank; for 'human development' aspects like schooling, health and housing, by the UN Development Programme and other UN agencies. They all share a commitment to social engineering.

The American psychotherapist Thomas Moore proposes to add another ailment to psychology's list of disorders:

> I would want to include the diagnosis 'psychological modernism', an un-critical acceptance of the values of the modern world. It includes blind faith in technology, inordinate attachment to the material gadgets and conveniences, uncritical acceptance of the march of scientific progress, devotion to the electronic media, and a life-style dictated by advertising. This orientation towards life also tends toward a mechanistic and rationalistic understanding of matters of the heart. (Moore 1992: 206)

Modern development has suffered from a severe case of 'psychological modernism', placing technological progress over human development. In Latin America, the work of the *cientificos* is not yet complete. In Asia, 'laboratory states' have used science as an instrument of power and reason of state (Visvanathan 1988). Even critical Marxist development thinking has been 'scientist' in temperament. As 'science became the integrating myth of industrial society' (Berman 1984: 187), so it became the guiding light of development policy. Rationalization was the key to modernization, so it became the master key to development. We now turn to the countermoves.

Shortcuts and other remedies

> *Do you think you can take over the universe and improve it?*
> (Lao Tsu 1973: 29)

Rather than another round of diagnosis, the situation calls for a scrutiny of remedies. Often presentations of the way ahead are no more than shortcuts – the ailment may be diagnosed correctly but the remedy is not examined. Some medicine turns a headache into a migraine, or provides only temporary or local relief. So in considering remedies for the culture of high modernism we may apply Vincent Tucker's recipe of remedying remedies. Among the problems are: the reproduction of dichotomous thinking, shortcuts and skipping levels, and framing contemporary dilemmas in anachronistic terms.

Positions and counterpositions in the development field often appear as simplistic dichotomies: modernity versus tradition, science versus indigenous knowledge, the impersonal versus the personal, the global versus the local. Critiques of development modernism also often take the form of dualisms which in effect replicate the thinking of modernism. Does it make sense to subject modernity to the same simplistic treatment to which the project of modernity has subjected social life? We need to distinguish between the *project* of modernity and *really-existing modernities* (or the sociology of modernity), which are far more complex than blueprint modernity. Opposition to modernization has been *part* of modern experience, and the dialectics of modernity include modernism (as a cultural politics which at times runs contrary to modernity), critical theory and reflexive modernity.

The world of postdevelopment ranges from militant development rejectionism to the New Age development thinking of the Schumacher College, which offers courses on 'Systems thinking and learning for change' and 'Buddhist economics'. At either end of the spectrum, adherents of postdevelopment use statistics to make their case. 'A single edition of the *New York Times* eats up 150 acres of forest land' (Rahnema 1997: 379). 'If all countries "successfully" followed the industrial example, five or six planets would be needed to serve as mines and waste dumps' (Esteva 1992: 2). Thus, postdevelopment also inhabits a mathematical universe. Opponents of abstraction, generalization, dichotomization and formalism often apply these techniques in order to make their own case. Some points of reference of postdevelopment, such as opposition to reductionist science and modernity (Nandy 1988; Alvares 1992), exhibit a polarized and dualistic thinking similar to that in modernization theory (which dichotomizes 'tradition' and 'modernity') and thus fall into the trap of *modernization in reverse*. The problem, however, is to *overcome* dichotomies, and not merely to change the direction of the current.

Majid Rahnema criticizes 'compulsory actomania' and the 'mask of love' in development aid. In his view, behind solidarity or 'charity' is 'the great fear we have of becoming fully aware of our powerlessness in situations when nothing can be done' (Rahnema 1997: 392, 393). Who are we to intervene in other people's lives? He recalls the Chinese notion *wu-wei*, which is variously translated as 'non-intervention' or 'action through non-action' (Rahnema 1997: 397). What is odd in Rahnema's treatment is that he proceeds to explain this Taoist notion by setting forth the Confucian 'arts of governance' and 'aesthetic order', as if unaware of the tensions between Taoism and Confucianism (which run as deep as those between mysticism and official religion) and of Confucianism's comeback as an ideological crutch for authoritarian regimes. It may be argued that 'non-intervention' is a superficial translation of *wu-wei*. A relevant passage in the *Tao te Ching* is:

> Tao abides in non-action,
> Yet nothing is left undone. (Lao Tsu 1973: 37)

Again, what Rahnema offers as a road ahead is merely a shortcut. A synthesis that is too fast, too easy, that does not do justice to the multiple dimensions of existence each of which involves tensions which require engagement in their own right and appropriate to the level at which they are experienced, is holism *without* a critical edge.

A similar polemical polarization relates to globalization. Some critics of globalization opt, in reaction, for localization. In reaction to free trade, they opt for 'new protectionism'. In their 1966 volume *The Case Against the Global Economy and for a Turn Toward the Local*, Mander and Goldsmith reduce globalization to economic globalization, confuse opposition to neoliberalism with opposition to globalization, and thus mix up the current *form* of globalization with the underlying *trend* of globalization. They set up a false dichotomy between the global and the local. Yet the global and the local require and sustain one another in many ways. Examples of 'interpenetration' of the global and the local are the thesis that transnational corporations can enter foreign markets effectively only if they become insiders ('insiderism'); the argument that flexible specialization leads towards the relocalization of operations so as to be close to consumers, suppliers, competitors and high-skilled labour ('glocalization'); the dialectics of globalization which show, for instance, that transnational corporations may well end up as active promoters of localism (Miller 1997); and a host of cultural studies that show that the global and the local are embedded in one another. A further argument is that 'the local' is itself a construction which owes its meaning and dynamics to its relationship to wider units, including the global (Boon 1990). On several counts, the contrast between the global and the local does not work as a clear-cut distinction or as a dichotomy because either requires the other to function.

'Identifying with the whole' is a formidable challenge, and taking shortcuts is tempting. Part of the remedy for modernism is to recover lost sensibilities or, 'rediscovering traditional knowledge' (Fals-Borda 1985). This may involve reconnecting with spiritual sources bulldozed by the incursions of colonialism and modernization, such as reinvoking the shaman (Nandy 1989). A recourse to cults is another option, with obvious limitations: 'cults can have either a tranquilizing or a liberating effect on people, depending, among others, on the leadership's inspiration and the social context' (Huizer and Lava 1989: 15). Morris Berman's point about the 'flip side of Cartesianism', even if overstated, is still valid:

> Why not abandon Cartesianism and embrace an outlook that is avowedly mystical and quasi-religious, that preserves the superior monistic insight that Cartesianism lacks? Why not deliberately return to alchemy, or animism, or number mysticism? ... The problem with these mystical or occult philosophies is that they share ... the key problem of all nondiscursive thought systems: they wind up dispensing with thought altogether. To say this is not, however, to deny their wisdom. ... My point is that once the insight is obtained, then what? These systems are, like dreams, a royal road to the unconscious, and that is fine; but what of nature, and our relation to it? What of society, and our relationship to each other? ... In fact, it is but the flip side of Cartesianism; whereas the latter ignores value, the former dispenses with fact. (Berman 1984: 188)

'The commitment toward the difficult whole' is ill-served by binarisms. It requires a combination of wholeness and difference, as in Vincent Tucker's synthesis. Shortcut holism may just produce Neolithic nostalgia – revisiting Arcadias that yield only temporary comfort, island paradises that provide only local relief, politics of ecstasy that produce hangovers. Recovering the wisdom of ages is needed, but not as a shortcut. Rather, what is needed is a new sense of balance, between science and art, fact and value, analysis and meaning. This means bridging the development gap and crossing sensibilities ranging from Neolithic to postindustrial settings. It involves recognizing multiple levels of existence and, accordingly, multiple modes of cognition which should coexist rather than compete. The assumption that only a single mode of cognition should prevail implies skipping levels.

Towards the Tao of development

Vincent Tucker's critical holism cannot be readily translated into a general theory of development because, unlike in health, there is no holistic practice in development. Alternative development practices tend to be local and short of a holistic approach. While there is a mysticism of the body, both a theory and a practice (holistic medicine), there is no equivalent holism of the social body. There are, so to speak, 'a thousand points of light', but they are scattered about like 'ten thousand things' – local alternatives, cultural and spiritual alternatives, rival theories, counterpoints and countercurrents.[5] There is no unifying, overarching paradigm. The appeal of critical holism is that it places holistic theorizing and practice about collective existence on the agenda, thus rendering it imaginable so that steps may be taken in its general direction.

Since social science in its epistemology has followed natural sciences, would it not be logical for it also to follow *new* developments in science? One problem with this is that specialization has narrowed the nexus between the two. The present situation in social sciences and development studies is an uneven combination of trends – towards polemical antagonisms, partial recombinations, and occasional syntheses.

Critiques of Cartesian science have deep roots in the South. Both science and critique-of-science movements have played a role in development activism and popular movements (Zachariah and Sooryamoorthy 1994). One trend is to view science as a religion[6] and as power. Suspicion of Enlightenment science is also a leitmotiv in ecological thinking (Shiva 1988). Science here stands for Cartesianism, Newtonian mechanics, positivism, an instrument to achieve mastery over nature. At times this critique presents a caricature of science which ignores ongoing developments in science and new science. Why should developing a critique of science and of science-as-power mean being anti-science? At times such 'anti-development' comes across as twentieth-century Luddism. Meanwhile science, of course, is a major instrument of ecological monitoring. Statements on the 'limits to growth' take the form of a mathematical argument. 'Green accounting' uses scientific measures to arrive at a realistic costing and pricing. The critique of science is part of reflexive modernity. What this means is there is a need to integrate multiple knowledges within a larger framework.[7]

Positivism is no longer the dominant temperament in social science except in economics. In social science, the lead paradigm is constructivism. In development, one-sided disciplinary perspectives are gradually in retreat and are being relegated to the status of partial knowledge. A development economist can no longer afford to ignore politics, sociology, gender, ecology, culture. Nor can a political scientist or sociologist afford to ignore economics. Most *problems* now faced in development – structural adjustment, currency instability, corruption, the environment, gender, poverty, conflict prevention, complex emergencies, postconflict reconstruction – require a combined approach. Many *policies* that are now initiated involve partnerships of government agencies, social organizations and firms. Many new *concepts* in development imply a combination of disciplines: good governance, accountability, human development, institutional development. New theoretical perspectives, such as new institutional economics, are likewise interdisciplinary. We witness both a return to and renewal of political economy, and new combinations such as ecological economics (which is more than simply resource economics) and economic sociology. The latter shows that markets are socially embedded and politically constituted and vary culturally, and yields such novel notions as social systems of production (Hollingsworth and Boyer 1997).

At the same time these reorientations tend to be *ad hoc* and only dimly reflected in general theoretical reorientation or in everyday research, which remains empiricist. Disciplinary knowledge still ranks as foundational knowledge. Interdisciplinary research is more widely applauded than practised. A multidisciplinary approach refers to a combination and an interdisciplinary approach to an interaction of disciplines; a holistic approach is a step further. Holistic means in-tegrated from the outset, which implies revising each discipline and not just an adding up.

Considering that one of the problems of conventional development thinking is linearity, a relevant option is the application of chaos theory to development. In social science, chaos theory is used as the basis of a nonmodern social theory (Lee 1997) and with a view to public policy (Elliott and Kiel 1997; Anderla, Dunning and Forge 1997). A preliminary point is that there is no ready translation of chaos theory from natural to social systems (Elliott and Kiel 1997: 72). Also chaos does not mean randomness or the absence of order; it refers to the unpredictability of the outcome of processes on account of small differences in conditions (Gleick 1988: 23). Chaos theory suggests a need to distinguish between different spheres of collective existence: those in which Newtonian dynamics prevail, and where robust policy interventions may be effect-ive; and those in which nonlinear dynamics predominate and where 'gentle action' is appropriate. In addition, chaos theory suggests an ecological perspective: 'If chaos theory is right, a myriad of interactions in the nonhuman world is required to support and sustain the human world. Perhaps the Gaia hypothesis is undergirded by the mathematics of chaos to a degree even its originator might be surprised to learn of' (Eve 1997: 279–80).

Thus, some social spheres lend themselves to intervention: 'In those cases where a stable and predictable response is known, related policy is eminently sensible. In areas such as tax expenditures where consumers and corporations do behave as Newtonian machines in response to interest rates or tax abatements, public policy is quite effective in altering behavior' (Elliott and Kiel 1997: 77). Whether this would apply in countries in the South with 'soft states' is an open question. Yet neoclassical economics, with its assumption of atomistic individuals exercising rational choice, proceeds as if this rational sphere is the only sphere. In reality this sphere is quite circumscribed and complexity is by far the more common condition, North and South. In the North this has led to an awareness of the limited effectiveness of social engineering (Elliott and Kiel 1997: 76), yet this insight has barely penetrated development thinking. Efforts at modernization remain surgery with a chainsaw, poverty alleviation remains a matter of advanced arithmetic. Chaos theory confirms what anthropologists have known all along: that 'Complex adaptive systems often exist on the edge of chaos' (Eve 1997: 280; an example given is the irrigation system in Bali). Many so-called traditional ways of life involve a sophisticated, time-tested social and ecological balance, and the harvest of several development decades confirms that outside interventions can do more harm than good.

Where nonlinear dynamics prevail, the counsel for policy is 'gentle action'. This might be a more faithful approximation of *wu-wei* than 'non-intervention'. Thus, chaos theory yields a complex range of action orientations. Consideration for the ramifications of small differences can be translated in different ways: as sensitivity to local conditions and cultural differences, or as an antidote to abstract models that gloss over local conditions and the actual implementation of development interventions. This is the point of the 'cultural turn' in development, the return of anthropology to development. It also suggests regard for the organizational and managerial dimensions of development on the ground and points to institutional analysis.

A related consideration concerns the *reflexivity* of development as a form of applied cybernetics. Reflexivity here involves the self-referential character of development thinking, which in effect represents layer upon layer of reflexive moves, each a reaction to and negotiation of previous development interventions, as an ongoing trial-and-error motion. It also involves the importance of subjectivities in the development process, of the reactions of people on the ground to development plans, projects, or outcomes, which should be built into the development process. Steps in this direction include popular development (Brohman 1996) and public action theory (Wuyts *et al.* 1992).

The contributions of chaos theory to social science are preliminary and schematic. The distinction between linear and nonlinear dynamics is too sketchy to be of much use. Already at times development processes are regarded as curvilinear, rather than linear.[8] Development refers both to a *process* (as in 'a society develops') and an *intervention* (as in 'developing a society'). For Cowen and Shenton, this produces an intrinsic tension in development: 'Development defies definition ... because of the difficulty of making the intent to develop consistent with immanent development' (Cowen and Shenton 1996: 438).

Considering this kind of difficulty, would it make sense to think of the *Tao of development?* While 'the Tao of physics' refers to a combination of physics and mysticism, the Tao of development is a more difficult combination because development is not merely a science or analytics (development theory) but also a politics. Taoism evokes an association of inaction, quietism. It is not clear whether this really applies to Tao, but there is no historical example of really-existing Taoism that disputes this, and historically there is a dialectic between Taoism and Confucianism.[9] Still this does not close the issue. For instance, by analogy, even if really-existing socialism has not met expectations, Marxism remains a relevant method.

One of the core problems of development is its pretentiousness, the insurmountable arrogance of intervening in other people's lives. This may be balanced by an equal but entirely different kind of pretension – the Tao of development. Setting a high goal for development may be better than setting no goal at all or, worse still, declaring development over and done with while in the meantime development business goes on as usual. Setting an elusive goal for development may be better than carrying on with development as a positivist politics of measurement. The Tao of development means acknowledging paradox as part of development realities: such as the antinomies between measurement and meaning, between intervention and autonomy, or the field of tension between the local and the global. These antinomies are part of the perplexities of the human condition. Development participates in these perplexities and is not in some fashion outside or beyond them. The Tao of development may be asymptotic, never entirely approachable, like an ever-receding horizon. It would involve a subtle and sophisticated sense of balance across different dimensions of collective existence.

'Balanced development' in a conventional sense refers to a balance between economic growth and redistribution, and between growth across different sectors. Critical holism involves balance in a wider and more fundamental sense, across dimensions of collective existence, from the epistemological to the practical, which may take several forms.

- A *multidimensional* approach, or a balance between the horizontal and vertical dimensions of collective existence. The horizontal refers to the worldly and social spheres; the vertical refers to the inner dimension of subjectivities and meanings, to the depth of the social field, its layered character, which Anouar Abdel-Malek (1981) referred to as the 'depth of the historical field'.

- A *multifaceted* approach or a 'diamond' social science, which reflects or shines light upon relations and dynamics across sectors (economy, politics, the social, cultural) and levels (local, microregional, national, macroregional, global) and achieves a balance between them.[10] This might be termed a Gestalt sociology.

- A *chiaroscuro* social science which abandons the assumption that society is fully transparent. The assumption of transparency is what lent the Enlightenment its totalitarian bent, as in Foucault's pan-opticism and also in socialist state ideology (Laclau 1990). This is a matter of modesty, a sense of the contingency of knowledge, or self-limiting rationality (Kaviraj 1992).[11] It is a sense of balance between what is known and unknown, conscious and unconscious, light and dark – between the day and night sides of life.

- A distinction between and combination of objective and subjective dimensions of development. Development thinking is now increasingly anchored in people's subjectivities rather than in overarching institutions – the state or international institutions. Development thinking has become more participatory and insider-oriented, as in the actor-oriented approach to development (Long 1994). On the other hand, development practice, particularly when it comes to macroeconomic management, has not been democratized, so there is a growing friction between development thinking and practice.

- A trend in local (and increasingly also in large-scale) development towards social partnerships across sectors, or *synergies* between different development actors – government, civic associations and firms. This may be referred to as a holistic approach.[12] This is a marked departure from times when development was seen as either state-led, or market-led, or civil-society-led (discussed in Nederveen Pieterse 1998).

- A more complex awareness of time in development, what is needed is combining *multiple time frames* and a balance between 'slow knowledge' and the 'fast knowledge' of instant problem-solving. 'Slow knowledge is knowledge shaped and calibrated to fit a particular ecological context' (Orr 1996: 31). Since development is concerned with the measurement of desirable change over time, it is chrono-centric. The conventional time horizon of development policy – the mid-term time span of a generation (or five years or so in the case of planning, development projects and project-based lending) – has changed with sustainable development and the implied notion of intergenerational equity, and 'coevolutionary development'. It is changing also as a consequence of the duration of the development era and the failures of 'development decades', which gradually brings to the foreground the *longue durée* of development. Evolution, a silent partner of development, is coming to the foreground.

On the whole, this sense of balance is in some respects better achieved in social science than in development studies. It is comparatively more developed in relation to situations that are geographically and socially near than in relation to those that are distant (as a function of insider knowledge). And it is more developed in relation to the past (where hindsight makes it easier to acknowledge complexity of motive, action and result) than in relation to the present or the future. In forecasting and future projects, one-dimensional treatments are almost the norm, except in science fiction.

There is an affinity between spatially wide and temporally long approaches, or between globalization and evolution. Both are forms of holism, spatial and temporal. With evolution making a comeback, older ideas are also coming back. Terhal has translated Teilhard de Chardin's ideas of 'evolutionary convergence', the noosphere and the dawn of collective reflection into perspectives on world development and compared them with those of Kuznets and Wallerstein.[13] He finds that Teilhard de Chardin underestimates social stratification and inequality in human evolution (1987: 228) and that there are elements of Eurocentrism to his work (Terhal 1987: 266–7), which makes it another instance of shortcut holism. Goonatilake (Terhal 1987: 1991), on the other hand, introduces the notion of 'merged evolution' to characterize the situation in which cultural evolution, which hitherto has run a separate course, merges with and impacts on biological evolution through biogenetic engineering. The advantage of this perspective is that it distinguishes *and* combines: rather than positing a shortcut 'evolutionary convergence' it confronts the dilemmas of really-existing convergence.

As to globalization, critical holism calls for a perspective on world history and globalization beyond conventional disciplinary methodologies (for example, Mazlish and Buultjens 1993). There is no doubt that the future lies with visions of cooperative globalization (as in Arruda 1996), in contrast to competitive globalization. Only shortcut holism, a holism that ignores or underrates inequality and difference, falls short as a remedy.

This sense of balance means treating development as a high-wire tightrope act. The source of critical holism is the field of health and healing, a field in which individual and collective concerns typically come together. Another field in which personal and social concerns are combined is feminism, by rethinking the boundaries between the private and the public, and by merging the personal and the political. Such combinations, along with the idea of Gestalt sociology, raise a further option: viewing social science not merely as explanation or as critique (the standard assignments of social science) but as *healing*, as socio-therapy. As there is therapy in relation to the individual body and psyche, can there not be healing of the collective body? In popular culture the idea is not uncommon, as in Sinéad O'Connor's song 'Famine': 'And if there ever is going to be healing, there must be remembering, and then grieving, so that then there can be forgiving.' In development work this idea is not so uncommon. After all, what else is postconflict re-habilitation or conflict prevention, both of which have emerged in relation to complex emergencies and ethnic conflict? And yet the notion of development as healing sounds novel, presumably because it makes explicit that which has been implicit, and in doing so combines sensibilities that are usually kept neatly apart in separate boxes.

These, then, are elements of the Tao of development: a sense of balance across dimensions, a holistic approach, a notion of collective healing. Critical holism, in combining holism and difference, combines these sensibilities in a balancing act. Thus, critical wholeness in develop-ment should not be expected from a shortcut towards an undivided whole in a divided world, but should be sought in a new balance. The counsel for development studies and social science is to distinguish between multiple spheres and levels, all of which require engagement in their own terms, and not merely to contrast but to combine knowledges. This involves implications for action and policy. It involves a case-by-case, contextual assessment of whether linear or nonlinear dynamics prevail, and whether robust or gentle action is appropriate. It also exceeds local alternatives. Critical holistic development should include macroeconomic management. Holistic politics should encompass global democratization. Holistic politics means planetary ethics. Identifying with the whole means that development can no longer be geared simply to material aims and achievements but should include nonmaterial dimensions, as in cultural development. It means that development can no longer be anthropocentric but must encompass the planetary ecology. Accordingly, stretching the meaning of development to its fullest extent, it may be summed up as a collective learning process and humanity's self-management according to the most comprehensive conceivable standards.

Notes

1. This is a shortened version of the Inaugural Vincent Tucker Memorial Lecture given at the University College of Cork, Ireland, in February 1998. For references I would like to thank Stuart Todd and for comments on an earlier version Ranjit Dwivedi, Lily Ling and other participants at an Institute of Social Studies seminar.

2. 'The computerization of the world represents an advanced stage of Cartesianism. Within that stage, programs become autonomous. We have even been given intimations of automated concept formulation and of action instigated as a consequence of such automation' (Davis and Hersh 1986: 303). Current developments in global currency trading are an example of such automated action: triggers built into trading programmes set in motion series of financial operations whose ripple effects can upset financial systems. For a more developed argument see Yurick 1985.

3. A standard omission in representations of the Enlightenment is that it was an epoch not only of rationalism but also of romanticism and, besides, that these also occurred in combination. Without this understanding, what is one to make, for instance, of these statements of Diderot: 'what makes me angry is that the passions are never regarded from any but the critical angle. People think they do reason an injury if they say a word in favor of its rivals. Yet it is only the passions, and the great passions, that can raise the soul to great things' and 'The language of the heart is a thousand times more varied than that of the mind, and it is impossible to lay down the rules of its dialectics' (Diderot, quoted in Gay 1977: 188, 189).

4. The complementarity between new physics and mysticism is disputed among others by Wilber, who deems it a false complementarity and at most concedes that new physics *accords* with mysticism (Wilber, 1982b: 166–79). While mysticism addresses all levels – physical, biological, mental, subtle, causal and ultimate – physics only pertains to a single level (Wilber 1982b: 159).

5. Besides alternative development literature (Nederveen Pieterse 1998) see for example Henderson 1996, Whitmyer 1995, Roszak 1976.

6. 'Positivism is just a crank religion' (Chris Mann in Dunn 1986: 2).

7. Capra gives another example of this integration of multiple knowledges: 'From the very beginning it was clear to me that there was no reason to abandon the biomedical model. It could still play a useful role for a limited range of health problems within a large, holistic framework, as Newtonian mechanics was never abandoned but remains useful for a limited range of phenomena within the larger framework of quantum-relativistic physics' (Capra 1988: 171).

8. For example, the view of Cowen and Shenton on Hegel's views on development: 'Unlike the linear image that the idea of progress evoked, the course of development was curvilinear or spiral-like, always impeded or arrested within its own logical structure' (Cowen and Shenton 1996: 130).

9. As to Taoism: 'It is inconceivable to a Taoist that Tao should be actualized in this world by human efforts because the core of Taoist doctrine is to

teach its followers to transcend merely human affairs and psychologically dwell in "nothingness" (*wu*) so as to be in line with the "nonaction" (*wu-wei*) of the great *Tao*' (Wei-ming 1979: 10–11). More generally, while there have been episodes of a working balance between mysticism and official or state religion – between Buddhism and governance, Qabbala and Judaism, Sufism and Islam, Christian mysticism and Christendom, etcetera – none is readily accessible that has a sustainable example function.

10. Several of the significant books in social science achieve this in different ways. It applies to the oeuvre of Max Weber, Gramsci and Braudel and to books such as Wertheim's *Evolution and Revolution*, Stavrianos's *Global Rift*, Worsley's *The Three Worlds*, David Harvey's *The Condition of Postmodernity*, or *Reworking Modernity* by Pred and Watts.

11. 'I plead not for the suppression of reason, but an appreciation of its inherent limits' (Gandhi in Parekh 1997: 68).

12. This is the theme of a report in the *Irish Times* on social partnerships particularly in disadvantaged areas. The partnerships include 'business, trade unions, farming organisations, schools, health boards, state agencies ... and representatives from the local community' (Catherine Foley, 'The holistic way of solving problems', *Education and Living* supplement, *Irish Times*, 17 February 1998, pp. 2–3).

13. For instance, according to Teilhard, 'Although mounting demographic pressure causes quite a number of evils at one level of human interaction', in principle it leads to 'social unification and a higher level of collective consciousness' (in Terhal 1987: 176).

References

Abdel-Malek, Anouar (1981) *La Dialectique sociale*. Paris: Seuil. Published in English as *Civilizations and Social Theory*, Vol. 1 of *Social Dialectics*. London: Macmillan, 1981.

Adachi, Ikuro (1995) *The Law of Undulation*. Yokohama: EVHA.

Ahmed, Durre S. (1997) 'Women, psychology and religion', in *Women and Religion*. Lahore: Heinrich Böll Foundation, pp. 23–58.

Alvares, C. (1992) *Science, Development and Violence: the Revolt Against Modernity*. Delhi: Oxford University Press.

Anderla, G., A. Dunning and S. Forge (1997) *Chaotics: an Agenda for Business and Society for the Twenty-first Century*. London: Adamantine Press.

Arruda, M. (1996) 'Globalization and civil society: rethinking cooperativism in the context of active citizenship', Rio de Janeiro: PACS (Alternative Policies for the Southern Cone).

Ayto, John (1990) *Bloomsbury Dictionary of Word Origins*. London: Bloomsbury.

Bateson, G. (1973) *Collected Essays in Anthropology, Evolution, and Epistomology*. St Albans: Paladin.

Benedict, Ruth (1935) *Patterns of Culture*. London: Routledge and Kegan Paul.

Berman, Morris (1984) *The Reenchantment of the World*. New York: Bantam.

Bhalla, A. and F. Lapeyre (1997) 'Social exclusion: towards an analytical and operational framework', *Development and Change* 28(3): 413–34.

Bhaskar, Roy (1991) *Philosophy and the Idea of Freedom*. Oxford: Blackwell.

Bohm, D. (1980) *Wholeness and the Implicate Order*. London: Routledge and Kegan Paul.

Boon, J.A. (1990) *Affinities and Extremes*. Chicago: University of Chicago Press.

Brohman, John (1995) 'Economism and critical silences in development studies: a theoretical critique of neoliberalism', *Third World Quarterly* 16 (2): 297–318.

— (1996) *Popular Development*. Oxford: Blackwell.

Capra, Fritjof (1988) *Uncommon Wisdom*. London: Century Hutchinson.

— (1996) *The Web of Life*. New York: Doubleday.

Cowen, M.P. and R.W. Shenton (1996) *Doctrines of Development*. London: Routledge.

Craig, Betty Jean (1992) *Laying the Ladder Down: The Emergence of Cultural Holism*. Amherst, MA: University of Massachusetts Press.

Davis, P.J. and R. Hersh (1986) *Descartes' Dream: The World According to Mathematics*. Boston: Houghton Mifflin.

Dunn, David (1986) 'Synchronisms: toward a phenomenological science', *International Synergy Journal* 1: 2–8.

Elliott, Euel and Douglas Kiel (1997) 'Nonlinear dynamics, complexity and public policy', in R.A. Eve, R. Horsfall and M.E. Lee (eds), *Chaos, Complexity, and Sociology*, London: Sage, pp. 64–78.

Esteva, G. (1992) 'Development', in W. Sachs (ed.), *The Development Dictionary*. London: Zed, pp. 6–25.

Eve, R.A. (1997) 'Afterword', in R.A. Eve, R. Horsfall and M.E. Lee (eds), *Chaos, Complexity and Sociology*. London: Sage, pp. 269–80.

Eve, R.A., S. Horsfall and M.E. Lee (eds) (1997) *Chaos, Complexity and Sociology*. London: Sage.

Fals-Borda, O. (1985) 'Wisdom as power', *Development: Seeds of Change* 3: 65–7.

Gay, Peter (1977) *The Enlightenment: An Interpretation*. New York: Norton.

Gleick, James (1988) *Chaos: Making a New Science*. London: Heinemann.

Goonatilake, Susantha (1991) *The Evolution of Information: Lineages in Gene, Culture and Artefact*. London: Pinter.

Harrod, J. (1997) 'Social forces and international political economy: joining the two IRs', in S. Gill and J.H. Mittelman (eds), *Innovation and Transformation in International Studies*, Cambridge: Cambridge University Press, pp. 105–14.

Henderson, Hazel (1996) *Building a Win–Win World*. San Francisco, Berrett-Koehler.

Hollingsworth, J.R. and R. Boyer (eds) (1997) *Contemporary Capitalism: the Embeddedness of Institutions*. New York: Cambridge University Press.

Huizer, G. and J. Lava (1989) *Explorations in Folk Religion and Healing*. Manila: Asian Social Institute.

Huxley, Aldous (1946) *The Perennial Philosophy*. London: Chatto and Windus.

Kaviraj, Sudipta (1992) 'Marxism and the darkness of history', in J. Nederveen

Pieterse (ed.), *Emancipations, Modern and Postmodern*. London: Sage, pp. 79–102.

Kothari, M.L. and L.A. Mehta (1988) 'Violence in modern medicine', in Ashis Nandy (ed.), *Science, Hegemony and Violence*, New Delhi: Oxford University Press, pp. 167–210.

Kuhn, T.S. (1962) *The Structure of Scientific Revolutions*. Chicago: University of Chicago Press.

Laclau, Ernesto (1990) *New Reflections on the Revolution of Our Time*. London: Verso.

Lao Tsu (1973) *Tao te Ching*. London: Wildwood House, translated by Gia-fu Feng and Jane English.

Lee, Mary E. (1997) 'From Enlightenment to chaos: toward nonmodern social theory', in R.A. Eve, S. Horsfall and M.E. Lee (eds), *Chaos, Complexity and Sociology*. London: Sage, pp. 15–29.

Long, N. and A. Long (eds) (1994) *Battlefields of Knowledge*. London: Routledge.

McHale, Brian (1992) *Constructing Postmodernism*. London: Routledge.

Mazlish, B. and R. Buultjens (eds) (1993) *Conceptualizing Global History*. Boulder, CO: Westview.

Mehta, P.D. (1989) *Holistic Consciousness*. Longmead, Shaftesbury: Element Books.

Meurs, M. van (1997) *J.C. Smuts: Staatsman, Holist, Generaal*. Amsterdam: Suid-Afrikaanse Instituut.

Miller, Daniel (1997) *Capitalism: An Ethnographic Approach*. Oxford: Berg.

Minter, William (1986) *King Solomon's Mines Revisited*. New York: Basic Books.

Moore, Thomas (1992) *Care of the Soul*. London: Judy Piatkus.

Nandy, Ashis (ed.) (1988) *Science, Hegemony and Violence*. New Delhi: Oxford University Press.

— (1989) 'Shamans, savages and the wilderness: on the audibility of dissent and the future of civilizations', *Alternatives* 14: 263–77.

— (1995) 'Modern medicine and its nonmodern critics', in Ashis Nandy, *The Savage Freud*, Delhi: Oxford University Press, pp. 145–95.

Nederveen Pieterse, Jan (1990) *Empire and Emancipation*. London: Pluto.

— (1994) 'Unpacking the West: how European is Europe?', in A. Rattansi and S. Westwood (eds), *Racism, Modernity, Identity*. Cambridge: Polity, pp. 129–49.

— (1998) 'My paradigm or yours? Alternative development, post development, reflexive development', *Development and Change*, 29: 343–73.

O'Connor, Sinéad (1994) *Universal Mother*. London: Ensign Records.

Orr, David (1996) 'Slow knowledge', *Resurgence*, 179: 30–32.

Parekh, Bhikhu (1997) *Gandhi*. Oxford: Oxford University Press.

Passmore, John (1978) *Science and Its Critics*. London: Duckworth.

Peters, Tom (1988) *Thriving on Chaos*. New York.

Pompa, L. (1990) *Vico: A Study of the 'New Science'*. Cambridge: Cambridge University Press 2nd edn.

Pred, A. and M.J. Watts (1992) *Reworking Modernity: Capitalisms and Symbolic Discontent*. New Brunswick, NJ: Rutgers University Press.

Rahnema, M. (1997) 'Towards post-development: searching for signposts, a new language and new paradigm', in M. Rahnema and V. Bawtree (eds), *The Post-development Reader*. London: Zed Books, pp. 377–404.

Roszak, Theodore (1976) *Unfinished Animal*. London: Faber and Faber.

Quigley, C. 1966 *Tragedy and Hope: A History of the World in Our Time*. New York: Macmillan.

Sampson, A. (1987) *Black and Gold: Tycoons, Revolutionaries and Apartheid*. New York: Pantheon.

Schumacher College (1997) 'Course programme 1997–1998', Dartington, Devon.

Shiva, V. (1988) 'Reductionist science as epistemological violence', in Ashis Nandy (ed.), *Science, Hegemony and Violence*, New Delhi: Oxford University Press, pp. 232–56.

Siu, R.G.H. (1957) *The Tao of Science: An Essay on Western Knowledge and Eastern Wisdom*, Cambridge, MA: MIT Press.

Skolimowski, Henryk (1994) *The Participatory Mind*. London: Penguin/Arkana.

Terhal, P. (1987) *World Inequality and Evolutionary Convergence*. Delft: Eburon.

Todd, Stuart (1997) 'Actualizing personal and collective health: questioning how development policy meets innate human needs'. The Hague, Institute of Social Studies, MA research paper.

Toulmin, S. (1990) *Cosmopolis: The Hidden Agenda of Modernity*. Chicago: University of Chicago Press.

Tucker, Vincent (1996a) 'Critical holism: towards a new health model'. Mimeo, Cork, University College.

— (1996b) *Cultural perspectives on development*, London: Frank Cass.

— (1996c) 'Health, medicine and development: a field of cultural struggle', in Vincent Tucker (ed.), *Cultural Perspectives on Development*, London: Frank Cass, pp. 110–28.

— (1997) 'From biomedicine to holistic health: towards a new health model', in Anne Cleary and Margaret P. Treacy (eds), *The Sociology of Health and Illness in Ireland*. Dublin: University College Dublin Press, pp. 30–50.

Visvanathan, Shiv (1988) 'On the annals of the laboratory state', in Ashis Nandy (ed.), *Science, Hegemony and Violence*. New Delhi: Oxford University Press, pp. 257–88.

Vries, J. de (1963) *Etymologisch woordenboek*. Utrecht: Spectrum.

Weber, R. (1982) '*The Tao of Physics* revisited: a conversation with Fritjof Capra', in Ken Wilber (ed.), *The Holgraphic Paradigm and Other Paradoxes*. Boulder, CO: Shambola, pp. 215–48.

Wei-Ming, Tu (1979) *Humanity and Self-Cultivation: Essays in Confucian Thought*. Berkeley, CA: Asian Humanities Press.

Whitmyer, C. (ed.) (1995) *Mindfulness and Meaningful Work: Explorations in Right Livelihood*. Berkeley, CA: Parallax Press.

Wilber, Ken (ed.) (1982a) *The Holographic Paradigm and Other Paradoxes*, Boulder, CO: Shambala.

— (1982b) 'Physics, mysticism and the new holographic paradigm: a critical appraisal', in Wilber (ed.), *The Holographic Paradigm and Other Paradoxes*, Boulder, CO: Shambala, pp. 157–86.

Wuyts, M., M. Mackintosh and T. Hewitt (eds) (1992) *Development Policy and Public Action*. Oxford: Oxford University Press.

Yurick, Sol (1985) *Behold Metatron the Recording Angel*. New York: Semiotext(e).

Zachariah, M. and R. Sooryamoorthy (1994) *Science for Social Revolution? Achievements and Dilemmas of a Development Movement: The Case of Kerala*. London: Zed Books.

PART TWO

Political Economy

Reintegrating Production and Consumption, or Why Political Economy Still Matters

Diane Perrons

The development of postmodernism and the interest in cultural issues provide intellectual challenges to political economy, by questioning its epistemological foundations, the issues analysed and the methods used. In particular, political economy approaches have been criticized for being trapped within a productivist paradigm and for failing to recognize the significance of consumption in shaping everyday life and in the formation of individual identities. In some cases this critique enriches the political economy framework by building upon its key analytical concepts and exploring their materialization in particular contexts. For example, consideration has been given to the way our images of social groupings by class, gender or ethnicity are rhetorically and ideologically constituted in daily life and how these social divisions become naturalized through the perpetuation of ideas (Gill 1993). Attention has also been given to the importance of social and cultural factors and to institutions in promoting and shaping development, for example, in the discussion of new industrial districts (Granovetter 1992; Amin and Thrift 1994). Furthermore as employment in manufacturing continues to decline, reflecting in part the way that basic needs can be more efficiently provided, it is important to analyse new forms of economic activity including services of all kinds and the consumption spaces within which they are provided. By drawing attention to these practices and processes the cultural perspective increases understanding of how social relations and economic practices are initiated, reproduced and sustained through the ideas and practices of daily life as well as through the power relations of capitalist and patriarchal societies. One question raised in this chapter is whether these insights require a fundamental shift in the conceptual framework of political economy, or whether this critique adds new insights into an approach that is philosophically sound but practised inadequately. Other studies within the postmodern tradition, however, question the very roots of the political economy approach by challenging its materialist epistemology. This more fundamental challenge is only briefly considered in this chapter, but see Sayer (1993, 1997) for a realist critique.

Political economists have always been clear about the purpose of their analyses: to understand the world in order to change it. There are no parallel claims in the cultural/postmodern tradition, so this chapter begins by outlining a role for academic inquiry. It then rejects the idea that political economy approaches are inherently reductivist and restates the main elements of a historical materialist methodology. The third section expresses reservations about the new interest in consumption and specifically the way in which it has been said to represent the 'structuring principle' of modern or postmodern societies (Falk and Campbell 1997). In particular I argue that analysis of production and consumption cannot be separated or separately prioritized in this rather binary way. Consumption opportunities are profoundly shaped by material well-being, which in turn remains dependent both on an individual's positioning within the social relations of production, including the gender division of labour, and on their societies' position within the international division of labour. Thus, constraints on individuals arising from their social class, gender and ethnicity as well as from the overall level of social development remain important for understanding individual and social practices, including consumption. In rejecting the importance of production and indeed social theory more generally, the postmodern tradition has neglected these social constraints. Instead, it has switched the emphasis to cultural explanations and cultural theory in an attempt to understand the meaning of consumption for individuals and the way consumption patterns shapes individual identity (see, for example, Bell and Valentine 1997 for a discussion of the relationship between food consumption and identity). In the final section of the chapter, some of these arguments are illustrated by reference to a case study which integrates an analysis of production and consumption through a particular commodity chain, the production of fresh fruit in Chile and its sale in Britain.

Subjects and objects of social scientific inquiry

The world can be construed as 'a concrete set of problems that people have to solve practically' (Pile and Thrift 1995: 15). Intellectuals can and should assist this resolution. However, Pile and Thrift believe that intellectuals instead tend to construe the world as 'a set of significations that need to be interpreted' (Pile and Thrift 1995: 15). Perhaps this view arises from the cultural turn taken by some academics as a consequence of their own particular reified standpoints, rather than some inherent tendency among intellectuals. Ken Saro-Wiwa, for example, argued that while many writers in the literary tradition are concerned with 'the angst of the individual', for him there were too many immediate problems to be solved to afford this luxury (interview on BBC *Panorama* programme 1995).[1] Nevertheless, there is a tendency within postmodernism to avoid analysing problems confronting societies and their practical resolution.

It is sometimes useful to explore the purpose of social inquiry. Most academic inquiries generate intrinsically interesting findings and it is difficult to know in advance whether such knowledge will be of any practical consequence. From a radical perspective, however, any evaluation and ordering of priorities has to depend on whether such work is likely to increase understanding of the social world, its underlying processes and capacity to effect change. My concern is that the recent turns in academic inquiry are becoming increasingly esoteric, substituting either rigorous models or, in the cultural tradition, the uninterpreted voices of the researched. As a consequence, explanation of practical social problems has been displaced. If these traditions of thought become dominant within the academic community, as seems to be the current fashion, then a wealth of intellectual inquiry, talent and effort could be wasted. As Jean Baudrillard (1998) argued, it could be that change in fashions in the field of knowledge is just as arbitrary as in the world of consumer goods and similarly 'adds nothing to the intrinsic qualities of the individual [/knowledge] ... but does however impose thoroughgoing constraints' on what studies are acceptable. In the field of knowledge, this arbitrary pursuit of fashion produces a 'non-rational social process of consumption' rather than an 'accumulation of scientific knowledge'. This would not disturb postmodernists, as the idea of an accumulation of knowledge is part of the Enlightenment project that they reject. However, if it is recognized that the academic community is subject to changes in fashion then at least it is important to reflect on the subjects, objects, methods and purposes of academic inquiry and resist the abandonment of ideas simply because they are of long standing.

There is always a danger of caricaturing opposing intellectual positions. In the current intellectual climate, however, I think it is timely to restate the central ideas of historical materialism, which has always sought to address social problems and understand social processes (see Dunford and Perrons 1983; 1995). This approach has been heavily criticized in recent years but, in my view, has been caricatured or at least inaccurately presented.

Methods of analysis: the role of theory and real abstractions

Methods based on historical materialism are often criticized for their determinism and overstatement of the role of the economy and production. But feminist analyses within a materialist perspective have been particularly important in widening the scope of inquiry beyond the workplace, even if sometimes with a view to understanding workplace relations more satisfactorily (see for example Cockburn 1991; Pollert 1996). It is important to remember that the historical materialist understanding of the economy is a much richer one than is sometimes supposed and that the outcomes of such analyses are rarely deterministic. Within this perspective, analysis of social development requires an understanding of the way material needs and wants have been and continue to be produced and satisfied. Thus, this approach has always in principle sought to link production and consumption, most noticeably within the regulationist approach (Aglietta 1979; Dunford and Perrons 1983; Lipietz 1987; Jessop 1991; Peet 1998).

Production and consumption are simultaneously physical and social activities and take place in given social contexts, which are organized in particular ways. In the contemporary world, most societies are capitalist and exhibit gender and ethnic inequalities. These social relations strongly influence the ways in which production and consumption are organized and as a consequence structure the nature of everyday life. They do not, however, determine each and every happening or the exact forms in which social processes are reproduced. Indeed, one contribution of the historical materialist approach is to identify tensions between social processes; the purpose of empirical enquiry is to analyse particular concrete situations in which these social processes are simultaneously embedded and embodied in different ways in different social, historical and geographical contexts.

Within capitalist societies the profit motive or the self-expansion of capital underlies the production and distribution of social output. Indeed, this motive forms the internal dynamic of capitalist society independently of the will of its agents and is crucial to an analysis of social change. In particular, the profit motive underlies the decision-making strategies of the major capitalist organizations which still shape the trajectory of social development within and between localities (Schoenberger 1991). This motive also underlies the related processes of globalization, the organization of work and relations between employees and employers, and the forms through which commodities are advertised, marketed and sold. The majority of people in capitalist society are still employees or work for others in order to obtain their survival needs – they engage in production activities of one form or another. They simultaneously form part of a reproductive unit, either singly or with others, so the relations between members of such units also need to be considered. These relations include the intra-household division of labour and gender roles, relations that are also influenced by prevailing social norms such as patriarchy, gender systems, orders, contracts or arrangements (Sen 1991; Walby 1990; Pfau-Effinger 1995). Whatever their form, these relationships are important characteristics of the society in question. The state also plays a part in influencing and being influenced by these relationships, as does the society's level of development within the global division of labour and its international political relations. Regulation theory has tried to encapsulate some of the interrelations between the regime of accumulation and the mode of regulation. Yet it has tended to overlook the way such systems are also shaped by gender relations (but see McDowell 1991) and how systems of regulation are experienced differently by different people according to their gender, ethnicity, age and stage in the life course.

At a fundamental level the logic of social change is composed of ideal and material causality. Ideal causality refers to the way in which human beings are able to shape their own destinies. They are able to conceptualize their future or elements of their future and either individually or collectively seek to bring their ideas into being. Human beings are not entirely free agents, however, but subjects who have to act in pre-given, natural, technological and social conditions (Marx 1973a). Structural constraints on capitalists define certain boundaries within which they can act.[2] Material causality refers to the effect of these natural and social conditions on human action and of natural and economic laws which shape the way nature and society can be modified. Since the external world that conditions human beings has increasingly been shaped and altered by human activity, human beings are increasingly conditioned not simply by natural conditions and processes but by what they have made of these conditions (Dunford and Perrons 1983). Paraphrasing Marx, human beings make history but not in circumstances of their own choosing. Thus, although constraints are recognized within a historical materialist analysis, so too is the role of human agency. This is why the argument that such analyses are deterministic is difficult to sustain.

Within this perspective – which can be seen as totalizing not because it necessarily seeks to explain everything at once but because any aspect of the system has to be contextualized within the whole – it can be difficult to know where to begin. As Marx argued:

> It seems to be correct to begin with the real and the concrete, with the real precondition, and thus to begin, in economics, with e.g. the population, which is the foundation and the subject of the entire social act of production. However, on closer examination this proves false. The population is an abstraction if I leave out, for example, the classes of which it is composed. These classes in turn [are] an empty phrase if I am not familiar with the elements on which they rest, e.g. wage labour, capital etc. These latter in turn presuppose exchange, division of labour, prices, etc. For example, capital is nothing without wage labour, without value, money, price, etc. Thus, if I were to begin with the population, this would be a chaotic conception of the whole and I would then, by means of further determination, move analytically towards even more simple concepts, from the imagined concrete towards ever thinner abstractions until I had arrived at the simplest determinations. From there the journey would have to be retraced until I had finally arrived at the population again, but this time not as the chaotic conception of the whole, but as a rich totality of many determinations and relations. ... The concrete is concrete because it is the synthesis of many determinations, hence the unity of the diverse. (Marx 1973b: 100–101)

This quotation together with the previous comments about analysing events within their specific social context makes it clear that a historical materialist perspective recognizes diversity and specificity. At the same time, however, it maintains that various analytical categories or abstractions are necessary in order to make sense of the diverse nature of the concrete world. Empirical events or instances are not reduced to theoretical abstractions; rather, these theoretical abstractions are employed to make sense of the otherwise chaotic world around us.

It is important to recognize, however, that prevailing social relations also shape the production and consumption of knowledge.[3] As a consequence, there has been an uneven development of ideas, with class analysis being of longer standing than gender. It is also possible that these analytical categories are of a different order (Pollert 1996). Sophisticated concepts relating to the organization and development of capitalist society have been developed in Marxian political economy and more recently within the French regulation school. The tensions between social classes in capitalist society – e.g., the wage relation or the capitalists' desire to retain their class position – can be shown to provide a motor of change leading to the development of the forces and social relations of production in particular directions, if not in precise ways. So far, analogous concepts for specifying how tensions between genders give rise to social change have not been developed to the same degree.[4] There are, however, analyses that link the form of gender relations with the development of capitalism or social, historical and political change more generally (Walby 1990; Cockburn 1991; Glucksmann 1990; Pollert 1996).

Despite this neglect of gender relations, there is nothing within the historical materialist epistemology that would prohibit such an analysis of gender's role in effecting social change. Capitalist society is structured by social class but simultaneously also by gender, ethnicity and other forms of social differentiation. The wage relation forms the 'simplest determination' of capitalist society, the essential concept that forms the starting point for analysis. But it is crucial to analyse how this structure interweaves with other forms of social differentiation in specific societies at particular moments, and these relations can only be explored empirically.

Thus, in principle the historical materialist method provides a solution to the question of how to recognize and analyse

> the structures that continue to influence the position and experiences of many (if not all) women at some level with an analysis that recognises that these structural processes may be experienced differently and indeed analysed differently by women from different ethnic and class standpoints. (McDowell 1993)

Linda McDowell advocates the view put forward by Sandra Harding (1987) and Donna Haraway (1988) which recognizes that the kind of work carried out and the knowledge produced by people is influenced by their ethnic, class and gender backgrounds.

This is a valuable and important recognition in the world of literary criticism and the philosophy of science. Within the social sciences, however, radical critiques of empiricism – and among them especially Marxist political economy – have always questioned the existence of objective universal knowledge. This is why the methodology has been referred to as historical materialism. There are no universal laws. Any law is specific to a particular kind of society at a particular historical moment.

The criticism that historical materialism is deterministic is misplaced because even within a given context the 'laws' of political economy are not laws in the positivist sense: they do not generate specific testable predictions. While Karl Popper saw this as a fundamental flaw, which he termed historicism (Popper 1966), Herbert Marcuse argued that in reality few scientific laws are capable of predicting specific outcomes

(Popper, Marcuse and Stark 1976). The law of gravity predicts that apples will fall to the ground but cannot say from which tree on which day; and if someone put a net up to catch them they would remain suspended. Hence, within Marxian political economy, laws identify directions or processes generating change but they cannot be deterministic precisely because people respond to and try to influence the course of events. Hence Marx's use of dialectical reasoning.

Within a feminist political economy perspective, concepts such as class, wage labour, capital and gender are the simplest determinations, whose role is to provide a starting point from which to understand the processes taking place in the world. The relationships between these concepts deriving from differing theoretical traditions and the ways in which they can be integrated, combined, enmeshed or materially constituted is far from problematical and was discussed extensively in the single-versus-dual system debates of the 1980s (see Delphy 1984; Phillips 1987; Perrons 1988; Cockburn 1991; Pollert 1996). Nevertheless, use of these concepts contributes towards explanation – they can never be substitutes for explanation, which has to be grounded in specific situations.

This brief résumé of historical materialism indicates that it contains a much greater richness than some critics have recognized. If specific predictions cannot be made within political economy, are there any advantages to be gained by using theoretical conceptions such as gender or class? Or do the preferences of discrete atomistic individuals in the case of neoclassical economics or the multiple and fluid identities of individuals in the cultural perspective make better starting points? There are two related answers to this question, one methodological and one more policy- or politically-oriented. I will discuss these in relation to recent debates in the analysis of consumption.

Contemporary analyses of consumption

Theoretical categories or abstractions provide a simple determination or characteristic that contributes to understanding the way particular individuals/entities fit into a society. As Sartre stated, 'Valery is a petit bourgeois but not every petit bourgeois is a Valery' (Sartre 1976). In other words, knowledge of someone's class position provides some insights but cannot explain a whole person's identity or mode of behaviour. Parallel remarks could be made in relation to gender, ethnicity and even age or a stage in the life course.

There is, however, a marked difference between (a) analyses of the opportunities open to individuals differentiated by social class, gender and ethnicity and (b) cultural analyses, which focus mainly on issues of individual identity and the meaning of events for individuals (because, they argue, the social constraints have weakened). For example Paul Glennie and Nigel Thrift argue that we 'increasingly live in an individualized world' and support the view that:

> Each person's biography is removed from given determination and placed in his or her own hands. ... The proportion of life opportunities which are fundamentally closed to decision-making is decreasing and the proportion of biography which is open and must be constituted personally is increasing. ... Individualisation of life situation and processes means that biographies become self-reflective. Socially prescribed biography is transformed into biography that is self-produced and continues to be produced. (Beck, quoted in Glennie and Thrift 1996: 232)

It is not clear exactly to which past Beck refers, but I would argue that individuals have always been able to shape aspects of their identities if not their destinies but that this freedom has been and continues to be shaped by important social structures or constraints. No organizing structure will ever be able to predict with certainty the 'biography' of the individual. Even when this structure forms a simple determination to be constituted with all the others in a specific context, this is unlikely.

But, then, is the biography of the individual a proper object of social inquiry? In other words, as social scientists, precisely how much detail and what aspects of social behaviour do we actually need to know about? It seems to me that the cultural turn has generated many studies that are highly idiographic, the purpose of which is unclear. The issues in some recent studies of consumption would seem to fall more appropriately within business studies, marketing or advertising than social science.

What, for example, is the social significance of 'hearing' Malcolm state 'my mother gets me Next underwear' or of knowing that Laura prefers shopping with her sister (who has taste) to shopping with her mother who seems to prioritize value for money. The inference drawn by the researchers is that the experience of shopping differs for Laura depending on who she is with and also that the meaning of skilful shopping is contested (Jackson and Holbrook 1995). These views of shoppers may well be of interest to market researchers and advertisers who will gain a clearer idea of whom they should target, but it is less clear that such findings are of interest to a social scientist. Documenting this research finding may overcome the criticism that social research has too often ignored the voices of the researched, but perhaps not all statements made by these voices are of social interest.[5]

Such criticism may be dismissed as reflecting the failure of Marxian political economy to 'engage with the pleasures of consumption' and 'the very ironies and ambiguities that give contemporary consumer culture so much of its power and dynamism' (Jackson and Thrift 1995: 220).[6] Political economy approaches to consumption are also criticized for their determinism. 'Relations of class, gender, sexuality and race are too often seen as unbending lines of force manifested in consumption spaces rather than as actively negotiated constructions of what counts as consumption spaces' (Jackson and Thrift 1995: 210). Specifically in this instance, what is being objected to is the view that shopping malls have been designed to 'persuade, even bully consumers into consuming' (Jackson and Thrift 1995: 210, referring to the ideas of Goss). Jackson and Thrift argue that this perspective neglects the active role of consumers in shaping consumption space, in particular the way shopping spaces may be used for purposes other than shopping and thus embody contested meanings.

However, there is probably a greater consensus between the cultural perspective and political economy than is apparent from the cultural criticisms of political economy reviewed above. The gulf perhaps derives more from reductivist readings of political economy or from particular deterministic applications than from a fundamental opposition. For example, Jackson and Holbrook conclude from their study of shoppers in north London that consumers are neither 'hapless dupes nor superhumanly empowered subjects'. Rather, 'a more nuanced picture begins to emerge of situated human subjectivity and meanings that vary according to social positioning'. Furthermore, they maintain that 'shopping encompasses a wide range of social activities, whose meanings vary with the dynamics of class and gender, ethnicity and generation (among many other mutually constitutive aspects of our human identities)' (Jackson and Holbrook 1995: 1928). This perspective would seem to be in principle consistent with a historical materialist approach as outlined above, although the way in which these different determinations are grounded would be of interest. More fundamentally, however, the issue chosen for analysis would probably differ not only because these analyses might more properly belong in the realm of market research but more funamentally because severe methodological and political problems arise from taking the consumer as the unit of analysis.

This is because there is apparent equality between consumers just as there is between voters; each pound, drachma or dollar in principle carries equal weight.[7] Jon Binnie argues that, while it is a myth to regard all queers as white, middle-class and affluent, nevertheless 'many queers enjoy going shopping ... because shopping offers us the opportunity to assert at least some kind of power' (Binnie 1995: 187). Thus, to some extent the pink pound and pink dollar have led to the creation and promotion of male gay consumption spaces. However, not all gay people can participate in these consumption activities, and few equivalent lesbian spaces exist as the gay community is likewise structured by class, race and gender inequalities. Furthermore although Binnie recognizes that 'the real source of power in society is money' he nevertheless points to the significance of other factors – 'you cannot "consume" yourself out of being sacked purely because of your sexuality' (Binnie 1995: 187–8). Thus, relations of social class have to be interwoven with other determinations to explain diverse reality in particular contexts but, as indicated earlier, this is precisely what empirical studies cast within a historical materialist framework should attempt to do.

Thus, one explanation for the apparent reluctance of political economists to focus on consumption is that the foundations of social inequality lie in the social relations of production and reproduction. Unless the social processes that lead to differentiation of the amounts of money different consumers possess are explained, there is a danger that they may be forgotten, sidelined or taken as given. Neglecting the social processes leading to differentiation is not a problem for marketing people, who can differentiate their products accordingly, but it does not provide a very satisfactory basis for social explanation as it excludes key issues from analysis. Specifically, priority is given to the distribution between pre-given classes or groups rather than explaining their differentiation.[8] John Urry, for example, argues that 'Everyone in the "West" is now entitled to engage in visual consumption, to appropriate landscapes and townscapes more or less anywhere in the world, and to record them to memory photographically. No one should be excluded except for reasons of cost' (Urry 1995: 176). This would seem to me to be a fairly vital form of exclusion but not the only one (see Massey 1993).[9]

Further differentiation between consumers arises from the amount of time at their disposal and the purpose of their shopping. There is a difference between doing the (regular weekly) shopping and going shopping (Bowlby 1997: 102). Given the prevailing division of domestic labour between women and men, women predominate in the former, as well as predominating among the sales workers, while both men and women may 'go shopping'. Despite the wealth of recent studies on the shopping mall, only a partial reading has been produced (Gregson 1995). The mall has been presented as a 'communicative text', and as a 'carnivalesque location ... of iconisation and simulation' (Gregson 1995:

137). The presence of more mundane shops and the shopworkers – predominantly women, except the security guards – have been overlooked. Nicky Gregson attributes this neglect to the difference between 'who is doing the shopping, who is working in retailing and who is writing about the mall'. The geographical writers that she refers to are all male and she argues that once again it is only a male gaze that is being portrayed and what we find are 'masculine and masculinist representations masquerading as universal and homogenizing tendencies in the world of consumption' (Gregson 1995: 137). Given that there are also security guards in these locations, probably more mixed by gender, the class and age location of these writers as well as their philosophical stance within postmodernism are probably equally significant in influencing their objects and methods of inquiry. The partial reading of the shopping mall might in part reflect the authors' identification with 'the middle youth ... sad "adultescents" who parade around Covent Garden and Harvey Nichols in thirtysomething skatewear, deluding themselves that they are down with the kids' (Peretti 1998: 16), rather than simply a male gaze.

Integrating production and consumption: commodity chains, gender and class

Consumption is, however, a vital part of social reproduction, and the products sold are also produced. One person's consumption/reproduction is another person's production. Thus, one way of grounding consumption within its social context is to examine commodity chains (see Fine 1995). Stephanie Barrientos and I have examined one commodity chain, the production of fresh fruit in Chile and its sale in Britain (Barrientos and Perrons 1996, forthcoming).[10] Our main focus was on the increasing integration of women into flexible paid employment at both ends of the commodity chain and on how gender relations have shaped and in turn been shaped by this involvement in the different national and social contexts. This study was, however, set within an analysis of the complex structure of the commodity chain, the relations between the different elements within it (including the processes giving rise to a landless proletariat in Chile) and the changing patterns of retailing and shopping in Britain. These developments in turn are also linked in part to the concentration and centralization of capital within the retailing sector, which in turn has driven the development of the commodity chain. This study goes some way to addressing the changing mode and social relations of production together with undertaking an analysis of changing consumption practices.

Between the mid-1980s and the mid-1990s the application of advanced technologies, including biotechnologies and electronic information systems, has contributed to the rapid increase in the global supply of a wide range of temperate and tropical fruit. Increasingly, commodity chains are driven by supermarkets, which have rapidly increased their share of final sales. Supermarkets in Britain accounted for 64 per cent of fresh fruit sales in 1994 compared to 34 per cent in 1980 (EIU Retail Business 1991, *Fresh Produce Journal* 1994; *Eurofruit*, 1995). By 1996, the big four supermarkets alone accounted for 63 per cent of all grocers' sales (Cowe 1998). Underlying these technological developments and organizational changes are the processes of the concentration and centralization of capital in retailing and fruit production and distribution, along with related changes in forms of consumption and shopping patterns.

Despite the application of new technologies, however, natural and social constraints remain. Fruit remains perishable and markets remain uncertain. The scheduling of production and distribution is therefore crucial to profitability. At one end of the chain the fruit has to be picked and packed at exactly the right moment and within the allotted time frame; at the other, the flow of fruit has to be maintained to ensure sale before it perishes. Labour supplies are adjusted accordingly, generating a demand for flexible female labour at both ends of the chain. Women, who are traditionally associated with the preparation and handling of food in the home, have been increasingly integrated into paid employment through the extension of commercial food production (Goodman and Redclift 1991; Wrigley and Lowe 1996). The sex-typing of work and the gender division of labour within the household encourage women to offer themselves on the labour market for short periods of time and to accept wages below the costs of reproduction (Bruegel and Perrons 1995).

In the case of Chile the new type of non-traditional export requires a greater input of labour than domestic fruit production, particularly in pruning and packing. Women are perceived to have the 'nimble fingers' necessary to prepare the fruit in the pristine presentational form demanded by supermarkets, to be more compliant than the traditional male rural labour force and to be employable flexibly on a seasonal basis. In the space of little more than a decade, paid female labour has became an integral part of this key export sector making up over 50 per cent of the temporary fruit workers (approximately 150,000 women) (Barrientos 1996). From being providers of household subsistence through the domestic cultivation of food they now provide household subsistence through earned income from specialized commercial cultivation of fruit (Barrientos and Perrons forthcoming).

In Britain, multiple retailing has also generated a rapid expansion of flexible female workers. The extended opening hours, including Sunday opening, mean that labour needs cannot be met from a full-time work-force working standard hours. Indeed, in many cases staff are constantly overlapping and people are working in the stores twenty-four hours, seven days a week. Investment in new technology that provides detailed information on both trading patterns and employee availability has also permitted employers to match labour supply with customer demands as they vary throughout the day (Rubery, Horrell and Burchell 1994; Usdaw 1996).

About 10 per cent of all British employees (2.25 million) work in retailing. Almost half of these are women, but in the food supermarket sector the proportion is much higher (Penn and Wirth 1993) and in-creasingly part-time. Just over 55 per cent of women checkout-operators work fewer than sixteen hours a week (Usdaw 1996). In Britain, part-time work is associated with low-income, low-status jobs with little opportunity for progression (a situation shared by part-time workers in the retail sector in other European countries; Perrons 1998).

Thus, the global fruit chain has generated a shift of female work from the household to paid but highly flexible female employment in different but interconnected 'developed' and 'developing' regions. Despite differences in national location, culture, history and religion, unequal gender relations are pervasive even though the forms of work are different and the experience of work varies between women – both within and between countries. An analysis of gender and gender relations is necessary in order to understand the form taken by this supply chain. Similarly, analysis of the processes of capitalist development is necessary to explain the development of the commodity chain itself.

To gain a full understanding of the commodity chain, however, one must also analyse consumption. As Ian Cook (1994) argues regarding exotic fruits, 'just because they are produced and packed in one place and shipped, ripened, and delivered fresh to a store in another, it does not necessarily follow that anyone will buy them'. Besides having to have a use value, commodities have to be symbolically constructed. 'Consumption involves a relationship between the physical and social properties of the commodity' (Fine 1995). Various meanings have been ascribed to fruit and these meanings then have to be matched by their material form to ensure sale (Dowling 1993). Thus it is also necessary to examine how both shopping patterns and the demand for different types of goods have changed.

The pattern and nature of Western food consumption have changed in contradictory ways, which contribute to the sale of fruit. Social scientists have never counted how often people eat with their families so there is insufficient evidence to know whether the general belief that family meals have declined is in fact correct (Murcott 1997). However, it is certain that separate eating, 'eating on the hoof', and snacking form a significant part of contemporary patterns of food consumption in the West and a greater emphasis is placed on 'fast food' but also higher-quality and healthy food. Fruit is perceived to provide health and vitality, is easily prepared, and can form part of a meal, packed lunch or snack and so helps reconcile the potentially conflicting demands of quick preparation and food value. Furthermore, shopping patterns have changed, with daily shopping trips replaced by once-weekly one-stop shopping, especially for dual-earning, car-owning households. This development is made possible by and in turn stimulates the extended opening hours of the supermarkets which, together with their ability to obtain cheaper products on a regular basis throughout the world, contributes to their rising share of the market.

Thus, with the global commercialization of fruit production and retailing, processes of production and consumption that would formerly have taken place within a particular household or locality now extend across the globe. The impact of this new global division of labour on the lives of women both within and between different locations has been varied and contradictory depending on their domestic situation and the specific form of their involvement in the food chain. While there are vast differences between the lifestyles of the fruit packers and the lifestyles of the supermarket workers, they are nevertheless linked by their exploitation as women (independently of their ethnicity, which may form another source of exploitation) and as workers. In some instances, alliances may even be formed with consumers, albeit indirectly. For example, some supermarket chains are involved with Fair Trade, which is designed to improve the conditions of workers engaged in export production.[11] Furthermore, some consumers want to find out more about circumstances of production, such as the hormones and pesticides that are necessary to ensure that the fruit arrives in a 'fresh' state. By drawing upon their common experiences the possibility of forming alliances is more likely. One of the respondents in our study, for example, stated that they had never really thought about the people producing the goods they sold. The bifocal case study in the context of the social processes governing the commodity chain enables the groundwork to be established for setting alliances.

Despite the diversity of experiences among the workers in the fruit chain, the concepts or structures of gender and class remain central to any analysis of new patterns of production and consumption taking place within the global economy. These analytical concepts are crucial for understanding social processes and for recognizing common experiences, both of which are preconditions for the development of transformative politics and policies. This recognition does not deny that in their daily lives people have different experiences of shopping or that shopping has different meanings for people or that shopping spaces are used for a multiplicity of purposes. However, to take people's perceptions as the starting point for analysis could lead to a neglect of the wider processes which shape the overall patterns within which these perceptions are formed.

Given that the meanings of commodities, use and understandings of shopping spaces, and preferences for different shopping partners may vary, and that modern identities are not singular and fixed but dynamic and multiple, it would be very difficult to construct policies or politics to accommodate this fluidity. Thus, it is important to identify commonalties that perhaps have a greater degree of stability. The structural inequalities or cleavages in society can be addressed by common rather than individually tailored policies. As Jasmin Alibhai-Brown argued:

> At different parts of the day, I am a Muslim, a woman, Asian, black, left wing. And I don't want to be told that I am 'the same'. I want my children to learn the languages, their religious identity, to have at their core something different. But when it comes to fighting for political rights – justice, equality – these things ought not to matter at all. (Alibhai-Brown 1996)[12]

While concepts of justice and equality may have different meanings, unless efforts are made to construct shared meanings any form of politics will be extremely difficult. At the same time, recognition of a common project does not mean that individual identities must subsumed in a common struggle. A transformative project would have to build upon diverse identities and people's conception of themselves. However, without any recognition of social processes it will be hard to formulate any common identity of interest necessary to effect social change. As Heidi Mirza (1997) has argued, the problem with identity politics is that it focuses too much on finding out who we are rather than on how we came to be 'located in the racialised and sexual space where we reside' (to this I would add class). Correspondingly, solutions are sought more in terms of changing personal behaviour rather than of challenging wider structures. Central organizing concepts such as gender and class are important for policy and political purposes.

Conclusion

Some of the work on consumption in the cultural tradition has led to a valuable critique of political economy, in particular, of the tendency among some writers in this tradition to substitute social concepts for detailed analysis. To refer back to the long quotation from Karl Marx on page 96, these studies have completed only half of the journey. They have identified simple determinations or cornerstones of social processes but have not considered how they intermesh with each other or with the prevailing social, historical and geographical context. This calls for a greater sensitizing of political economy rather than rejecting it and retreating into the discovery of fragments and contingencies.

To begin analyses with individuals and their identities, to focus on consumption alone and on diversity rather than commonalities, is to overlook the social origins of inequality. Such analyses do not contribute to the establishment of shared understandings and meanings that form the necessary foundations for social change. The analysis of female employment in one food chain suggests that, while the form of gender inequality changes, gender inequality remains. Thus, the concept of gender needs to be retained. The cultural project has a valuable contribution to make in terms of analysing the ways in which the structures are effectively sustained and reproduced in the daily lived experience of people (Wetherell and Potter 1992; Jackson 1992). By drawing on work in different traditions of thought which focus on different but related issues, not only might reality be understood in its entire complex determinations and diversity, but the foundations for social change might be laid.

Notes

1. Ken Saro-Wiwa, a writer, was active in the protests against the way environmental, health and human rights standards were being ignored in the exploitation of oil resources in the Ogoni lands in Nigeria. He was executed on 10 November 1995.

2. At a conference of polytechnic lecturers in economics in the late 1970s the economist Laurence Harris described how, when he lost his job at the London School of Economics following the student disturbances in the late 1960s, he worked at his father's furniture factory in the East End of London. He tried hard but found it impossible to be a benevolent capitalist in a competitive market.

3. Similarly, the prevailing knowledge and ideas of a society are shaped by the material conditions of life. Indeed, there are parallels between the argument that socal constraints have weakened and that people are free to shape their

own identities and the no-liberal project, which has emphasized that individuals are responsible for their own welfare, epitomized perhaps by Mrs Thatcher's remark that there is no such thing as society, only individuals.

4. While it is important to recognize that there are different forms of capitalist society, Anna Pollert points out that 'capitalists could not become "good capitalists" by ceasing to exploit wage labour; they would cease to be capitalists and if they did it en-masse (and we know no system has ever committed collective suicide), capitalism would disappear with it. By contrast, men can and do alter their gender as do women, and they can alter their material and ideological relationship into different gender systems without social production grinding to a halt, or abolishing all gender relations between men and women' (Pollert 1996: 643).

5. These writers are also critical of some cultural approaches for not grounding their analyses in appropriate ethnographic research and for failing to study what people actually do when they go shopping (Jackson and Holbrook 1995: 1, 914). In the case of supermarkets, the shops themselves closely monitor actual sales but now increasingly monitor what people do not buy. While it is probably wrong to see shoppers simply as 'pawns in the hands of faceless hidden persuaders', the knowledge-gathering activities of the managers of mass consumption should not be forgotten. The attention given to common forms of persuasion such as the spatial organization of produce on display should also be recognized. Fruit and vegetables are placed near the entrance, as they not only provide a fresh and healthy image to the store but are also said to be impulse purchases. Drinks, which are bulky, are situated at the opposite end because if they were selected first the shopping carts would have less room for other items (see also Bowlby 1997).

6. This is a clear example of how perceptions vary with standpoint: 'the pleasures of consumption' are restricted to those with time and money.

7. Again, this is more of an apparent than a real equality as the purchasing power of lower-income groups is often reduced by their inability to buy in quantity or to reach lower-cost retail outlets.

8. It is to be hoped that the shift from analyses of production to analyses of consumption will not develop in a parallel way to the marginalist revolution in economics, where the analysis of markets and consumption became the focus of the analytical project. Thus, questions of production within political economy which are linked to the origin of social class were replaced by questions of consumption and the distribution of the social product between pre-given consumers or social groups whose origins and income differences remained external to the analysis.

9. From the quotation it is not entirely clear whether John Urry thinks people without money should be excluded or simply that they are excluded. He goes on to argue that few in the West are formally excluded from tourism, which has become a right of citizenship. The problem of focusing on consumption and the markets in which it takes place remains. Within these markets there is formal equality but substantive inequalities remain, arising in part from different roles in production which to a large extent determine income but also

from gender, ethnicity and sexuality, which in part influence production roles but also place other constraints on freedom of movement. Demonstrating the ways in which these substantive inequalities arise and are perpetuated is an important element of the radical critique of contemporary society, something that seems to be neglected in studies of consumption, which too often slide into studies of the abstract consumer.

10. The case study was based on semi-structured interviews and focus groups with women supermarket workers and managers in the Southeast of England (ranging from highly urbanized outer London to rural mid-Sussex) and with fruit workers in the V, VI and VII regions of Chile; plus interviews with professionals working in the trade. In Chile, Stephanie Barrientos conducted three in-depth interviews and three focus groups, of between five and eight women temporary workers, as well as ten interviews with professionals working in the field. In Britain, Diane Perrons carried out twelve in-depth interviews and two focus groups with women workers, and five in-depth interviews with human resources managers. Subsequently, she carried out further interviews with employees in the retail sector in the context of a comparative project for the European Union (Perrons 1998).

11. The reason for the supermarkets' involvement is largely to protect their reputations but also because the fruit products are regarded as own-brand products for which the retailer is legally responsible under the 1990 Food Safety Act (Doel 1996).

12. Jasmin Alibhai-Brown goes on to criticize young people in Muslim communities who claim rights simply as Muslims; she argues that this overlooks the possibility of forging alliances with other groups. She points out that there is no need to subsume individual identities in a common struggle. While the diversity of culture and identity should not be denied, neither should the existence of common objectives. Otherwise, the people of one group or region may simply be exerting their rights at the expense of others.

References

Aglietta, M. (1979) *A Theory of Capitalist Regulation*. London: New Left Books.

Alibhai-Brown, J. (1996) 'In defence of diversity' (Rosemary Belcher talking to Jasmin Alibhai-Brown), *New Times*, 20 July, p. 2.

Amin, A. and Thrift, N. (1994) *Globalization, Institutions and Regional Development in Europe*. Oxford: Oxford University Press.

Barrientos, S. (1996) 'Flexible work and female labour: the global integration of Chilean fruit production', in R. Auty and J. Toye (eds), *Challenging the Orthodoxies*. Basingstoke: Macmillan.

Barrientos, S. and Perrons, D. (1996) 'Fruit of the vine – linkages between flexible women workers in the production and retailing of winter fruit'. Paper presented to the Conference on the Globalization of Production and the Regulation of Labour, University of Warwick (September).

— (forthcoming) 'Gender and the global food chain: a comparative study of

Chile and the UK', in H. Afshar and S. Barrientos (eds), *Women, Globalisation and Fragmentation in the Developing World*. London: Macmillan.

Baudrillard, J. (1998) *The Consumer Society: Myths and Structures*. London: Sage (originally published in 1970).

Bell, D. and G. Valentine (1997) *Consuming Geographies: We are Where We Eat*. London: Routledge.

Binnie, J. (1995) 'Trading places. Consumption: sexuality and the production of queer space', in D. Bell and G. Valentine (eds), *Mapping Desire*. London: Routledge.

Bowlby, R. (1997) 'Supermarket futures', in P. Falk and C. Campbell, *The Shopping Experience*. London: Sage.

Bruegel, I. and D. Perrons (1995) 'Where do the costs of an unequal treatment for women fall? an analysis of the incidence of the costs of unequal pay and sex discrimination in the UK', *Gender, Work and Organisation*, Vol. 2, No. 3, pp. 113–24.

Cockburn, C. (1991) *In the Way of Women: Men's Resistance to Sex Equality in Organizations*. London: Macmillan.

Cook, I. (1994) 'New fruits and vanity: symbolic production in the global economy,' in A. Bonannon *et al.*, *From Columbus to ConAgra: The Globalization of Agriculture and Food*. Kansas: University of Kansas Press.

Cowe, R. (1998) 'Grocers suffer cold feet', *Guardian*, 26 August, p. 23.

Delphy, C. (1984) *Close to Home: A Materialist Analysis of Women's Oppression*. London: Hutchinson.

Doel, C. (1996) 'Market development and organizational change: the case of the food industry', in N. Wrigley and M. Lowe (eds), *Retailing, Consumption and Capital: Towards the New Retail Geography*. London: Longman

Dowling, R. (1993) 'Femininity, place and commodities: a retail case study', *Antipode*, no. 25, pp. 259–319.

Dunford, M. and D. Perrons (1983) *The Arena of Capital*. Basingstoke: Macmillan
— (1995) 'Structural change, theories of regional development', in G. Benko and U. Strohmayer (eds), *Geography, History and Social Sciences*. London: Kluwer Academic Publishers.

EIU Retail Business (1991) *Fresh Fruit and Vegetables, Parts 1 and 2*, Market Reports 1 and 2, No. 401 and 402, July and August.

Eurofruit, various issues.

Falk, P. and C. Campbell (1997) *The Shopping Experience*. London: Sage.

Fine, B. (1995) 'From political economy to consumption', in D. Miller (ed.), *Acknowledging Consumption*. London: Routledge.

Fresh Produce Journal, 1994 and 1995.

Gill, R. (1993) 'Justifying injustice: broadcasters' accounts of inequality in radio', in E. Burman and I. Parker (eds), *Discourse Analytic Research: Repertoires and Readings of Text in Action*. London: Routledge.

Glennie, P. and N. Thrift (1996) 'Consumption, shopping and gender', in N. Wrigley and M. Lowe (eds), *Retailing, Consumption and Capital: Towards The New Retail Geography*. London: Longman.

Glucksmann, M. (1990) *Women Assemble: Women Workers in the New Industries in Inter-war Britain*, London: Routledge.

Goodman, D. and M. Redclift (1991) *Refashioning Nature, Food, Ecology and Culture*. London: Routledge.

Granovetter, R. (1992) *The Sociology of Everyday Life*. Boulder, CO: Westview Press.

Gregson, N. (1995) 'And now it's all consumption?' *Progress in Human Geography*, Vol. 19, No. 1, pp. 135–41.

Haraway, D. (1988) 'Situated knowledges: the science question in feminism and the privilege of the partial perspective', *Feminist Studies*, Vol. 14, No. 3, pp. 575–99.

Harding, S. (1987) *Feminism and Methodology*. Bloomington: Indiana University Press.

Jackson, P. (1992) *Maps of Meaning*. London: Routledge.

Jackson, P. and Holbrook, B. (1995) 'Multiple meanings: shopping and the cultural politics of identity', *Environment and Planning* A, Vol. 27, pp. 1913–32.

Jackson, P. and N. Thrift (1995) 'Geographies of consumption', in D. Miller (ed.), *Acknowledging Consumption*. London: Routledge

Jessop, B. (1991) 'Fordism and post-Fordism: A Critical Reformulation', Lancaster Regionalism Group Working Paper 41.

Lipietz, A. (1987) *Mirages and Miracles: The Crisis of Global Fordism*. London: Verso.

McDowell, L. (1991) 'Life without father and Ford: the new gender order of post-Fordism', *Transactions of the Institute of British Geographers*, Vol. 16, No. 4, pp. 400–19.

— (1993) 'Space, place and gender relations: Part 2. Identity, difference, feminist geometries and geographies', *Progress in Human Geography*, Vol. 17, No. 3, pp. 305–18.

Marx, K. (1973a) *A Contribution to the Critique of Political Economy*. London: Lawrence and Wishart.

— *Grundrisse: Introduction to Political Economy*. Harmondsworth: Penguin.

Massey, D. (1993) 'Power-geometry and a progressive sense of place', in J. Bird *et al.* (eds), *Mapping the Futures*. London: Routledge.

Mirza, H. (1997) 'Mapping a genealogy of black British feminism', in H. Mirza (ed.), *Black British Feminism: A Reader*. London: Routledge.

Murcott, A. (1997) 'Family meals – a thing of the past?' in P. Caplan (ed.), *Food, Health and Identity*. London: Routledge.

Peet, R. (1998) *Modern Geographical Thought*. Oxford: Blackwell.

Penn, R. and B. Wirth (1993) 'Employment patterns in contemporary retailing: gender and work in five supermarkets', *Service Industries Journal*, Vol. 14, No. 4, pp. 252–66.

Peretti, J. (1998) 'Middle youth ate my culture', *Modern Review*, No. 5, pp. 15–19.

Perrons, D. (1988) 'Flexible accumulation, gender and space', City of London Polytechnic Working Paper No. 12.

— (1998) 'Flexible working – the reconciliation of work and family life or a new form of precariousness. Comparative Report'. Produced for the European Union, DGV Brussels.

Pfau-Effinger, B. (1995) 'Social change in the gendered division of labour in cross-national perspective'. Paper given to the Second European Conference of Sociology, working group on Gender Relations and the Labour Market in Europe, Budapest, September.

Phillips, A. (1987) *Divided Loyalties: Dilemmas of Sex and Class*. London: Virago.

Pile, S. and N. Thrift (1995) 'Mapping the subject', in S. Pile and N. Thrift (eds), *Mapping the Subject: Geographies of Cultural Transformation*. London: Routledge.

Pollert, A. (1996) 'Gender and class revisited; or the poverty of patriarchy', *Sociology*, Vol. 30, No. 4, pp. 639–59.

Popper, K. (1966) *The Open Society and Its Enemies*. Vol. 2. *The High Tide of Prophecy – Hegel, Marx and the Aftermath*. London: Routledge and Kegan Paul.

Popper, K., H. Marcuse and F. Stark (1976) *Revolution oder Reform?: Herbert Marcuse und Karl Popper. Eine Konfrontation*. Munich: Kusel-Verlag.

Rubery J., S. Horrell and B. Burchell (1994) 'Part-time work and gender inequality in the labour market', in A.M. Scott (ed.), *Gender Segregation and Social Change: Men and Women in Changing Labour Markets*. Oxford: Oxford University Press.

Sartre, J.-P. (1976) *Critique of Dialectical Reason*. London: New Left Books.

Sayer, A. (1993) 'Postmodernist thought in geography: a realist view', *Antipode*, Vol. 25, No. 4, pp. 320–44.

— (1997) 'The dialectic of culture and economy: the economization of culture and the culturalization of the economy', in R. Lee and J. Wills (eds), *Geographies of Economies*. London: Arnold.

Schoenberger, E. (1991) 'The corporate interview as a research method in economic geography', *Professional Geographer*, Vol. 43, No. 2, pp. 180–89.

Sen, A. (1991) 'Gender and co-operative conflicts', in I. Tinker (ed.), *Persistent Inequalities: Women and World Development*. Oxford: Oxford University Press.

Urry, J. (1995) *Consuming Places*. London: Routledge.

Usdaw (1996) *Women in Usdaw – An Integral Role: The Agenda for 1996*. Manchester: Usdaw.

Walby, S. (1990) *Theorizing Patriarchy*. Oxford: Blackwell.

Wetherell, M. and J. Potter (1992) *Mapping the Language of Racism: Discourse and the Legitimation of Exploitation*. Hemel Hempstead: Harvester-Wheatsheaf.

Wrigley, N. and M. Lowe (eds) (1996) *Retailing, Consumption and Capital: Towards the New Retail Geography*. London: Longman.

CHAPTER 6

Tigers and Transnational Corporations: Pathways from the Periphery?

Denis O'Hearn[1]

Part of the so-called impasse in development studies involved a negative reaction to modernization and critical political economy approaches alike. This took many forms, often including a move away from political economy and towards culture and the dismissal of both modernization and dependency as 'Eurocentric' in their approval of conceptions of development that included technology, innovation and growth. Some experts even pursued *anti*-development arguments like those in Sachs's *Development Dictionary* (1992), which began with a call to 'write [development's] obituary'. Esteva argued that the marginalized 'common man' had, in practice, *marginalized development* by creating new forms of survival based on community-embedded strategies for provisioning, where orthodox conceptions of the 'economic' were irrelevant (Esteva 1992). Such talk, along with other culturalist analyses, struck a chord at a time when postmodernism was making its mark in all social studies, including development studies, and when many adherents of the 'impasse' thesis proclaimed that dependency-type approaches were dead. Culturalists like Vincent Tucker, however, went beyond mere anti-developmentalism to argue for a new synthesis of critical cultural and political economy approaches based on dialogue (see Chapter 1).

A critical political economy of development remains vital today. Even 'socially-embedded' economies require resources and can benefit from the technologies and productivity that have been centred in increasingly global economies. Using Sutcliffe's terminology (Chapter 7), this puts the 'attainability' and 'desirability' critiques on their heads: is a community-based social economy possible or desirable without elements of products, practices, and technologies that have been developed largely in the core regions of a global economy?

Access to material resources and to the products of human labour is crucial in 'communities' and 'economies' alike. The lessons of works by Polanyi (1957), Granovetter (1985) and others on embeddedness is, surely, *not* that 'the economy' does not exist or should be marginalized but that 'economy' in its substantive sense *cannot* be marginalized because it pervades every aspect of our existence. Yes, we must reorder our priorities and revalue many activities of provisioning that are not 'marketable' today. But even social economies require resources and technologies – what a difference the laptop computer and the mobile phone have made to marginalized communities and indigenous movements from Chiapas to Nigeria!

Despite their Eurocentricity, it could still be argued that concepts like productivity and innovation have an important place in any of our hopes to create new forms of society that can genuinely improve cultural and material living conditions. Historically, however, the control of key innovations and technologies by core capitals and their allied states has been crucial to their establishment of global economic power and the maintenance of global inequality (O'Hearn 1994). Under such conditions, the *development* of social economies requires fairer access to and control of such resources and technologies than exist in today's global economy.

For these reasons, I believe the subject of unequal control of key economic activities and innovations is still at the heart of a critical development theory. Unfortunately, the real world transition to (or intensification of) globalization has made access to, and control over *meanings* of, technologies and resources more unequal than ever. The rise of supranational global institutions and market-oriented 'global networks has increased the power of core capitals to subjugate peripheral regions in the age of 'postmodernism' and 'postdevelopmentalism'. If we hope to achieve the socialization of economy, that is, the demarginalization of what has not been valued in orthodox economics, we *still* require an understanding of how a small minority of people within a minority of regions of the world control the vast majority of material resources and technologies. In doing so, they not only reproduce uneven development, they also compel underdeveloped regions to participate in a system that prioritizes commercialistic exchange-value considerations over popular well-being.

Ironically, while globalization intensified core power and control over resources it also created new 'miracles' that purport to show the opposite. The so-called tiger economies have powerfully reinforced the conception that upward mobility is possible in the global system. The perception that there are 'pathways from the periphery', to use

Haggard's (1990) phrase, was enhanced by the arrival of wider groups of Southeast Asian countries as the new 'tiger cubs'.

It could be argued that globalization has created a new image of development through global integration that is, in many ways, even more attractive than the old model of national development and growth centred on transnational corporations (TNCs). Former critics of TNC-centred growth can now be found to argue that dependency theory 'has been rendered obsolete by the rise of a growing number of developing countries to NIE [newly-industrialized economy] and near-NIE status, in part through the vehicle of foreign investment and increased participation in international trade' (Lim and Fong 1991: 180). Although the authors of this statement are generalizing from the limited experiences of East and Southeast Asia, this perspective has been strengthened by the rise of new tiger economies outside Asia, such as southern Ireland[2] and Chile, which have attained growth on the basis of the neoliberal orthodoxies of export orientation, maximum global integration, and market-friendly policies for macroeconomic stability (McMichael 1996: 151–2). Clearly, modernizationism has yet to be put to rest.

A most challenging aspect of these countries' recent rise to tigerhood is that they, unlike the original East Asian tigers, appear to demonstrate that the most reliable contemporary 'pathway' from the periphery is a neoliberal one that eschews any notion of a 'developmental state'. That is so, at least, in Peter Evans's (1995) sense of a state that continues to be involved in the 'husbandry' of economic units and not just as a 'midwife' at their birth. The Southeast Asian tiger cubs, several of which had decidedly statist elements in their economic growth strategies, liberalized substantially during the late 1980s by privatizing, cutting back on public expenditures, and enhancing their attractions to foreign investors. The result, arguably, was an acceleration of their economic growth. Moreover, the most popular interpretation of the Asian crisis of the late 1990s reinforces the positive view of neoliberalism, since Southeast Asia and Korea are seen to have reached their limitations because they did not sufficiently cut back state management of their economies and, as a result, they have been induced to liberalize on the basis that 'developmental states' are inevitably inefficient and corrupt.[3]

In this sense, while globalization has made the image of development more rather than less attractive, it has also raised neoliberalism to a hegemonic position. The rise of Asia, and the replacement of the rapacious beast of imperialism by the more benign Asian *flying geese* model (discussed below), renewed the promise that regions could achieve material development, this time by becoming integrated into global networks. And in the newer tiger economies not only did it appear that transnational corporations could help regions become richer rather than impeding them, it also appeared that this promise was available to more regions rather than fewer. In this context, development is decidedly not dead for many regions of the former Second and Third Worlds. As a result, we have a greater need than ever for understanding of the political economy of globalization if we hope to transform the system.

Despite the appearance that some regions of the globe are now more upwardly mobile than hitherto with respect to their possibilities of creating material wealth, however, the reality of development is still that 'many are called ... few are chosen' (Cumings 1984). Economic tigerhood is limited to a few regions; recent rapid-growth economies are increasingly dependent and unsustainable; localities have lost economic instruments resulting in reduced abilities to build developmental states; and economic tigers are increasingly excluded from innovative high-profit activities that are still carefully monopolized by capitals from core regions.

Moreover, although the latest phase of globalization makes new promises for semiperipheral regions that succeed in achieving high growth, it carries new dangers of severe economic marginalization for peripheral regions and unsuccessful semiperipheral ones. Although neoliberalism has swept away some of the more corrupt state practices of the former Third World, it has also left peripheral states without instruments to achieve positive economic changes.

In many ways, these contentions parallel and develop critiques of earlier phases of modernization/development. I will finish the chapter, however, by asking whether tigers can use their relatively advantageous positions within the global division of labour and within major regional groupings to create new possibilities for change.

From 'development project' to 'globalization project'

In a recent book, Philip McMichael (1996) analyses how the 'development project' of the 1950s and 1960s gave way to a 'globalization project' which prevails to this day. Where the first project advanced the hope of national development through economic management, the second integrated regions into the world market in ways that were primarily determined at the global level. Where the first gave hope for progress through 'developmental states' which regulated markets, the second emphasized strict adherence to self-regulated markets. Where the first promised social entitlement and welfare as an aspiration, the second promised only the right to participate in the world market.

Ironically, this 'postdevelopmentalism' enhanced the promise of development in many parts of the world.

The old 'developmental project' viewed growth-related development with relative optimism. There was widespread agreement that *nations* could follow the Western route to development through industrialization. Orthodox modernization theories assumed that societies could become 'modern' by acting in modern ways and, specifically, by inducing and/or allowing 'enterprising men' to come forward and forgo current pleasure for future gain. Such behaviour would eventually but inevitably lead to a 'take-off to self-sustained growth' for each country around the globe (Rostow 1960). Many Marxists and other critics agreed in principle with the desirability of industrialization but argued that the behaviour of developed capitalist states and firms barred other countries from achieving it. Therefore, late developers required special tools: interventionist states to overcome barriers to development, or a new international order to level the playing field. Both approaches held that national development through industrialization was possible and desirable, and it was this that people like Sachs rejected.

Yet 'globalization' was already changing the discourse in ways that presented new challenges to critical development theory. Many of us would argue that 'globalization' is, in many ways, little more than a repackaging of 'development'. The nature of global hegemony is less clear than it was under Pax Americana, but new international institutions provide even greater protection for core 'property' than before. An 'open door' policy that was backed primarily by US force turned into 'neoliberalism'. After a decade, in the 1980s, of 'disciplining' through debt and disinvestment, this new regime is most powerfully enforced by getting less developed states themselves to agree that markets provide the most rational way of doing things. More and more countries 'voluntarily' joined the General Agreement on Tariffs and Trade (GATT) and subsequently came under the new rules of the World Trade Organization (WTO) including, most crucially, the rules protecting Northern technology under the guise of 'intellectual property'. Thus, McMichael and others (Arrighi *et al.* 1993; Arrighi 1995) argue that countries participate in the 'globalization project' not as nations inevitably on their way to modernity, but as pragmatic and strategic actors in a much more restricted game that is governed by free trade, specializing in what can be done without the aid of protection, privatization, and 'living within one's means'. One could argue that, from the point of view of the industrialized core, the 'development project' was always a 'globalization project'. But its global character has been strengthened by several decades of core penetration of all regions of the globe, by

TNC investments, and by the restructuring of world trading and investment patterns after capitalism's crises of the 1970s and 1980s. Most
important, as alternative localized strategies have been discredited,
globalization appears more and more to be the 'only game in town'.

Within the broad globalization discourse, the rise of Asia as a
powerful economic region has been one of the most widely discussed
and debated development phenomena. The organization of Asian production and trade, and the demonstration effects of this organization
on economic restructuring worldwide, is at the centre of globalization.
East Asia's rise from the periphery where other regions failed appears
to challenge critical approaches to development such as dependency
and world-systems.

Furthermore, in the newer tigers such as Ireland and Chile, and
tiger cubs such as Thailand, Malaysia and Indonesia, fresh opportunities
for upward economic mobility were associated with new patterns of
outward movement by TNCs. Even US-based TNCs appeared to be
making investments that were less clearly *under*developing than the old
imperialism. This apparent widening of economic success, then, raises
questions about whether regions can now attain upward *dependent*
mobility under capitalist globalization and what this bodes for their
populations. Under what conditions is tigerhood possible? And is such
rapid growth a sustainable phenomenon or merely transient like the
promised 'bonanza development' of earlier decades (Becker 1987)? A
first step towards answering these questions is an examination of the
original tiger economies of East Asia and the characteristics that made
them 'successful'.

Old tigers

Experts widely agree that the original four tiger economies were
South Korea, Taiwan, Singapore, and Hong Kong. They all achieved
rapid and sustained economic growth over several decades, along with
even higher annual growth rates of manufactured exports. Orthodox
economists turned this association into a purported relationship: export
growth *causes* economic growth. Moreover, the World Bank (1993) tried
to attribute economic growth to the four tigers' strict observance of
the 'market friendly' approach by 'getting the prices right' so that
markets could be left to do their job of creating growth and prosperity.
The World Bank's message for other countries that aspire to growth is
clear: dismantle protection in favour of free trade, privatize, open your
economies to the free movement of foreign investments, and export
(or let TNCs do it for you).

Contrary to the World Bank, however, most experts found that the East Asian tigers 'succeeded' primarily because their states *intervened* in their economies. With the exception of Hong Kong, each state intervened heavily to promote local industry, exports and economic growth; they oppressed their populations and popular movements to control wages and maintain stability; they actively controlled markets through public policy; and they developed state-owned industries (Lim 1983; Grice and Drakakis-Smith 1985; Huff 1995). State policies also encouraged rapid demographic transitions to highly urban, low-fertility, low-mortality societies; dynamic agricultural sectors; high levels of education and training; and rapid growth in personal savings and investment (Page 1994: 616–17). According to Amsden (1994: 627), the East Asian states *created* competitiveness through 'pervasive intervention'. Along with Japan, these states have been largely responsible for the popularity of the concept of the 'developmental state' among sociologists and political scientists (Evans 1995).

Other late-industrializing states intervened less successfully. Most encountered opposition from global forces such as the US government and the World Bank, which coerced them into liberalizing their economies (George 1992). But the East Asians, until recently, avoided such coercion for geopolitical reasons (Cumings 1984; So and Chiu 1995). Moreover, East Asian states intervened *effectively*. Some experts credit the special nature of Japanese colonialism with transforming 'corrupt and ineffective' East Asian states into highly authoritarian but effective developmental states, while clearing out class interests that corrupted other postcolonial states. Once Japan reintegrated East Asia into its regional economy during and after the 1960s, these developmental states were further encouraged (Kohli 1994).

Most important, Japanese expansion differed from Western imperialism. Hill and Fujita (1995) argue that major differences between US and Japanese corporate strategies caused differences in their foreign investment strategies which, in turn, affected developmental outcomes in countries they integrated into their regional divisions of labour. Where oligopolistic US firms tried to maintain profits by secretly protecting technologies and products, by controlling markets and by cheapening labour costs, Japanese corporations competed by constantly upgrading their products and ways of producing them, that is, by *shortening* product life-cycles in order to capture monopoly profits from introducing new products and production processes.

As they shifted into new higher-value-added activities, Japanese companies shed their more standardized products and components to subcontractors, often non-Japanese. Akamatsu Kaname called this a 'flying geese' model of regional development: the countries of Asia form an inverse V formation, like wild geese, with Japan in the lead. As Japan advanced and concentrated in higher-tech industrial activities, it shed the next-lower echelon of activities and technologies to the East Asian countries in its wake. As the East Asian economies took on these new activities, they in turn shed the next lower rank of activities and technologies to Southeast Asia in their wake. As leading countries advanced, they brought along 'new industrializers' behind them. In this guise, it appeared, a new Asian 'modernization' actually worked.

Japan corporate structures also differed from those in the West. The typical Western multidivisional firm (Chandler 1962) moves abroad through fully- or majority-owned corporate affiliates to gain access to raw materials, cheap labour, and/or markets. The resulting 'global corporation' has many subsidiaries that sell inputs to each other and assemble products for markets throughout the world (Jenkins 1987). Japan, however, is at the centre of a regional 'multilayered sub-contracting system' that extends into East and Southeast Asia (Arrighi *et al.* 1993: 49). Where the typical Western firm sources inputs internally through its subsidiaries, Japanese corporations like Honda or Mitsubishi source most of their inputs externally from hundreds of small and medium-sized firms, who in turn subcontract from thousands of smaller firms, and so on down the line to tens of thousands of the smallest producers (Arrighi *et al.* 1993: 51). From the mid-1970s onwards, large Japanese firms embarked on joint ventures and subcontracting agreements in Asia, encouraging local suppliers from outside Japan.

These Japanese investments were far more agglomerated geographically than Western direct investments. Arrighi *et al.* (1993: 60) suggest that this was particularly important in the 1960s and early 1970s, when the four East Asian economies received more than half of Japanese investments in textiles and 80 per cent in electronics. Western investments did not really agglomerate until the restructuring of the late 1980s and 1990s, and even then less so than Japanese investments. Moreover, the rapid and sustained growth of East Asia is explained not just by the number of Japanese investments, but by the fact that they created networks of linked economic activities and, most important, encouraged the rise of strong domestic industrial sectors.

This pattern of industrial upgrading and 'shedding' created a different regional economy in Asia from the wider US-led world economy. Technological learning and upgrading occurred as a matter of course in larger Korean *chaebol* (conglomerates) like Samsung and smaller companies in Taiwan and Hong Kong (Hobday 1994a, 1994b). The Japanese arguably found such development desirable because East Asian corporations became some of the most important customers for Japanese high-tech products. Where US firms saw vibrant electronics industries in other countries as competitors, Japanese corporations and state bodies like the Ministry of International Trade and Industry (MITI) saw them as potential customers (Arrighi *et al.* 1993).

Thus, Japanese foreign investment allows considerably more scope than the Western variety for industrialization by its semiperipheral junior partners. Yet it also has limitations, perhaps especially for later waves of 'new industrializers' in Indonesia and Malaysia, or China and Vietnam. As Bello (1993) points out, East Asian regional integration is still based on an unequal division of labour. Compared to Japan, even South Korea and Taiwan are still mainly sites for relatively labour-intensive production, such as electronic assembly of Japanese components. Their 'heavy' industries like shipbuilding, steel, or machine tools are relatively less high-tech and bring fewer profits than associated Japanese nodes of the same commodity chains of which they form a part. And even their leading sectors, like computers or cars, are still heavily dependent on Japanese technology (Smith 1997; Hobday 1994a, 1994b). Thus, although being an economic tiger has been a 'pathway from the periphery' in one sense for the East Asian economies, it has also limited their access to technologies and resources.

Krugman has taken this lack of real innovation in East Asia to deliver the most stinging critique of the East Asian 'miracle', which he calls simply a 'myth'. 'What is miraculous about more inputs yielding more output?' he asks, adding, 'Economies cannot forever keep increasing labour and capital inputs at such high rates' (Krugman 1994: 64). From an ecological point of view, such extensive growth could be considered especially shocking because it is so dependent on the added use of resources, without even the typical 'technology fix' that First World champions of economic growth have called upon to justify their depletion of scarce resources.

New tigers and old tigers: the role of TNCs

Up to this point, the discussion has given little support to the neo-liberal ideology of contemporary globalization. East Asia developed by virtue of special conditions and strong state intervention rather than through liberalization, adherence to 'market principles' and, especially, transnational corporate investments. Japanese firms invested in South Korea and Taiwan, but mostly to encourage the kinds of regional subcontractors and consumers the new upgraded Japanese industries desired. Domestic industrial sectors thrived in these economies under

Pacific regional integration. Even in Hong Kong, whose success has concentrated more in its financial sector than that of either South Korea or Taiwan, industrial successes were largely domestic and integrated into regional subcontracting networks.

Another East Asian tiger, however, appears to offer a more optimistic view of foreign direct investment. Singapore based its economic growth on concentrated investments from targeted foreign sectors, exploiting its cheap labour and its historical role as entrepôt for trade within the region and between several continents. It set up an economic development board (EDB) in 1959 to create the necessary infrastructure for industry and to identify the most promising sectors to attract foreign investments. The EDB targeted electronics TNCs after 1966 and, as a result, the electronics share of assets in manufacturing grew rapidly, from less than 2 per cent in 1965 to nearly 30 per cent in 1980 (Lee 1997: 60). The EDB also targeted financial and business services, based on Singapore's own historic 'comparative advantages' as entrepôt and banker to trade, and Singapore soon became the centre of Asian financial services.

In apparent neoliberal style, the state avoided restrictions on the entry of foreign capital or personnel, or on their activities in Singapore. There is no restriction on the removal of capital or profits, dividends and interest. The state provided TNCs with tax incentives; duty-free importation of equipment and materials; and various subsidies and grants. It also guaranteed political stability, peaceful industrial relations, and orderly wage increases, while suppressing labour movements (Lee 1997).

These policies made Singapore, in one expert's words, 'the world's most globalized economy' (Ramesh 1995). It was the biggest recipient of foreign direct investments outside of the developed core during the 1980s, receiving nearly 13 per cent of such investments (Huff 1995: 738, 739). The foreign share of manufacturing investments in Singapore grew from 43 per cent in 1965 to 75 per cent in 1994, and the foreign share of GDP doubled from 18 per cent in 1970 to 36 per cent in 1990 (Lee 1997). Foreign companies today account for three quarters of manufacturing output and 85 per cent of manufactured exports (Huff 1995: 740).

But several things keep Singapore from being a model of neoliberal development. Most obviously, a city-state can maintain rapid growth much easier than a larger country, where rapid manufacturing growth in cities is often achieved at the expense of rural stagnation and poverty. Singapore manipulates surrounding countries to attract migrant labour when necessary, leaving problems of underdevelopment and unemployment to them.

Moreover, as in South Korea and Taiwan, Singapore's state intervenes heavily in the economy. It is directly involved in key support sectors for export industries and in traded services such as shipping, banking, transport, and trading. It forces workers to save a part of their incomes, which it has invested in infrastructure and public enterprise, both of which helped to attract foreign investments. And government directives replace market mechanisms in the labour market. In short, the 'Singapore model' of economic growth is based on strict control of labour, heavy state investment in infrastructure financed by forced savings, extensive state enterprise, *and* high dependence on TNC investments in manufacturing and financial services (Lee 1997; Huff 1995).

Even more than South Korea and Taiwan, however, Singapore faces barriers to technological development. High-profit stages like R&D and product design remain in the home countries of TNCs. The state has been notably unsuccessful at restructuring the economy toward higher-tech activities since it has little influence over the kinds of projects provided by TNCs. Huff contends that 'the reliance on foreigners, together with Singapore's lack of an indigenous technological contribution to manufacturing, marks the Republic as not being a developed country' (Huff 1995: 741). Krugman's stinging critique of the East Asian 'miracle' applies doubly to Singapore, whose 'success' lies primarily in its ability to attract a continuous enough flow of foreign investments to maintain high economic growth rates and ensure full employment.

It is not surprising, therefore, that the next wave of tiger cubs were states around Singapore that began to attract TNCs directly instead of exporting cheap labour to Singapore to work in them. Malaysia had welcomed foreign investments before 1985, but they were not aggressively pursued; the high degree of foreign ownership of Malaysian business was mostly a legacy of its colonial past (Lim and Fong 1991: 40). And before 1985, local Thai business elites had managed to limit foreign investments to parts of the automobile and textiles industries, where Japanese capital was quite active. But after the recession of the 1980s, these and other countries of the region rapidly liberalized their economies. They privatized public agencies, turned their development priorities towards exports, liberalized rules on foreign ownership, cut corporate taxes, and expanded investment incentives. As a result, foreign investments soared. TNCs accounted for nearly half of Malaysia's fixed capital investment in 1985–90 (UNCTAD 1997). Thailand made a conscious decision to 'upgrade' its export profile from textiles to electronics, helped by trade liberalization. It secured major foreign investments in electronics after 1985 and was considered the most attractive investment location in Southeast Asia (Lim and Fong 1991: 25). Consequently, the growth rates of each country rose, nearly doubling in Thailand during 1985–90 to 9.9 per cent. Foreign electronics investments accounted for one third of the growth of value added in Thai manufacturing during this period, rising to 40 per cent in the 1990s. One company alone, Seagate, increased its Thai employment from 5,000 to 20,000 in just two years after 1986. Both Malaysia and Thailand, in turn, were hailed as the 'fifth Asian tiger'.

Unsurprisingly, the result of such high inflows of foreign capital was rapid economic growth in Southeast Asia, soon to be followed by China. Worldwide, moreover, the wave of new foreign investments in the 1990s – largely driven by a desire of TNCs to gain access to the main Asian, North American and European markets – created other new tigers whose rapid growth rates were based primarily on direct TNC investments and subsequent rapid growth of TNC-based exports to crucial markets.

Southern Ireland – the 'Celtic tiger' as Morgan Stanley put it (Gardiner 1994) – is a prime example of rapid growth driven by TNCs in pursuit of market access. In the 1980s, the southern Irish economy was the failure of Europe, with stagnant growth rates, rapid foreign disinvestment, unemployment rates exceeding 20 per cent, and rapid emigration. Yet it achieved a stunning turnaround in the 1990s. US computer firms such as Intel and Microsoft wanted to locate plants within the European Union so that they could increase their share of the European Union (EU) market. They had learned lessons of flexibility from the Japanese experience – especially, the benefits that could come from locating close to one another to reduce transactions costs and create flexible networks of purchase and supply. The Irish Industrial Development Authority attracted Intel to southern Ireland as the base of their European operations, at huge costs in terms of grants, special loan packages and, most important, nearly tax-free status for their profits. Nearly every major player in the computer industry followed Intel to Ireland. Within a few years, the TNC sector in southern Ireland was practically a *Who's Who* in computers, peripherals, software and teleservicing centres.

The foreign share of fixed capital investment in the south of Ireland rose to 75–80 per cent in the 1990s. Dependence on US investments became particularly acute, rising from 40–50 per cent of foreign investments during the mid-1980s to more than 75 per cent in the 1990s. TNC exports skyrocketed, accounting for up to three quarters of southern Ireland's economic growth in the 1990s. Most of the rest of this growth was in associated service and construction sectors. And all of this took place within a context of fiscal austerity, privatization, and maximum integration into the EU with its single market. Ireland became a showpiece of globalization, a prime example of how a region could turn around from economic laggard to tiger in just a few years, by integrating itself maximally into the global division of labour.

Because the source of economic growth in the new tigers is TNC-driven exports, growth has been concentrated in industry, especially in manufacturing. These economies are significantly more industrialized today than they were in 1980. During 1970–93, the share of industry in GDP grew from 20–25 to about 40 per cent in Thailand, Indonesia, and Malaysia, and from 38 to 48 per cent in China. Within manufacturing, growth was concentrated in so-called 'modern' sectors like computers, electrical machinery and pharmaceuticals. During 1970–92, the share of machinery and equipment in manufacturing output grew from 2 to 14 per cent in Indonesia, from 4 to 40 per cent in Thailand, from 8 to 34 per cent in Malaysia, and from 13 to 27 per cent in southern Ireland. Because they are export-oriented, merchandise exports became heavily concentrated in these sectors (World Bank 1995: 166–7; 190–91).

Many of these sectoral characteristics also applied to East Asia. But unlike these 'old' tigers (Singapore excepted), the 'new' ones depend more on direct TNC investments for their growth. During 1985–90, foreign debt investment (FDI) flows accounted for 43.7 per cent of fixed capital investment in Malaysia, 24 per cent in southern Ireland, 14.5 per cent in China and 10.2 per cent in Thailand (UNCTAD 1997: Annex Table B.5).

By contrast, not only was inward FDI far less important in South Korea and Taiwan, but outward investments there were about double the level of inward investments. South Korea and Taiwan were careful to avoid direct TNC investments and, in doing so, avoided some of the classic problems of dependency. Direct TNC investments contributed less than 2 per cent to South Korea's capital formation during 1976–95, and about 3 per cent to Taiwan's during the same period. To put the strength of East Asian local industry into perspective, Japanese and US FDI into the four tigers during the whole period 1980–88 amounted to $11.6 billion, which is just one fifth of Samsung's *annual* sales (Hobday 1994a: 336, 337; also UNCTAD 1997). This does not mean, however, that these economies avoided foreign investments altogether – indeed, foreign investments in these countries have been significant. Yet they have taken different forms, such as joint ventures and subcontracting networks, than in the later tiger economies.

Looking at how the different economies, new tigers and old, gained their reputations as economic miracles, perhaps the most striking difference is that East Asia's economic reputation was based on consistent rapid economic growth over several decades, while the sustainability of growth in the new tigers is already challenged by the economic crises in Asia and Latin America. Their rise in status has been meteoric, in southern Ireland's case over less than half a decade, resembling more the 'bonanza' development of other countries, especially in Latin America, during the 1970s.

Results: sustainability and desirability

Economic tigers have apparently achieved upward mobility in the world system. The original East Asian tigers are now among the richest countries in the world in terms of per capita incomes. The World Bank classifies them all as 'high-income economies', whereas as recently as 1980 they were nowhere near such status. In terms of per capita GDP, Singapore is now the eighth richest country in the world. Moreover, the tiger economies – and only they – have become significantly richer compared to the United States since 1987.[4]

But in what sense is this 'development'? Are these countries now more able to sustain their newly found positions of growth and higher wealth? Do they control or have greater access to key technologies / innovations and associated economic activities that characterize core economies? Are they much closer to acquiring resources that could, even if their regimes were of a mind, enable them to achieve the kinds of social economies that many of us would desire (and, of course, why should they be if already-'developed' capitalism cannot provide such economies)? Do the kinds of policies these states must pursue in order to achieve rapid economic growth – in this case TNC-dependency and neoliberalism – help or hinder them in introducing more humane forms of economic organization and sets of economic activities?

We have already seen that even Singapore and South Korea have been called 'underdeveloped' in technological terms because they are still dependent on core countries for access to the most innovative technologies and technicians. In the countries that I have called 'new tigers', TNC-dependency narrows the structure of economic activities even further – the technological basis of growth is even shallower than in East Asia. Although these countries produce more and more 'high-tech' industrial exports, they actually perform restricted and routine activities within those commodity chains. They have little control over what is produced, how it is produced, or for whom it is produced in the sectors in which they are so heavily involved. Nor are they particularly powerful relative to core regions as consumers of high technology. Rather, they respond to the strategic plans of leading TNCs and to technological imperatives that are formed in core regions and largely for core regions. Where Samsung is forced to take its product development to the US because it lacks the right kinds of skilled technicians, newer tigers have little product development in this sense to take anywhere. This is an important constraint on the sustainability of the tiger economies but, ultimately, the question of the distribution of technology and innovation is a crucial one because a project of building alternative socially based economies will require a technological order that can be turned to their needs.

In more immediate terms, rapid economic growth in the new tiger economies has not been matched by a comparable increase in the material standards of living of their populations (even aside from questions of distribution). Consumption is not necessarily 'good' in its present forms – we know, for example, that it is unequally distributed and also that it is most highly influenced by Western consumer cultures. Yet the resources that are given over to consumption roughly indicate what could be available to populations to increase their general well-being in a society with more acceptable priorities. It is remarkable, then, that all the new tigers have experienced rapidly decreasing consumption as a proportion of national income.[5]

This fall is directly associated with globalization. Because growth is export-led, it has comprised mainly the surplus of exports over imports, which has a high profit-content as opposed to wages. In the original East Asian tigers, such rapid growth of export profits could perhaps be justified on the grounds that they went to indigenous sectors who reinvested them locally. In the newer tigers, where growth is more a result of TNC exports, profits are not automatically reinvested to create further growth. Moreover, the consumption share has also fallen because of government spending cutbacks which are mandated by globalization. Thus, although tigerhood is defined by economic growth, it is not necessarily associated with factors that would lead to the sustainability of growth (reinvestment, dynamic indigenous sectors) or to increases in the material well-being of populations (consumption). The degree to which tiger economies have 'caught up' with core economies has been counterbalanced by the degree to which their popular consumption has been constrained.

The increasing concentration or agglomeration of TNC location in a few countries means that their economic 'successes' have a flip side: to the degree that a continual rapid inflow of foreign projects underpins rapid economic growth, upward mobility under globalization is available to only a few countries. The vast majority of countries that compete for foreign projects cannot attract enough of them to sustain rapid economic growth. Thus, the threat of economic marginalization has increased even while the apparent possibility of achieving tigerhood has been highly visible in a few noted cases. This is not to say that the problems of sustainability and unevenness that are raised by the tiger experiences could be solved if there were large enough flows of foreign investments to raise more regions to high economic growth. Rather, the problem is that globalization has eliminated alternative development strategies – for example, by limiting local options of creating developmental states – while simultaneously reducing the chances for 'success' of those who compete for foreign investments.

At the global level, the concentration of investments along with increasing competition to secure them by imposing more and more TNC-friendly neoliberal measures have made foreign investors big winners in the globalization game. Lim and Fong (1991) insist that the net result has been a win-win situation for the new tiger economies – unlike previous cases of dependency they have benefited unambiguously from hosting TNCs. But my own work on Ireland questions whether this is true, particularly when the limited benefits to one or two 'successful' semiperipheral countries in a region are compared to the marginalization of competing countries in the region (O'Hearn 1998). Moreover, TNC activities even in Southeast Asia are still characterized by a lack of linkages between foreign and indigenous sectors and by chronically low levels of technology transfer (Lim and Fong 1991: 86–90), which challenge the concept of these economies being 'winners'.

The Asian crisis of the late 1990s also casts doubt on whether the new tigerhood is sustainable. Even if East Asia and Japan re-emerge into a more powerful global position than they held before the crisis (Palat 1997), the later industrializers of Southeast Asia, at the tail end of the V of the flying geese, could find it difficult to recover their previous levels of dependent development. Similar concerns plagued southern Ireland in the late 1990s, as its major benefactors like Intel began to re-evaluate their international investment strategies and as the pending enlargement of the EU threatened increasing competition for TNC investments.

Yet these are, interestingly, still the questions of the old 'development' literature. TNCs have always been faulted for low technology transfer or inappropriate technology, lack of linkages, and being footloose in the face of global economic changes. In other words, they do not develop their host countries in the same ways as they have developed the regions from whence they came. Although such conclusions may seem old hat in the context of postdevelopment, I believe it is crucial to continue to discuss these issues. Most states, if not all of their populations, are still entranced by the vision of growth-related 'development', as is evidenced by the vast increase of countries that have signed on to GATT and liberalized their economies under the post-Uruguay global regime. The example of the tiger economies has helped keep the growth illusion alive, and this illusion still must be confronted both in terms of the degree to which it is generalizable and in terms of the internal contradictions of the tiger model itself.

But what of other questions of development? Have tigers or their surrounding semiperipheral neighbours attained new political or material resources that might give them more ability to challenge core power? Are there possibilities for solidarity between economic tigers and other regions to achieve new ways of providing material and nonmaterial things on a more equitable and sustainable basis, in ways that are more sensitive to community priorities and individual diversities? Can Western technologies be stripped of their Western meanings and functions and be combined with non-Western ('Southern', in Santos's metaphor) objectives and practices in order to transform societies and the ways people provision themselves and each other? If so, are there ways that a Malaysia or an Ireland, as postcolonial societies, can exploit their advantageous forms of integration into global divisions of labour to gain potential leverage and force change?

As 'economic success' has become more and more tied to a country's willingness to integrate into a liberalizing global regime, states and localities have less control over policy, and movements have fewer realistic opportunities to mobilize about policy. Not only are 'economic' policy options such as trade, exchange rates, interest rates and privatization limited by a country's participation in regional and global regimes and by what is necessary to attract foreign investments; so too social welfare options are limited by austerity programmes and structural adjustment. Moreover, nonparticipation has become less attractive to localities as global and regional institutions have become more powerful and policy options have become more restricted. In Ireland, for example, many activists on the left once considered leaving the EU as a viable option but few would now advocate withdrawal. Nor would there be much support for withdrawal in other semiperipheral countries like Portugal and Greece. The question for semiperipheral activists and movements, then, appears to have changed from withdrawal to renegotiation. But renegotiation around what issues?

One issue is fairer access to technologies and economic activities that are now monopolized by core regions. I have argued throughout this chapter that access to materials and technologies, even for the most basic social economies and community-based movements in peripheral and semiperipheral regions, continues to be important. Yet there is a rapid drop-off in access to or control of such resources and technologies in semiperipheral regions, perhaps especially in the economic tigers, despite their workers' relatively high skill levels and their presence in certain stages of high-tech commodity chains like computers, cars, and communications equipment. This shallowness of participation in the division of labour within commodity chains is especially apparent as one moves on from the 'old' to the 'new' tiger economies of Southeast Asia, southern Ireland and, perhaps, Chile. These are places that are very dependent on exports for their economic growth and whose insertion into commodity chains is quite limited to fairly restricted assembly-type operations and subcontracting.

Membership in regional associations, however, may offer movements from these countries key strategic positions from which to influence policies about the development and consumption of technology. The relative power of semiperipheral regions, some of which have important markets and some of which are players in major core economic blocs, may place them in strategic positions from which to mobilize for a change of the world technological order.

Analysis of this question is not entirely generalizable because, as Santos emphasizes, there are important social, historical and functional differences between semiperipheral regions in Europe, Asia and Latin America (Santos 1995: 287). Yet the experience of the European semi-periphery, at least, shows some reasons for hope. Like other core projects, the EU project has been a contradictory one, with capitalist competitiveness its primary objective but with 'social cohesion and inclusion' as a stated, if not consistently implemented, secondary objective. Peripheral European regions have not significantly converged towards the EU core in economic terms (despite southern Ireland's recent surge of growth). But their states have, in Santos's terms, been 'corefied' politically as a result of integration even as their economies have been further peripheralized (Santos 1995: 288). The contradictions arising from conflicting regional goals and national priorities will increase further with the expansion of the EU to take in the countries of the former Eastern Europe.

Under such circumstances, semiperipheral states that are members in regional groups that also contain core states have political leverage to promote change by demanding the expansion of social programmes (or the creation of new programmes) that weaken the hegemony of regional competitiveness as the *raison d'être* of the group. In the EU context, this could mean strengthening the Social Chapter, developing new demands for fairer regional access to technologies (including, for example, the placement of regional technology centres), and renegotiating terms of membership so that semiperipheral states can recover the economic instruments they require for developmental and social purposes.

Obviously, this requires mobilization in multiple directions. Strengthening social inclusion is a class project that transcends different regions in the core–semiperiphery–periphery hierarchy, while demands for regional economic inclusion are largely (semi)peripheral in character. Not only will it be tricky to mobilize class solidarity across regions for demands of regional inclusion, it is even difficult to create semiperipheral solidarity in conditions where different semiperipheral states compete for resources, whether they be TNC investments or transfers from the core of their regional groups. And this does not even take into account the problems of mobilizing support for social economies within semiperipheral states whose orientation is towards creating 'the right macroeconomic conditions' (that is, neoliberalism) to be competitive in the globalization game.

Yet new movements at the grassroots of the economic tigers, as elsewhere, have already begun to challenge the neoliberal order. Local groups have resisted corporate and state activities, from ecologically destructive chemical plants to state cutbacks and austerity plans. Grassroots development forums have encouraged small but important projects that aspire to reverse dependency, implement democratic structures and prioritize development for community needs. Even the unevenly distributed experience of recent 'economic success' is not all bad in this respect. Irish people have recently witnessed a remarkable transition, from a passive acceptance of the 'feel-good factor' that was broadcast with the coming of the 'Celtic tiger', to a rising tide of grassroots anger that the promise of development has not improved the lives of so many of Ireland's citizens. Similar experiences have informed the remarkable record of mass social resistance in South Korea, through decades of 'economic miracle'.

Perhaps this is where solidarity is most important. Many semiperipheral regions, especially the tiger economies among them, have strayed from their own histories of resistance in their desire to 'develop'. Yet they still have a memory of resistance and, mostly, a quite recent one at that. As Vincent Tucker believed fervently, solidarity with non-Western movements and ideas can help semiperipheral people to rediscover and re-create their histories of rebellion and knowledge of alternative ways. This dialogue is crucial for the process of imagining alternatives to the current growth-centred illusions of 'development', as well as for devising ways of achieving a transformation to economies and technologies that are not just socially embedded, but where 'economy' is subordinated to broader democratic social priorities.

Notes

1. I would like to thank Andrew Schrank, Stephen Bunker, and participants in the Sociology of Economic Change seminar at the Univeristy of Wisconsin-Madison for their comments on an earlier version of this chapter.

2. The discussion in this chapter refers to the southern Irish economy only, since the northern part of Ireland, which is still under British rule, has experienced neither the inflows of TNC investments, nor the rapid levels of growth attained in the south in the 1990s.

3. This raises the additional unanswered question of the role of states in economies (including 'social economies'). One would not, of course, want to downplay the repressive nature of actually existing states – not least the so-called 'developmental states'. Yet states are still clearly important as institutions that can implement anti-market policies where markets are repressive or, more precisely, that can attempt to defend local populations against the repressive powers of core states and capitals as expressed through their manipulation of markets. By insisting that states may still have a role to play in defending regional populations, one is not conceding the legitimate control of states to local power elites but instead maintaining that states can be arenas where popular movements struggle to capture power for useful ends.

4. In terms of purchasing power parities, southern Ireland rose from 44 to 58 per cent of US per capita income levels during 1987–95, Chile from 25 to 35 per cent, Malaysia from 23 to 33 per cent, Thailand from 16 to 28 per cent, Indonesia from 10 to 14 per cent, and China from 6 to 11 per cent. All of the East Asian tigers became at least 15 per cent richer compared to the United States. The only other countries that made significant gains relative to the United States during this period were the very small economies of Mauritius and Botswana.

5. Between 1980 and 1995, total consumption fell from 86 per cent of GDP to 72 per cent in southern Ireland, from 79 to 71 per cent in Chile, from 77 to 64 per cent in Thailand, and from 68 to 63 per cent in Malaysia.

References

Amsden, Alice (1989) *Asia's Next Giant: South Korea and Late Industrialization.* Oxford: Oxford University Press.

— (1994) 'Why isn't the whole world experimenting with the Asian model to develop?', *World Development*, Vol. 22, No. 4, pp. 627–33.

Arrighi, Giovanni (1995) *The Long Twentieth Century.* London: Verso.

Arrighi, Giovanni, Satoshi Ikeda, and Alex Irwan (1993) 'The rise of East Asia: one miracle or many?' in Ravi Palat (ed.), *Pacific-Asia and the Future of the World-system.* Westport, CT: Greenwood, pp. 41–66.

Becker, David (1987) '"Bonanza Development" and the "New Bourgeoisie":

Peru under military rule', in David Becker *et al.*, *Postimperialism: International Capitalism and Development in the Late Twentieth Century*. Boulder, CO: Lynne Rienner.

Bello, Walden (1993) 'The Asia-Pacific: trouble in paradise', *World Policy Journal* 10:2 (Summer), pp. 33–40.

Chandler, Alfred (1962) *Strategy and Structure: Chapters in the History of the Industrial Enterprise*. Cambridge, MA: MIT Press.

Cumings, Bruce (1984) 'The origins and development of the Northeast Asian political economy: industrial sectors, product cycles, and political consequences', *International Organization*, 38:1 (Winter), pp. 1–40.

Esteva, Gustavo (1992) 'Development', in Wolfgang Sachs (ed.), *The Development Dictionary: A Guide to Knowledge as Power*. London: Zed Books.

Evans, Peter (1995) *Embedded Autonomy*. Princeton, NJ: Princeton University Press.

Gardiner, Kevin (1994) 'The Irish economy: a Celtic tiger', in *Ireland: Challenging for Promotion*, Morgan Stanley Euroletter (31 August), pp. 9–21.

George, Susan (1992) *The Debt Boomerang*. London: Pluto.

Granovetter, Mark (1985). 'Economic action and social structure: the problem of embeddedness', *American Journal of Sociology*, Vol. 91, pp. 481–510.

Grice, Kevin and David Drakakis-Smith (1985) 'The role of the state in shaping development: two decades of growth in Singapore', *Trans. Inst. Br. Geogr.*, 10, pp. 347–59.

Haggard, Stephen (1990) *Pathways from the Periphery: The Politics of Growth in the Newly Industrializing Countries*. Ithaca: Cornell University Press.

Hill, Richard Child and Kuniko Fujita (1995) 'Product cycles and international divisions of labor: contrasts between the United States and Japan', in David Smith and József Borocz, *A New World Order? Global Transformations in the Late Twentieth Century*. Westport, CT: Praeger, pp. 91–108.

Hobday, Mike (1994a) 'Export-led technology development in the four dragons: the case of electronics', *Development and Change*, 35, pp. 333–61.

— (1994b) 'Technological learning in Singapore: a test case of leapfrogging', *Journal of Development Studies*, 30:3 (April), pp. 831–58.

Huff, W.G. (1995) 'What is the Singapore model of economic development?' *Cambridge Journal of Economics*, 19, pp. 735–59.

Jenkins, Rhys (1987) *Transnational Corporations*. London: Methuen.

Kohli, Atul (1994) 'Where do high growth political economies come from? The Japanese lineage of Korea's "developmental state"', *World Development*, 22:9, pp. 1,269–93.

Krugman, Paul (1994) 'The Myth of Asia's Miracle,' *Foreign Affairs*, Vol. 74, No. 2 (November/December), pp. 62–78.

Lee, William Keng Mun (1997) 'Foreign investment, industrial restructuring and dependent development in Singapore', *Journal of Contemporary Asia*, 27:1, pp. 58–70.

Lim, Linda (1983) 'Singapore's success: the myth of the free market economy', *Asian Survey*, 23, pp. 752–64.

Lim, Linda and Pang Eng Fong (1991) *Foreign Direct Investment and Industrialization in Malaysia, Singapore, Taiwan and Thailand*. Paris: OECD.

McMichael, Philip (1996) *Development and Social Change: A Global Perspective*. Thousand Oaks, CA: Pine Forge.

O'Hearn, Denis (1994) 'Innovation and the world system hierarchy: British subjugation of the Irish cotton industry, 1780–1830', *American Journal of Sociology*, 100:3 (November), pp. 587–621.

— (1998) *Inside the Celtic Tiger: Irish Economic Change and the Asian Model*. London: Pluto.

Ó Riain, Seán (1997) 'The birth of a Celtic Tiger', *Communications of the Association for Computing Machinery*, 40:3 (March), pp. 11–16.

Page, John (1994) 'The East Asian miracle: an introduction', *World Development*, 22:4, pp. 615–25.

Palat, Ravi (1997) 'A lost decade for Asia?' *Hindu*, 12 December.

Polanyi, Karl 1957. 'The economy as instituted process', in K. Polanyi, C. Arensberg and H. Pearson, *Trade and Market in the Early Empires: Economies in History and Theory*. Chicago: Henry Regnery Co.

Ramesh, M. (1995) 'Economic globalization and policy choices: Singapore', *Governance*, 8:2 (April), pp. 243–60.

Rostow, Walt (1960) *The Stages of Economic Growth*. Cambridge: Cambridge University Press.

Sachs, Wolfgang (ed.) (1992) *The Development Dictionary: A Guide to Knowledge as Power*. London: Zed Books.

Santos, Boaventura de Sousa (1995) *Toward a New Common Sense: Law, Science and Politics in the Paradigmatic Transition*. London: Routledge.

Smith, David (1997) 'Technology, commodity chains and global inequality: South Korea in the 1990s', *Review of International Political Economy* 4:4, pp. 734–62.

So, Alvin and Stephen Chiu (1995) *East Asia and the World Economy*. Thousand Oaks, CA: Sage.

UNCTAD (1997) *World Investment Report 1997: Transnational Corporations, Market Structure and Competition Policy*. New York and Geneva: United Nations.

World Bank (1993) *The East Asian Miracle: Economic Growth and Public Policy*. Oxford: Oxford University Press.

— (1995) *World Development Report*. Washington, DC: World Bank.

. . . .

CHAPTER 7

The Place of Development in Theories of Imperialism and Globalization

Bob Sutcliffe[1]

Development, imperialism and globalization are three ideas that have been designed to interpret and change the world. They can frequently be seen rubbing shoulders in discussions of international questions in the social sciences but what they mean to each other is often anything but clear. This chapter is written with the intention of finding out more about their interrelations. It produces a simplified map of each of the concepts, showing some main currents of thought, and then over-lays the three maps on each other in the hope of finding the areas where they coincide, overlap and conflict in their depiction of the same conceptual and empirical terrain.

Development: a model and three critiques

I find it helpful in looking at ideas about development to use the metaphor of a journey, with a starting point, a form of travel, and a final destination. The dominant and, despite apparently devastating criticisms, still prevailing idea of development is that it is an experience of nations which all start from roughly the same place (an under-developed country today or a European country in the fourteenth century). The form of travel is characterized by the transfer of labour from low-productivity agriculture to higher-productivity industry and modern services, and all nations end up at more or less the same destination, where high consumption matches the high productive capacity. Many other things follow more or less automatically in the wake of economic progress, including more education, urbanization, more access to medical services, longer lives, democracy and human rights – in short, modernization. The countries of the world are strung out along the route but, with the right policies, they will all arrive in the end at the destination and there, so far as development is concerned, history will stop.

This standard model has been buffeted by blasts of attack from different directions which for explanatory purposes can usefully be reduced to three, which I call the polarization critique, the attainability critique and the desirability critique.

The polarization critique, dating from the 1960s, was a fundamental denial of the linearity and potential generality of the process of development, at least under the prevailing capitalist social system. This critique took a number of forms (including dependency and world-systems theory) but they all shared the idea that the process of development was, when viewed globally, one not of homogenization and universal attainment but one of polarization and exclusion.

The first target of the polarization critique is the starting point of this journey. True, there was a common starting point, it argues, but it was not like today's underdevelopment. That has been created as a necessary by-product of development. From the common starting point, nations polarized into the developed and underdeveloped; that polarization became set and by the end of the nineteenth century virtually unalterable. Underdevelopment is, like Dorian Gray's portrait, development's negative *alter ego*. The other main argument of the polarization critique concerns the form of travel. It is not open to latecomers to take the same route to development since they are not starting from the same place and they face insuperable obstacles placed in their way by earlier travellers. Thus capitalism prevents the industrialization of underdeveloped countries whose only hope for development is to break from the polarized and polarizing international context in which they find themselves; such a disconnection requires national protectionism and probably some form of socialism.

Many things have undermined the polarization critique in recent years: the perceived failure of the relatively disconnected Communist economies, the perceived success of a number of relatively connected countries in East Asia, intellectual broadsides coming from the left which have been inadequately answered, and the critique's lack of an answer to the questions raised by more recent critiques of the original development model. These questions have been not at all about the starting point of development, very little about the form of travel but almost entirely about the validity of the destination, about which the polarization critique said virtually nothing. In general it endorsed the view of the original development paradigm that high productivity, urbanized, technologically sophisticated societies were developed. As Vincent Tucker said, 'The fundamental goal remained the same.

Dependency theorists were profoundly modern in their worldview' (see Chapter 1). In a way, the polarization critique even reinforces the validity of the standard destination since its central complaint is that under-developed countries have been prevented from attaining the same level of development as the developed ones. Nor does the polarization critique challenge the idea that development is essentially an experience of nations. Again it has tended to reinforce the nationalism that is characteristic of development ideas, something that has been a special target of some of its strongest critics.

The attainability critique of development argues that it is physically impossible for the whole world to reach the received destination. The stronger versions claim, though the claim hardly yet amounts to proof, that the per head levels of emission of greenhouse gases, and other contaminants and of use of nonrenewable resources typical of in-dustrialized countries cannot be generalized to the population of the world as a whole without causing an apocalypse. 'Actually existing development' is seen less as the accumulation of goods and economic welfare and more as the accumulation of burdens on the environment. The voracious pig that is happier the more it eats is replaced by the finely balanced camel whose back breaks if it is overladen. Universal development is therefore an unsustainable illusion: the received destina-tion of development has been part of a Faustian pact with the devil, allowing some to enjoy a brief material orgy destined to end in disaster.

This fundamental critique of the assumptions of the standard model redefines development as a state that cannot be ecologically sustained in the long term. But ecologically centred writing produces various conclusions about what happens along the route. These range from a 'light' version which sees a more advanced, cleaner technology as a saviour; through neo-Malthusian population reduction; to a more thorough-going anti-materialism and anti-consumerism, often combined with proposals for a 'return' to a society based on small, mostly self-sufficient communities. The ecological critique, therefore, can be a critique either of the route, or of the attainability of the destination, or of both. There is still, however, little agreement about the exact physical dimensions of this problem and even less about a possible way around it. The attainability critique also tends to displace the nation as the focus of development since the problems to which it draws attention are apt to be relevant to a space at once more local and more global (Sutcliffe 1995).

Even if the received destination were attainable, a growing number of critics have been saying that it is undesirable. After what economists call 'the golden age' (1950–73), when rates of economic growth were the fastest ever experienced, it was still apparent that not only people in poor countries but also many groups in rich countries did not regard their existential needs as having been met. Implicitly and explicitly the desirability of development was increasingly questioned. This is, I think, the significance of the 'new social movements' to the development debate. The demands of each of them (women, ethnic minorities, gays and lesbians, senior citizens, and so on) constitute, at least implicitly, a critique of the standard development destination, a denial that the supposed social benefits of development flow more or less automatically from high levels of productivity and material consumption. Because they come from so many quarters, the desirability critiques are even more diverse than the attainability critique. But they are no less fundamental. The concept of desirability, like attainability, tends to displace the nation from the centre of the development goal. It emphasizes how even rich, productive, 'developed' nations can be full of needy, oppressed and unfulfilled people.

As a reflection of such critiques, development specialists have tried to get beyond a purely economistic concept of development. The UN Development Programme's annual *Human Development Report*, originally conceived as a kind of retort to the focus of the World Bank although now somewhat muted, proposed new criteria for the measurement of development which are generally those that were thought by the standard model to be more or less automatic consequences of advances in national income per head. The philosophy behind the *Human Development Report* was Amartya Sen's notion of development as the expansion of the capacity of human individuals to live fulfilling lives. On another front there is an increasing tendency to present development goals in terms of human rights, especially to stress the relevance of the concept of human rights not only to civil and political life but also to material questions such as the human right to food, to education and so on. Others have proposed even more radical rejections of the standard destination, stressing the destruction caused by development and proposing various 'alternative development' schemes. An even more radical approach eschews any statements about the nature of the destination on the grounds that it must reflect the free choice of participant individuals or communities and so any attempt to prescribe it by others amounts to reprehensible 'trusteeship' or Eurocentrism (Cowen and Shenton 1996).

In both the desirability critique and the reactions to it, some idea of culture as an essential part of development has come to the fore. The form in which it has done so varies from the UNDP's stress on education and literacy as indicators of development, through prevailing political ideas and practices as emphasized by the human rights approach, to an insistence that real development does not have only one cultural expression but must be consistent with cultural pluralism, necessitating in particular the enfranchisement of non-Western cultures. This is one of the issues on which Vincent Tucker's work (Chapter 1) makes such a clarifying contribution.

Two waves of imperialism theory

Imperialism is essentially the idea that the world contains an undesirable hierarchy of nations in which some oppress or exploit others, or strive to do so. In this century there have been essentially two waves of thinking about imperialism, one before the First World War and one after the Second World War. Between 1890 and 1917, imperialism was mostly used to denote the aggressive expansion of Europe and the struggle for domination between its major powers. The later wave of theories was more concerned with inequality between developed and underdeveloped countries and its causes. This question, while never central to the early theories, was none the less touched on by them.

Marx took apparently inconsistent positions on the question of how imperialism affected the colonies. He clearly expected and hoped that capitalist colonialism would develop India, though he noted that it had underdeveloped Ireland and expressed grave doubts about whether it could or should develop Russia. Whether these positions represent inconsistency, the evolution of his opinions, or eclecticism in the face of different circumstances and pressures is difficult to say. Classic early theories of imperialism also had mixed views on the subject. Hobson saw the developed countries sacrificing their own development by exporting capital to the colonies. Hilferding, who seemed to say nearly everything in his impressive book *Finanzkapital*, produced a prototype of a polarization theory. Bukharin saw conflicts of interest between industrial and agricultural regions of the world. Kautsky foresaw a world in which a group of developed countries oppressed the rest. But it was Lenin who was to become the touchstone of Marxist orthodoxy on imperialism. To him, imperialism was capitalism once it had definitively ceased to be historically progressive – a world system characterized by unresolvable conflicts for dominance between its leading national powers, which would struggle to redivide the world and its markets and fields of investment until they were all replaced by international socialism. Lenin asserted as against Hobson and his like (the 'liberals') that imperialism was not a policy of capitalism but an integral part of its nature. Against Kautsky and his like (the 'revisionists'), he argued that it could not qualitatively evolve any further and change into something else.

Even though he accepted that capitalism, 'once the great liberator of nations had become their great oppressor', Lenin clearly expected that capital export would accelerate and not impede economic growth and industrialization in underdeveloped areas. He saw the threat to the development of the forces of production coming from interimperialist war and not from obstacles to the industrialization of poor countries. He saw capitalism as being congenitally unable to match its massive capacity for economic globalization with an equal capacity to globalize itself politically and escape from the armour of the nation-state in which units of capital were permanently enclosed.

Even Rosa Luxemburg, of the first wave of imperialism theorists the most sensitive to events in the Third World, expected capitalism to foment more industrialization there. Yet she was particularly attentive to the way in which the price of this kind of economic progress was paid by the peasantry of poor countries. Her theory of imperialism is in other ways in a different category from most of the others of the epoch. For her, imperialism was not an epoch of capitalism, let alone a new one; nor did it have anything to do with the development of monopoly or the union of finance capital with the state. It was a permanent expression of the rapacious primary accumulation that capitalism required due to its inherent underconsumption. Too much has been made of Luxemburg's mistaken argument for permanent underconsumption. That underconsumption is not necessary and permanent does not mean that it is not real and important. Primary accumulation (the absorption of non-capitalist areas and activities into the capitalist system) can be a feature of capitalism at any stage in its history, not only at its birth as emphasized by Marx. Perhaps the most arresting peculiarity of Luxemburg's theory is that, since she sees imperialism as the rapacious expansion of a system and not of nations, she completely rejects nationalism as an appropriate response to it (for an overall survey and bibliography see Brewer 1989).

There is a striking gap between the main concerns of most of these classical theories of imperialism and the great majority of more recent writings. The second wave of imperialism theory, often referred to as neo-Marxist, sees imperialism as the collective domination of a few industrialized countries who lord it over the Third World (or equivalent phrase) as a whole. Very little interest has been shown in the classic imperialist question of the relations between different industrial countries.

At the economic level, especially, there is a considerable and not very often mentioned gulf between the expectations of the 'first wave' theorists and those of the neo-Marxist writers. Numerous detailed analyses from the standpoint of imperialism have been done on trade and unequal exchange, on foreign investment and multinational corporations, on debt, the banks and the international organizations and on aid and political domination. A large volume of material concludes that the North exploits the South in the sense that it appropriates the surplus product of the South through unequal exchange, profit repatriation and debt repayment; in this and in other ways the North restricts the economic development of the South. The struggle to break the monopoly of development is by means of nationalism, socialism and solidarity. This does have more in common politically with what became the Leninist approach to the question but is far distant from the views of other classic imperialism theorists, particularly Luxemburg. The predominant currents in modern neo-Marxist theory regard capitalism as having been the dominant mode of production for a very long time and are therefore not very interested in relations between capitalist and precapitalist modes. One group of writers, however, has taken up this question, seeing things in a somewhat more Luxemburgian light (Brewer 1989: Chapter 10).

The second wave of imperialism theory is almost coterminous with the polarization critique of development. The word *imperialism* fits quite comfortably in the polarization theorist's view of the world as a planet divided between developed and underdeveloped or centre and periphery, where the former exploit, oppress and distort or halt the development of the latter. Imperialism is seen as a collective characteristic of the centre more akin to Kautsky's idea of ultra-imperialism than Lenin's imperialism. But some of the themes of the modern version of imperialism can also be found in the classical theories, even if with something of a different role: the importance of foreign investment, for example, which both Hobson and Lenin and later Baran, Frank and others all stressed; the role of debt as an instrument of surplus extraction of which Luxemburg made much and which then featured strongly in modern versions of imperialism especially after the debt crisis of 1982. But in general, for the polarization critique of development the theory and the vocabulary of imperialism were subordinate. I think that accounts for the relative disappearance of imperialism from the left's vocabulary, which Prabhat Patnaik (1995) recently lamented. As the polarization critique of development came under pressure and began to show its limitations, the imperialism vocabulary that had accompanied it also retired from the stage, although to return in a new form as part of other critiques.

Where did the idea that imperialism is an obstacle to development originate? The idea only became a basic tenet of the socialist movement after the 1927 congress of the Third International, at which it was stated baldly. The idea, like many other Stalinist dogmas of the period, was hardly based on theory, let alone empirical research. It was part of the theoretical apparatus designed to justify the class-against-class stance by which Stalin isolated his political enemies in the International and radicalized the international political stance of the communists. Once that justification had been done not much more was heard about the question from this quarter, although the forced industrialization of the Soviet Union was increasingly set up as the only way in which further industrialization could proceed. That idea clearly had an influence in the early years of economic planning in India and elsewhere in the newly liberated colonies after 1945. The proposition only became a real, almost universally accepted theory on the left after the publication of Baran's *The Political Economy of Growth* and the work of Gunder Frank and the *dependentistas*. It was, of course, strengthened by the disappointing economic performance of developing countries after their political independence (Brewer 1989, Chapters 7–9; Kay 1990).

One of the main criticisms of polarization theories is that they seem to fly in the face of evidence about the economic growth of parts of the world which, according to those theories, should not be growing. What is the truth about the claim that imperialism holds back the economic development of the Third World? The empirical evidence is not really very clear. In aggregate terms there has been growth and there has been decline. It is striking, however, that on many indicators of development (including the most used one, income per head) there is a persistent gap in the middle of the world distribution, implying that it is indeed very difficult to cross. Angus Maddison's recently perfected massive database in which he has calculated or estimated levels of income per head for all countries of the world since 1820 in consistent comparable units, produces a clear conclusion: income levels were much closer together in 1820 than they are today (Maddison 1995). The figures depict two hundred years of virtually continuous polarization, and, with very few exceptions, those countries that had the highest incomes in 1820 are the same as those that have the highest incomes today. There has been much more relative movement within the two groups of countries than between the groups. A few countries in Latin America (Argentina, Chile, Venezuela) have briefly attained Western levels of income per head only to fall back into the lower group. Doubts have even arisen about the Asian tigers, which appeared definitively to have crossed or to be about to cross the gap in the 1990s, after the financial crisis of late 1997 and early 1998. Symbolically and, perhaps, ironically in view of the crisis that broke out at the end of 1997, South Korea crossed the gap and was with much difficulty accepted into membership of the OECD. But how, even before the 1997 crisis, should South Korea's experience be interpreted: as the exception that proves the rule or the example which shows the way is open? While neoliberal international organizations claim that success came from market-friendly policies which would work anywhere else, a more convincing explanation is based on a weak version of the polarization theory, arguing that South Korea crossed the divide only with the help of strong state intervention and the insulation of the domestic economy from the outside through protectionism and a ban on foreign investment. But as to whether it was capitalism or state intervention that caused growth, no definitive conclusion has emerged in this debate any more than in earlier debates of the same kind, such as whether Latin America really began some independent industrialization during its partly accidental isolation from the main capitalist powers in the 1930s and 1940s. The partisans of both sides will no doubt slog it out, with no clear winner, like Alfredo and Olmo in Bertolucci's *Novecento*.

Meanwhile, however, imperialism has reappeared on the stage in a slightly new guise. The development of both the attainability and the desirability critiques of development have produced their own contributions to imperialism theory. In the first place the concept of 'ecological imperialism' has made its appearance. Partly this has arisen from new historical work on the ecological component of Western expansion and colonialism, which has illuminated the way in which Western capitalist imperialism made its impact not only on people and their social and economic life but also on their physical environment (Crosby 1993, MacKenzie 1990). But also a number of writers have analysed the way in which unequal and exploitative relations between nations have an impact on questions of environmental contamination. The phenomenon of relocating dangerous and polluting industrial activities in the Third World has been much commented on, especially in the wake of the Bhopal disaster. But it is the issue of global climate change and the international negotiations around it that raise new interesting issues relating to imperialism.

The economic polarization version of imperialism stressed that the developed capitalist countries prevented the industrialization of the peripheral ones. But if the attainability critique of development is correct, and the whole world cannot physically be developed along the standard model, then the complaint that the nonindustrialized are prevented from industrializing is beside the point. The point is more that the unequal international distribution of high consumption and high-productivity economic activity is a major factor propelling the world towards ecological disaster because it disguises the seriousness of the problem. The privileged can afford to *over* pollute because the underprivileged are *under* polluting. But that means that the privileged have even stronger interest in maintaining the differences because closing the gap will make their own lifestyle less sustainable and will damage many vested interests. Since it is the global level at which the problem exists, while the negotiation of relative levels of pollution is done via nation-states, then imperialism in this sphere is as alive and rampant as it ever was (Agarwal and Narain 1991). The evidence for this is clear enough in all the recent world conferences on climate change, especially in Kyoto in 1997 where the USA, the world's greatest polluter, refused to accept targets for the reduction of carbon dioxide emissions if developing countries did not do so. The United States was saying in effect: 'We will very slightly change our polluting lifestyle only if poor countries limit their economic growth.' Negotiating a global reduction in carbon dioxide emissions is now perhaps a more central arena of anti-imperialist struggle than the more traditional areas of debt repayment and the terms of trade.

The desirability critique is also partly responsible for generating new debates about imperialism. The process of changing the goals of development, as Vincent Tucker stressed, cannot be left to political economy but must incorporate questions of culture. And it is precisely in that hitherto ignored area where many recent contributions to imperialism theory have been made (Said 1993; Tomlinson 1991). Thus, new critiques of the destination of development appear to be enriching the theory of imperialism, although that theory at present tends to consist of several separate strands and there is as yet very little discussion of what is common between them and whether they can be unified in a way that allows imperialism once again to become an important theoretical concept.

One consequence of more discussions of cultural imperialism is a more rigorous analysis of Eurocentrism. And one of the most important expressions of Eurocentrism is the universalization of the present state of developed countries as the assumed destination for the whole world. The new critiques of this destination, although they are not necessarily devoid of Eurocentrism, none the less in general point away from it. To find actually existing development either undesirable or unattainable or both is already to break something of the Eurocentricity of the concept. If the destination is no longer defined as what now exists in the 'developed countries' then development becomes a task for all parts of the globe. Development has not yet happened anywhere.

In a related sense the two critiques of the development destination hint at ways in which some flesh can be placed on a common idea in theories of imperialism, as well as in other theories of oppression and exploitation, which is usually left skeletal and purely rhetorical. This is the idea that in a relation of oppression the oppressor is also not free. Unequal development has brought high production and consumption to parts of the world but at the cost of generating many by-products that make development undesirable even to many of those who are supposed to benefit from it. Culture and meaning can be destroyed for the inhabitants of developed as well as underdeveloped countries. And if development leads to global ecological disaster the inhabitants of developed countries cannot escape.

Globalization in different strengths

J.A. Hobson remarked early in the twentieth century that the word *imperialism* was on everybody's lips. If he were writing at the end of the century he would surely have substituted the word *globalization*. The idea of globalization takes off from the common observation that, in accordance with economic policies advocated by the major powers and international organizations, there has in recent decades been an expansion of international economic relations far in excess of the expansion of production. Between 1950 and 1992 the real value of the planetary product increased by a factor of a little over five while international trade expanded by a factor of about ten; between 1980 and 1995, the value of home investment doubled, but the value of foreign investment multiplied by six; and since the floating of exchange rates at the start of the 1970s, the volume of dealings in foreign exchange has increased several hundred thousand times (Maddison 1995, UNCTAD 1997).

These are impressive figures. The authors of hypotheses about globalization usually add a whole lot more to give further empirical backing. Here are three striking, and not atypical, examples:

> In fact, in 1990 more than half of America's exports and imports, by value, were simply the transfers of such goods and related services *within* global corporations. (Reich 1991: 114; the author continues in a footnote that 'By one estimate, 92 percent of US exports and 72 percent of US imports [in 1987] occurred within global corporations.')

> Thus, the share of transnational capital [the 200 largest transnational companies] in world GDP grew from 17% in the middle of the 1960s, to 24% in 1982 to reach more than 30% in 1995. (Clairmont 1997: 16)

> Some 400 transnational corporations own two-thirds of the planet's fixed assets and control 70 percent of world trade. (Robinson 1996: 20)

The trouble is that all three of these statements, and many other common ones, are either incorrect or misleading or both. So it is worth trying to put the empirical evidence in perspective before looking at what globalization might mean for imperialism and development.

In 1913, at the close of a previous globalization epoch, the value of international trade of the now developed countries was equal to about 16 per cent of the value of their total product. It fell sharply after that and by 1950 had only returned to a little over 10 per cent. By 1984, it had overtaken the 1913 level at 19 per cent and by 1994 it had fallen a little again to just over 18 per cent (about 15 per cent for the world as a whole). Since services, which are increasing their share of production, are less tradable than goods this figure may be close to the limit. In this sense the world is just a little more globalized than it was in 1913. According to the best estimates, 36 per cent of the exports and 40 per cent of the imports of the USA consist of intra-firm trade. These proportions continue to rise slowly. For Japan the percentages are much lower: 28 per cent and rising for exports, and 14 and falling for imports. Very rough but not implausible estimates put the value of all foreign investment at about 9 per cent of the world's stock of real capital in 1913 but less than 5 per cent in 1994, a long way below what is commonly believed. The value of the production of all multinationals (40,000 of them) as a share of the total global product was 22 per cent in 1990. Figures for other years are not available but the share is almost certainly rising. The output produced by all multinationals outside their home country rose from 4.5 per cent of world production in 1970 to 6.4 per cent in 1990 and 7.5 per cent in 1995 – slightly less, 6.3 per cent, for 'developing countries' alone. In China, the most important Third World destination of foreign investment in recent years, the share of foreign multinationals in industrial output is rising fast – from 5 per cent in 1991 to 13 per cent in 1995. But most of the multinationals involved are non-mainland Chinese-owned.

Without labouring the details, I think it is obvious that these figures give a very different picture from some of the extraordinary claims made by other writers for the quantitative degree of globalization. But they do show that international economic integration is considerable and for the most part still growing. They do not show that it has attained historically unprecedented levels (Maddison 1995; World Bank 1997; Glyn and Sutcliffe 1992; Sutcliffe and Glyn forthcoming; UNCTAD 1997).

The simplest or 'weak' version of the globalization hypothesis is that economic interrelations between countries, through trade and investment, have grown so fast that national economies are more inter-dependent than they have ever been. The world has become for the first time a single macroeconomic unit. All states have, therefore, lost some of their economic independence to this global economic space.

Stronger versions of globalization go on to argue that the power of individual states has been reduced (or has even disappeared), to be replaced by an overweening growth in the power of the multinational companies and some international organizations, which form a proto-state at the international level. The most radical versions go much further, arguing that the whole concept of 'nation' has lost its meaning, that the world is not only a single economic space but a single society with a single class structure. A single global ruling class has been formed based on the executives of the multinational corporations along with a few bureaucrats, politicians and intellectuals. So the world is now socially divided by classes alone and no longer by nations. Both eco-nomically and socially, and increasingly politically, the nation-state is being (or has been) euthanized. While the new ruling class has no formal world state, it is well on the way to constructing a pseudo-state apparatus at the world level.

The relationship between globalization and imperialism has not been very much discussed. The weaker versions of the idea simply see globalization as a new form taken by imperialism in the polarization/ dependency sense. Globalization in this account is simply seen as an increase in the power of the countries of the North over those of the South through the penetration of the multinational corporations and debt dependency supervised by the International Monetary Fund (IMF) and the imposition of neoliberal policies through the International Trade Organization and the World Bank. In this version, globalization is just more of the same. World systems and other polarization theorists have after all argued that a polarizing form of globalization has existed at least for centuries. Logically many of them see recent developments as simply one more turn of an epochally long screw.

Stronger versions of the globalization hypothesis, however, are often explicitly presented as replacements for all or parts of the concept of imperialism as an appropriate description of the world. An intermediate-strength version stresses that economic globalization means that eco-nomic interests now so completely straddle national boundaries that concepts such as 'centre' and 'periphery', or 'First World' and 'Third World', are completely obsolete. Globalization is seen as a denial of the polarization view of the world (Warren 1980; Harris 1990). The full-strength version argues specifically that class and not nation forms the only fundamental basis of division of the world social system. In this form, globalization as the complete de-nationalization of capital is in one important sense the opposite of the idea of imperialism. Nearly all theories of imperialism are about a supposed hierarchization of the world on the basis of nations. The full-strength globalization theories argue that the number of teams in the league has been reduced to one, so hierarchy and struggle on the basis of nation has passed. Lenin hypothesized that the state of the world was determined by the impossibility of globalization, despite the economic and technological logic behind it. So national capitalist classes and their representative states were destined to slog it out until social chaos gave way to socialism. He argued vehemently that capitalism would be incapable of achieving the desirable goal of globalization.

Thus, strong versions of globalization contradict early as well as late versions of imperialism. In fact, one of the earliest formulations of strong globalization did not use this term but 'postimperialism' (Sklar 1976), seeing it, as Warren and others have done, as a return to the concepts of classical Marxism before Lenin (and indeed, though this is not mentioned, before some of Marx himself). Even though it is not often explicitly appreciated, the growing tendency to accept strong versions of globalization is another reason for the scarcer appearance of theories of imperialism.

So is anything left of imperialism? First, it could be said that there would be a place for imperialism even if the world really were a single social and economic nation. In individual countries, hierarchies of regions have survived the establishment of unitary states. In the same way, distinct sociogeographical and cultural regions could be expected to survive as the afterimages of nations long after the world became globalized. But, second, the world is very far from being really globalized. The extent of globalization assumed by the radical globalization theorists is in fact exaggerated, sometimes ludicrously so. While there has been a fast expansion of international economic transactions in the past twenty-five years, these have not yet reached unprecedented proportions relative to the overall size of the world economy. No more of world production is traded across national borders than in 1913; foreign direct investment relative to production is considerably less than it was in 1913. There is little reason to suppose that markets, even stock markets, are more internationally integrated now than they were then. Admittedly, there is a very much larger international foreign exchange market, but it is not clear whether this represents a qualitative change in world capitalism compared with the nineteenth century. There are also many more firms that operate in more than one country, and there is no doubt that they have enormous power. They trade voraciously, they produce output in many countries, they even occasionally (but not often) fully integrate their productive units across national borders. But there is very little evidence that they have formed a transnational capitalist class. With only a handful of exceptions their top leadership is overwhelmingly composed of nationals of their country of origin, and nearly all of them look constantly for support to their own national state (Ruigrok and van Tulder 1995). Capitalist classes are still national. Present-day globalization is much less new than is claimed and is, to a considerable extent, the re-establishment of the international structure of capitalism typical of the period before the economic upheavals of two world wars and the Great Depression. To sum rather than mix metaphors, perhaps the globalization bandwagon is heading down a blind alley.

At least that is how it seems to me from a largely economic standpoint. One area, however, where it is argued that the winds of globalization blow particularly strongly is that of culture, a question that concerned Vincent Tucker very much. Here I do not feel qualified to argue but only to wonder. Developments such as satellite technology certainly give the impression that culture is an area where globalization is happening especially quickly. And the fact that the growth of this global medium, unlike the dawn of radio and television, coincides with an epoch of decontrol and private capitalist initiative makes one fear even more for its corrosive consequences. Dennis Potter, in a memorable interview shortly before his death, said that he had called the tumour that was killing him 'Rupert Murdoch', because what it was doing to his body was similar to what its namesake was doing to the culture of the world. The intrinsic power of the new media is enormous and it is easy to see how their effect can be to reinforce the old and much-criticized ideas about the destination of development.

On the other hand, I am impressed by the way cultural differences survive, often much more than independent economies; by the fact that the minimum melting point for foreign cultures in countries receiving immigrants seems to being going up rather than down; and how cultures that migrate without people are not always imposed or impoverishing. The cellist Julian Lloyd Webber recently interestingly remarked that the Western classical music tradition was now more firmly rooted in some East Asian countries than in Europe. Thus, I sometimes wonder whether the impression of cultural globalization may be as much an exaggeration as most versions of economic globalization.

Development, imperialism and globalization

In discussions of development three recent processes have tended to coincide and overlap: the growth of the attainability and desirability critiques of the standard development model; the displacement of economics from the centre of the debate on development by ecology, sociology and cultural studies, as well as social movements; and the relative decline of discussion of economic imperialism along with the rise of discussions of ecological imperialism and cultural imperialism.

The result thus far is not a clear escape from the impasse in development that many perceived a decade ago. But a positive step has been the rehabilitation of the role of practical utopianism in radical debate. Both ecological and cultural aspects of utopia are central to these new ideas, and in examining the prospects for utopias, new sightings of imperialism have also taken place. If the complaints of those who regretted the relative disappearance of imperialism from the vocabulary of the left have not been satisfied, at least the development debate has revealed some of the problems of imperialism theory and hinted at ways in which it needs to be revived.

All that, to me, seems positive. Yet, even though the world is fuller of resistance than we see or are told, the standard development model is still firmly in charge – in governments, international development agencies and even in many universities and non-governmental organizations. At the same time, there is a worrying side to some of the conclusions emerging from the critical utopian debate. The criticism of the standard development model seems at times too total. Because the old destination, which in the West we experience every day, seems so unsatisfactory, all aspects of it are often rejected as a whole. Along with consumerism out goes science, technology, urbanization, modern medicine, and so on. And in sometimes comes a nostalgic, conservative postdevelopmentalism.

A visceral, unreconstructed, rationalist economist's voice in me continues to ask nagging questions: although it is good to have a new, less human-centred, more respectful attitude to the rest of nature instead of regarding it as instrumental, is this really an answer? Is it not possible that even societies highly respectful of the rest of nature can irreparably, perhaps unknowingly, damage the environment? Do all the problems and only problems come from the modernization project? And while it seems important to talk increasingly of human rights to education, health and food is there not a danger of forgetting that rights have a material basis? What is the use of a fundamental universal human right to so many grams of protein a day when the productivity of human labour is still not sufficiently high to produce that quantity for everyone, even if it were all distributed equally?

In all projects, there is a danger of losing the baby when we throw out old bath water. In this case, the baby is the material, economic, productive basis of whatever satisfactory utopia can be, to echo Vincent Tucker's suggestive words, imagined and democratically negotiated among the inhabitants of earth. It is not enough to imagine and negotiate a new destination; we also have to construct a mode of travel that will get us to there from here. To this end are there not some elements of the reviled, economistic modernization project that, robbed of their unequal and imperialist form, must still form a part of the content of that journey? The power of the standard model's route and destination are hard to understand unless we recognize that they have positive aspects: not everything in them is imposed on passive consumers; parts of them are actively and unconstrainedly desired. And parts of them are necessary for almost any utopia to be possible.

Similar questions arise in relation to globalization. Whether it is seen either as imperialism in a new dress or a qualitatively different postimperialist phenomenon, the predominant reaction to it on the left is distaste and fear. To a left accustomed to think, especially politically, in purely national terms the globe seems too vast a stage on which to organize. The difficulty of contesting or effectively democratizing such an enormous economic space tends to produce either fatalistic despair or a heightened demand for a disconnection. There is little sign in current debates of the sense of promise and opportunity with which many socialists and revolutionaries greeted the signs of capitalist globalization in the nineteenth century, when the phenomenon was seen as a prelude to major advances to socialism and the elimination of the frontiers that held each national working class inside its own national prison. Marx's insight that capitalism, in spite of itself, prepares the way for socialism can still have relevance, even though not exactly in the way he expected. Nowadays, against that point, it is often objected that this globalization is of the wrong kind: it is the capitalists' globalization, dominated by the multinationals, destructive of the earth and offering nothing to the oppressed and exploited. But it was always necessarily the capitalists' globalization. Marx and his co-activists in the international socialist movement of the nineteenth century saw the globalization of their epoch as offering a chance to build a global workers' movement, a global working class for itself, at least as fast as, and preferably faster than, the capitalists could build their global class for itself. Many would claim that, this time, the capitalists are far ahead. But I have argued that that is an extreme exaggeration. What is lacking at present, I believe, is a strong current of opinion on the left that takes globalization as a new opportunity to build global responses. We could start with demands to redress the great absence in the current form of globalization: the right of all people to be allowed to cross national frontiers with at least the same facility as they are now crossed by goods and money.

Perhaps the preceding few paragraphs will seem like the concerns of an unreconstructed, modernist, incurably Eurocentrist economist. But they are also the worries of a gay man who is sure that it was not by coincidence that the modern gay liberation movement began in the middle of Manhattan, that island so emblematic of the modernist development destination, and those of an atheist who is frightened by the way in which culture is increasingly reduced to religion, and those of a music lover who would find it hard to find meaning in life without modern sound reproduction technology.

One way of rephrasing all these concerns would be to say that development and globalization are experienced in practice in conditions of profound inequality of wealth and power between nations (imperialism) as well as between classes and sexes (capitalist class exploitation and patriarchy). It is necessary to distinguish which of the rejected aspects of development and globalization are inherent to those concepts and which come about because of the unequal circumstances in which we experience them. If we reject them completely because of the form in which they arrive we will always be struggling against the wrong enemy.

Note

1. This article is part of what was for me an absorbing and stimulating debate about development with Vincent Tucker. His influence on it will be obvious, as well as the points he would have disputed. It was my good fortune to get to know Vince in the relaxed and intellectually fertile environment of the Sociology Department of the University of Wisconsin when we were both visiting scholars there in 1993. It was my bad fortune to have known him so briefly since I enjoyed this almost utopian state for only a month. I went there to give a series of lectures about imperialism and development on which Vince commented generously and tellingly, introducing me to writings I did not know and to ideas that made me come away rethinking many questions. I was looking forward to a proposed visit to Cork to continue to discuss our agreements and disagreements and to deepen our friendship, but it was not to be. His ideas and his way of expressing them made such a strong impact on me, however, that I can imagine what some of his comments would be; and so the debate does not have to stop; nor will the memory of a brief but significant friendship. My thanks as always to Andrew Glyn for comments on a draft of this paper.

References

Note: in general I have not given detailed references but have referred the reader to surveys with detailed bibliographies.

Agarwal, Anil and S. Narain (1991) *Global Warming in an Unequal World: A Case Study of Environmental Colonialism*. Delhi: Centre for Science and Environment.

Brewer, Anthony (1989) *Marxist Theories of Imperialism: A Critical Survey*, 2nd edn. London and New York: Routledge.

Clairmont, Frédéric F. (1997) 'Ces deux cents sociétés qui contrôlent le monde', *Le Monde Diplomatique*, No. 517, April.

Cowen, M.P. and R.W. Shenton (1996) *Doctrines of Development*, London and New York: Routledge.

Crosby, Alfred W. (1993) *Ecological Imperialism*. Cambridge: Cambridge University Press.

Glyn, Andrew and Bob Sutcliffe (1992) 'Global but leaderless? The new capitalist order', in Ralph Miliband and Leo Panitch (eds), *The Socialist Register 1992*. London: Merlin Press, pp. 76–95.

Harris, Nigel (1990) *The End of the Third World*. London: Penguin Books.

Kay, Cristóbal (1990) *Latin American Theories of Development and Underdevelopment*. London and New York: Routledge.

Maddison, Angus (1995) *Monitoring the World Economy, 1820–1992*. Paris: OECD.

MacKenzie, John M. (ed.) (1990) *Imperialism and the Natural World*. Manchester and New York: Manchester University Press.

Patnaik, Prabhat (1995) 'Whatever happened to imperialism?', in P. Patnaik, *Whatever Happened to Imperialism and Other Essays*. New Delhi and Madras: Tulika.

Reich, Robert B. (1991) *The Work of Nations: Preparing Ourselves for 21st Century Capitalism*. New York: Simon and Schuster.

Robinson, William (1996) 'Globalization: nine theses on our epoch', *Race and Class*, 38: 2.

Ruigrok, Winifred and Rob van Tulder (1995) *The Logic of International Restructuring*. London and New York: Routledge.

Said, Edward W. (1993) *Culture and Imperialism*. London: Chatto and Windus.

Sklar, Richard (1976) 'Postimperialism, a class analysis of multinational corporate expansion', *Comparative Politics*, October.

Sutcliffe, Bob (1995) 'Development after ecology', in V. Bhaskar and Andrew Glyn, *The North, the South and the Environment: Ecological Constraints and the Global Economy*. London: Earthscan.

Sutcliffe, Bob and Andrew Glyn (forthcoming) 'Still underwhelmed: measures of globalization and their misinterpretation', *Review of Radical Political Economics*.

Tomlinson, John (1991) *Cultural Imperialism*. London: Pinter.

Tucker, Vincent (1992) *The Myth of Development*. University College Cork, Department of Sociology Occasional Paper No. 6.

UNCTAD (1997) *World Investment Report 1997*. Geneva: UNCTAD.

Warren, Bill (1980) *Imperialism, Pioneer of Capitalism*. London: Verso.

World Bank (1997) *Global Economic Prospects and the Developing Countries 1997*. Washington, DC: World Bank.

PART THREE

Polemical Perspectives

CHAPTER 8

Is it Possible to Build a Sustainable World?

Richard Douthwaite

Defining sustainability

The goal of 'sustainability' owes much of its popularity to the freedom people have to define the term in whatever way they wish. Twenty-four different definitions appeared in *Blueprint for a Green Economy* (Pearce *et al.* 1989) and many more have been formulated since. Consequently, rather than choosing between existing definitions it might be better to develop one for ourselves. Here goes: in a sustainable world, all the processes by which things are produced, once established, would be capable of being carried on unchanged for an indefinite period without causing a progressive deterioration in any factor, human or environmental, that they affected or on which they relied.

'Capable' is the key word here. The definition does not mean that each process has to remain unchanged for the foreseeable future but excludes processes that we know will have to be changed at some stage, perhaps by a still-to-be-developed technological innovation, to overcome features like a build-up of pollutants or the exhaustion of mineral deposits that would otherwise make them unsustainable. On the other hand, processes that cause initial changes are sustainable so long as they can then be continued indefinitely without causing further changes. For example, a farming system that involves the clearance of a limited area of scrub is sustainable if, once the scrub is cleared, no further clearance is necessary, no species suffers a significant fall in numbers, and farming can continue for generations on the cleared section without its fertility declining or its soil being lost.

By our definition, the set of processes by which the needs of most of humankind is currently met, the world economic system, is seriously unsustainable. The most obvious reason is that these processes release into the atmosphere each year such large quantities of carbon dioxide and other greenhouse gases that they have overwhelmed the planet's natural absorption capacity and are causing the climate slowly to change in ways that are, on balance, almost certainly unfavourable. At best, severe storms are expected to become more frequent and tropical diseases to spread. At worst, a new ice age might be induced.

Another reason the world economy is unsustainable is that it employs agricultural methods that cause soil to be lost at up to thirty times the rate it is being created (Worldwatch Institute 1996: 83). In addition, the natural genetic resistance of crops to pests and diseases is being neutralized to such an extent that within a few years it could become impossible to grow one or more major food crops however much insecticide or fungicide is applied (Fowler and Mooney 1990: 89).

A third reason that the world economy is unsustainable is that some of the chemicals it employs mimic human hormones and disrupt the body's endocrine system. As a result, the sperm counts of European men have been falling at 3 per cent per year since these chemicals came into use after the Second World War (Swan *et al.* 1997). The same chemicals are also causing increases in testicular and breast cancer (European Workshop 1996) and are causing fewer boys to be born relative to girls. Moreover, a higher proportion of these boys than ever before have defective genitals. In short, the world economic system is undermining humanity's ability to reproduce itself. If the human race is not sustainable then neither is its economic system.

Many more examples of the unsustainability of the world economy could be mentioned but the three above are enough to make it clear that the processes by which most of humanity lives have to be changed radically before we can rely on being able to continue for very much longer without bringing one or more catastrophes upon our heads.

Most economists would agree the economic system is not sustainable in its present form, but would go on to argue that a definition of sustainability that precludes change, as ours does, is invalid because it prevents the economy responding to price signals and using changes in technology to correct its faults. They would point out that the economic system has been changing through the centuries and if at any time in the past five hundred years contemporary trends had been projected far enough into the future, the economy of that period would have been unsustainable by our definition. In this context, they would certainly trot out the anonymous nineteenth-century prediction that if the volume of traffic in New York continued to grow at the then-current rate it would not be long before the streets were six feet deep in horse manure.[1]

Until his death early in 1998, Julian Simon was one of the most prominent economists to argue along these lines. He believed that there is no need to establish sustainable systems now because human in-genuity will allow us and our descendants to invent our way around whatever crises we create, just as people appear to have been able to do in the past (Simon 1981). He stated this position clearly in a debate with Norman Myers at Columbia University in 1992. Myers, speaking of increasingly acute water shortages in many parts of the world, commented: 'Some people might say "Well, technology always comes up with a substitute." We haven't found a substitute for water yet.' To this, Simon replied:

> Here we have the difference in our basic views. Norman's view is: 'We cannot go on like this. The well must eventually run dry' ... Nevertheless, the evidence of history is that these positive trends [he had mentioned improvements in the quality of drinking water in the US, side-stepping the issue of the limits to the supply] have indeed gone on forever all throughout our history. And there's no reason I know of why this cannot continue to go on forever. Three hundred years ago, people used to worry terribly in England about smoke in the air. And for good reason: it was awful in London. Now look at the average smoke levels ... from 1922 to 1970–71. The smoke levels have been going down, down, down. The air was awful early on but became less and less awful. (Myers and Simon 1994: 151–2)

Very few economists have opposed this view. One of the pioneering exceptions was E.J. Mishan of the London School of Economics who pointed out that just because technology had rescued us in the past did not mean that it always would: 'A man who falls from a hundred-storey building will survive the first ninety-nine storeys unscathed,' Mishan wrote in 1977. 'Were he as sanguine as some of our technocrats, his confidence would grow with the number of storeys he passed on his downward flight and would be at a maximum just before his free-fall abruptly halted' (Mishan 1977: 82).

Herman Daly, a colleague of Simon at the University of Maryland, is the leading economist today to attack the idea that constant economic expansion is sustainable. He argues that a sustainable society has three characteristics: it does not use renewable resources faster than they regenerate; it does not use nonrenewable resources faster than re-newable substitutes are developed for them; and it does not release pollutants faster than natural systems can break them down (Daly 1992).

The many definitions of sustainability can be grouped into two categories: those that accept the existence of limits, like Daly's and the definition that opened this chapter, are 'strong'; those that do not, like Simon's, are 'weak'. Tim O'Riordan terms weak sustainability definitions 'technocentric' because they rely on technology to remove constraints that would otherwise make them untenable. He calls strong sustainability definitions 'ecocentric' because they accept ecological limits. I would argue that there is no middle ground: either one accepts that there are limits or one does not.

The essential difference between weak and strong sustainability is ideological. If one believes in free markets and thinks that the effects of government planning are usually bad, one is intellectually unable to accept a strong sustainability approach. Once one accepts that the level of resource use is limited, one has to have some way of sharing the right to use those limited resources not only among the earth's present population but also among future generations, who cannot stake their claim to use them through free-market mechanisms. Indeed, a large segment of today's human population is currently too poor to register its resource use needs in the marketplace, and if the acceptance of limits causes hopes of providing higher incomes and extra resources for them to be abandoned, the fact that they are deprived while others consume resources profligately becomes ethically unacceptable. As Henry Wallich put it, 'Growth is a substitute for equality of income. So long as there is growth there is hope, and that makes large income differentials tolerable' (Wallich 1972: 62).

In short, the acceptance of limits means that the role of the market must be curtailed and not only must value-based judgements be made about who is to get how much and when, but planners must be involved in sharing things out. As both of these are anathema to economists trained to regard their discipline as 'positive' and value-free rather than normative, it is scarcely surprising that, despite all the evidence, they insist on believing that growth can continue indefinitely.

The clash between the strong and weak definitions of sustainability is in fact between two paradigms: the conventional, growth-based one and an emerging ecological rival. The latter holds that sustainability is closely related to stability and that fiercely competitive markets and the completely free movement of goods and of capital stand in the way of the development of a socially, culturally, economically and environmentally sustainable future.

Problems of 'weak sustainability'

Obviously, a very different world would emerge if there was a general insistence on a strong definition of sustainability rather than a weak one. Weak definitions, such as the World Bank's 'non-declining per capita utility' (Pezzey 1989) lead to rapid and accelerating rates of social and economic change while strong ones lead to economic systems, and thus societies, that change very slowly. Some people oppose strong definitions for this reason alone. As John Maddox, a former editor of the British science magazine *Nature*, wrote: 'Widespread acceptance of what the doomsday men are asking for could so undermine the pattern of economic life as to create social stagnation' (Maddox 1972).

But is the choice of definition a simple matter of one's political persuasion or ideological taste? Do left-wingers and pessimists choose strong definitions while right-wingers and optimists pick weak ones with no one able to prove either right or wrong? I argue that the weak sustainability approaches are so deficient on four grounds that they must be rejected. These are:

Complexity. The interactions between humans and the natural world are now so complex and far-reaching that we cannot rely on having the knowledge and means to correct the consequences of unsustainabilities before catastrophic damage is done. Instead, a safety-first policy needs to be adopted and known unsustainabilities need to be eliminated as quickly as possible. However, as I explain below, removing one unsustainability can aggravate another, so we need to proceed with care.

Reaction time. Every year, economic growth increases humanity's impact on the planet and thus reduces the time available to implement solutions to any unsustainability crises that arise. The only forms of economic growth that do not require faster reaction times are those rare types that reduce human environmental impact rather than increase it. However, countries cannot prevent forms of growth that make their economies less sustainable while at the same time maintaining their international competitiveness and obeying the rules of the world trade system; nor can they deal with sustainability crises by themselves. International agreement is required before action can be taken to deal with sustainability crises. The need to secure such agreements makes the achievement of increasingly fast (ultimately, infinitely fast) reaction times impossible.

Absence of limits. Weak sustainability says, in effect, that there are no constraints and anything might happen, and thus makes it impossible to imagine a desirable future and to work out the steps required to move towards it. Technocentrism removes any basis for citizens to say that an unsustainability has become sufficiently serious to require an immediate, costly, legal remedy because they cannot know whether or not a marvellous innovation is just around the corner that will enable the problem to be solved cheaply overnight. In other words, although weak sustainability postulates a reaction mechanism to remedy the unsustainabilities in the economic system, its refusal to accept fixed limits means that there is no point at which a legal correction mechanism is certain to kick in. Moreover, the price mechanism only makes it profitable to develop solutions if those affected have enough cash to create significant market demand and can ignore a barrage of propaganda from vested interests and express their fears through the market before the problem becomes insoluble. This absence of a guaranteed correction mechanism invalidates the whole weak-sustainability approach.

Efficiency. Allowing a crisis to develop and then seeking a solution is generally a much less efficient way of using resources than attempting to eliminate the problem at the design stage. But since technocentrists believe that there are no limits to the earth's resources, they do not consider it necessary to be efficient in the way those resources are used. However, I show in this chapter that inefficiencies of resource use are already so large in several industrialized countries that the cost of remedying them now consumes more goods and services than each year's economic growth. In other words, the free-market system has gone into reverse as a way of generating benefits for the many rather than the few. There could be no more powerful reason for rejecting it.

Let us look at these four objections to the weak sustainability approach in more detail.

Complexity Those urging a technocentric approach seem to know little about current technologies and their consequences. Consider, for example, the problems created by the growing use of chemicals alone. According to the UN (1997), 'The increasing, pervasive use and spread of chemicals to fuel economic development is causing major health risks, environmental contamination, and disposal problems. ... Environmental emergencies involving chemicals appear to be steadily increasing.'

Surprisingly little is known about the health and environmental effects of most of the high-volume chemicals in commercial use, let alone the obscure, low-volume ones. A recent sample of 100 chemicals out of 486 that are produced in large quantities and that are already the subject of environmental concern found that: 63 per cent had no published carcinogenicity data; 53 per cent lacked reproductive toxicity test data; 67 per cent lacked neurotoxicity test data; 86 per cent lacked immune system toxicity test data; 90 per cent had not been tested for their impact on children; 58 per cent lacked recent chronic toxicity test data (Roe *et al.* 1997).

Just identifying those chemicals that present a threat to human fertility by acting as endocrine disrupters would involve an immense amount of work. Removing the offenders from use would require even more, as international legislation would have to be enacted and safe substitutes found. About fifty chemicals have been identified as endocrine disrupters to date, most of which are still in use, but roughly 70,000 commercial chemicals are still untested. An American commentator recently outlined what thoroughly testing this number would involve:

> To understand the problem of endocrine-disrupting chemicals, we must study the interactions between combinations of chemicals; we must study these interactions on at least two generations of live animals; we must expose these animals at different moments in their lives (different times prior to birth and after birth). And of course, the animals must be exposed to various concentrations of the chemicals to see if a dose–response relationship becomes evident. (*Rachel's Environment and Health Weekly*, 22 May 1997)

The need to test combinations complicates the picture enormously. For example, to test the thousand most common toxic chemicals in unique combinations of three would require at least 166 million different experiments. To do this in just twenty years would require 8.3 million tests each year. The USA presently has the capacity to conduct only a few hundred such tests each year.

The task of establishing whether or not our present economic system is building up insuperable problems for humanity before taking corrective action is therefore huge. Indeed, since the unforeseen effects of chemical use are only one potential source of unsustainability among many, the job possibly could not be completed before a serious breakdown occurs. The reason that the majority of economists seem happy to think otherwise might well be that they are working at a theoretical level without the faintest idea of the practical problems involved.

Reaction time A minimum response to the complexity problem is to adopt the principle, 'if you are in a hole, stop digging'. For chemicals, this would mean freezing the output of untested chemicals until adequate safety data were gathered and making it illegal for new chemicals to be put into use without being properly screened. More generally, it would involve stopping forms of economic growth that increase the human impact on the environment and make that impact more complex.

Unfortunately, halting almost all forms of growth and refraining from doing anything new until existing unsustainabilities have been identified and corrected is not a viable strategy. That would itself cause the system to collapse. The world is in a classic Catch-22: we cannot make its free-market economic system sustainable because it is so unsustainable that it breaks down if we try.

This is why. Each year, industrialized economies plough back roughly one fifth of the goods and services they produce in order to increase their capital stock, the national collection of machines, factories, roads, houses and so on. If a single government introduced legislation to ensure that the only projects that went ahead made the country more sustainable by reducing the impact its citizens were having on the environment, most investment projects would be ruled out, causing job losses among builders, machinery suppliers, architects, lawyers and financiers. Investment funds would flow abroad, newly unemployed people would have less to spend, and businesses dealing with them would be forced to make layoffs. Job losses would lead to further layoffs and the economy would spiral downwards into an ever-deepening depression. There is no way that a country that works alone while allowing the free movement of goods and capital could avoid such a collapse.

Neither does collective international action offer a way ahead. In the unlikely event that an international treaty was signed to restrict growth, it would probably prove unenforceable since governments would collude with companies operating within their borders to ignore the treaty's provisions and steal a march on their neighbours. Even if an international agency policed the treaty, the result would probably be the same. After all, the UN has not been able to confirm that Iraq is not making chemical weapons despite having inspection teams there.

Even if governments supported the treaty and there was little evasion, the introduction of more stringent project-approval criteria might cut the proportion of world output being ploughed back into investment and cause an international slump, unless demand for consumer goods was increased by shifting spending power to the poor to compensate. Such a shift would require global planning, which would be rejected by free-marketeers.

It is thus almost impossible to stop the growth process increasing the level of international economic unsustainability if policies protecting the free movement of goods, services and capital are maintained. As a result, human pressure on the environment will almost certainly increase since the only mechanism in the technocentric model that could prevent it from doing so, the price system, does not operate effectively with regard to resource use.[2] On optimistic assumptions, an annual growth rate of 3 per cent will double the levels of pollution and resource extraction in less than fifty years.[3] This would be equivalent to doubling the speed of a car which has already been battered and scratched by being driven too rapidly at night along an unknown, narrow road. If the headlights are not adapted to reach any further ahead, drivers of the future will have half the time to see obstacles and take avoiding action.

If the world economy is going to grow, it cannot be sustainable in the long term because centuries of exponential growth would make the annual increase in the value of world output approach infinity. If this output had any resource content at all, the resource requirements of growth would also approach infinity and would quickly exceed the weight of the planet. Only if one postulates that growth can be completely dematerialized, so that increases in sales value would be entirely the result of improvements in quality rather than increases in volume, could one pretend that growth can go on for ever.

In the short term, a growing world economy is sustainable only if the international speed of response to potential crises is rapid enough to head off problems before they cause it to break down. Either the ability to anticipate obstacles (the distance the headlights reach) or the response rate to them must improve each year by at least as much as the environmental impact of economic growth. As the discussion of complexity has already showed, our scientific knowledge is inadequate to anticipate many problems. How rapid, then, has the response time been in previous crises?

The best example is the ozone layer. On the face of it, the response time looks remarkably good. The first scientific paper demonstrating that chlorofluorocarbons (CFCs) were destroying ozone in the upper atmosphere was published in 1985. An international agreement to phase out CFCs was signed in Montreal two years later.

A closer look, however, shows that luck and unusually good head-lights produced this result. The luck was the chance discovery in 1969 by James Lovelock, a maverick scientist who could not get funding for his work, that CFCs (which were already being used on a large scale in many industries) were accumulating in the atmosphere. Had Lovelock not bought a holiday cottage in the west of Ireland and been puzzled about the haze in the air, this discovery would not have been made until much later. Although Lovelock realized that CFCs were a potential threat to the ozone layer he did not see them as an immediate one. He was sceptical when a paper in *Nature* in 1974 suggested a possible threat. Fortunately, however, the suggestion was taken seriously by the UN Environmental Programme, which organized an investigation by other UN agencies in 1975 and, disturbed by the results, got twenty countries to sign the Vienna Convention for the Protection of the Ozone Layer ten years later. As a result, an international mechanism for handling the problem was already in place when in May 1985, a month after Vienna, an atmospheric scientist working for the British Antarctic Survey, Joe Farman, published conclusive evidence that CFCs were eating a hole in the ozone layer above the Antarctic (Farman *et al.* 1985).

The unsustainability caused by the use of CFCs could scarcely have been more serious. Ultra-violet (UV) light is used for sterilization in the food and pharmaceutical industries because it breaks down living cells. When more of it reaches the earth's surface unblocked by ozone it destroys cells there too. In the surface layers of the ocean, even a small rise in UV light is enough to kill plankton cells, the basis of the marine food chain and the sea's ability to convert carbon dioxide back into oxygen. On land, UV damage to leaf cells at best cuts crop yields, at worst kills the plants. In short, the survival of most life on earth was at risk.

In these circumstances, one would have expected a rush to halt CFC production within a month or two. But industrial states signing the Montreal agreement merely agreed to cut their production in half by 1999, leaving American firms free to promote new uses for CFCs and to equip a factory in India to make refrigerators using CFCs. In 1989, another agreement, signed in Helsinki, committed all industrialized countries to end CFC production by 2000. By the end of the phase-out period, 30 per cent more CFCs than had already been made would have been produced.

In fact, industrial countries ended CFC production by 1996 but production continues in 'developing' countries until 2010. Moreover, HCFCs, the main CFC substitutes, deplete ozone themselves, albeit much less rapidly. In addition, methyl bromide, which is used to fumigate fruit and vegetables for export, is now recognized to be as serious a threat as CFCs. Although the US and Canada demanded a world ban on this chemical by 2001 at a meeting in Caracas in September 1997, major fruit-exporting countries objected. A compromise was worked out under which the industrial countries will phase it out by 2005 and the developing world will do so ten years later.

The net effect of these delays was that in 1997, ten years after the Montreal agreement, the destruction of the ozone layer was still going on although at a reduced rate. The World Meteorological Organization (WMO) predicted that ozone would continue to weaken until the year 2000. If so, the system will have taken twenty-five years from the time that the possibility of CFC damage to the ozone layer was noted to stop it, and fifteen years from the time destruction was proved. The WMO says that it will be at least 2050 before the hole over the Antarctic ceases to open up annually – provided the international agreements are kept.

This episode shows that if governments bow to commercial pressure it greatly lengthens the response time before international action is taken. At present, even in situations of acute danger, commercial considerations are given much more weight than environmental ones. Thus, it is difficult to be confident that human common sense and ingenuity will always enable human beings to defuse sustainability crises before catastrophic damage is done, particularly if economic growth increases unsustainability as it did with CFCs. As Joe Farman told his radio audience in 1990: 'It's very worrying – industry can grow so fast these days. How many times can we stop them?'

Absence of limits Why, even though the impossibility of achieving infinite exponential economic expansion in a finite world would seem to be a matter of common sense, do so few economists consider that economic growth is unsustainable? A mainstream economist might answer that there are no limits to economic growth in a market economy because a combination of new technologies and price changes will enable the system to cope with whatever shortages of raw materials or pollution its functioning creates.

This counterintuitive argument has been exposed to surprisingly little public debate. The only time it was widely discussed was after the 1972 publication of *The Limits to Growth*, a report by seventeen experts at the Massachusetts Institute of Technology (MIT) led by Dennis Meadows (Meadows *et al.* 1972). They used computer projections to show that if growth continued in its conventional form there would be a sudden and uncontrollable decline in world population and industrial capacity within the next hundred years.

The Limits to Growth advanced two main arguments. One, which mainstream economists queued up to attack, was that as fossil fuels and minerals became increasingly scarce, the growth process would progressively grind to a halt. The mainstream economists simply denied that increasing levels of real resources would be required to extract minerals as lower-grade ores and more difficult sources had to be brought into use until, eventually, the resources expended on extraction would almost equal the additional production and further growth would become impossible. They were denying their own concept of diminishing returns.

Robert Solow was one of the more influential economists to claim that a lack of natural resources would not constrain economic growth. In the text of a lecture published in the *American Economic Review* two years after *The Limits to Growth* appeared, he argued that, provided humankind had access to unlimited energy (from, he suggested, nuclear breeder reactors), it would always find substitutes for natural resources as they ran out. 'At some finite cost, production can be freed of dependence on exhaustible resources altogether,' he wrote (Solow 1974). He ignored the fact that nuclear reactors require large quantities of exhaustible resources for their construction, perhaps because he felt that, with enough energy available, sea water or ordinary rocks could be processed for the mineral traces they contain. His view, in fact, was simply a restatement of the modern economic principle that if you have enough of one factor of production, it is infinitely substitutable for all others.[4]

By natural resources, Solow meant raw materials. His analysis completely overlooked the importance of another type of natural resource, the natural systems and sinks that break down or absorb wastes produced by human activities and which can only handle a limited amount in any given period before they become overloaded and pollution becomes a problem. This omission was inexcusable because the second major argument made by the *The Limits to Growth* team was that if growth continued indefinitely, pollution levels would eventually cause a population crash. Even if steps were taken to reduce pollution, they showed, the cost associated with such steps would rise as industry continued to grow because higher and higher standards would be required to prevent pollution increasing to life-threatening levels. Eventually, all the income produced by industrial expansion would go towards additional anti-pollution measures. In a well-regulated world, this would bring industrial growth to a halt but in one such as ours, where the economic system has to be allowed to grow to prevent its collapse, the necessary restrictions would not be introduced, pollution would rise, and the sicknesses it brought would cause the world population to fall.

Pollution is an insurmountable problem in any economic growth scenario. However much emissions of heat or anything else from an industry are cut, there will always be some. Consequently, if industrial growth takes place year after year, emissions will eventually grow by enough to outweigh the cuts. Even the escape of heat from the use of Solow's vast and perpetually increasing amounts of energy from non-solar sources would cause problems. Indeed, the *The Limits to Growth* team presented projections for waste heat in the Los Angeles basin showing that it could amount to 18 per cent of absorbed solar energy by the year 2000. Even at its 1970 level, 5 per cent of absorbed solar, it was affecting the local climate. Solow was either sloppy or dishonest in not taking this point on board.

Paul Romer, Solow's anointed heir, believes that growth can be limitless because ideas are limitless. 'Old growth theory says we have to decide how to allocate scarce resources among alternative uses,' he says. 'New growth theory says "Bullshit" ... all that stuff about scarcity and price systems is wrong' (quoted in Kelly 1996). Likewise, Julian Simon believed that agricultural land 'is not a fixed resource ... and it is likely to continue to increase where needed'. Similarly, natural resources 'are not finite in any economic sense', and population growth 'is likely to have a long-run beneficial impact on the natural-resource situation'. With energy, 'finiteness is no problem here either' (Simon 1981: 5–6).

This absence of limits is one of the most powerful objections to the technocentric position. Because it says, in effect, that there are no constraints, it is impossible to imagine what form a desirable future might take and then work out the steps required to move towards it. Imagining the future in the absence of limits is like trying to design a house without knowing the site, what building materials will be available, how many people it is required to accommodate, the budget, and even the climatic conditions the building will have to face. In such circumstances one can do nothing. One cannot even say when pollution levels have gone too far because a technology might be just around the corner to overcome the problem.

Perhaps we are not meant to try to work towards an appealing possible future. Such a course implies interference with the self-regulating free market, which is the essence of the technocentric approach. It is on auto-pilot, thus leaving the individual, the community and the country totally disempowered in many areas of life.

Efficiency Most unsustainabilities have been overcome by treating their symptoms technologically rather than removing their cause. When the growing volume of garbage threatens to exhaust landfill sites, few people examine how the economy might be made more efficient to produce less waste. The preferred remedy is usually to recycle whatever bulk components can readily be separated out of the waste stream and to incinerate the rest. This approach adds activities and costs to the system and thus makes it less sustainable in the longer term. For example, incineration might release dioxins which cause illness, a problem which in turn will be solved by costly medical treatment rather than tackling the root cause. Round and round the cycle goes, activity being added to activity, solution to solution, and because the solutions consume fossil energy themselves and introduce new technologies, they create new unsustainabilities and aggravate existing ones. They build an increasingly complex economic edifice which is likely to collapse more catastrophically when it eventually breaks down.

Joseph Tainter believes previous complex societies broke down because they solved their problems in ways that led to greater complexity, higher costs, and diminishing returns. He writes:

> In time, systems that develop this way are either cut off from further finances, fail to solve problems [and] collapse or come to require large energy subsidies. ... Energy has always been the basis of cultural complexity and it always will be. ... In the days before fossil fuel subsidies, increasing the complexity of a society usually meant that the majority of its population had to work harder. (Tainter 1996: 72–3)

The increasing levels of research and regulation required to anticipate and avoid the undesirable consequences of a growing economy can themselves be unsustainable. 'Bureaucratic regulation itself generates further complexity and costs,' Tainter writes. 'As regulations are issued and taxes established, those who are regulated or taxed seek loopholes and lawmakers strive to close them. A competitive spiral of loophole discovery and closure unfolds, with complexity continuously increasing. ... Such a strategy is unsustainable' (Tainter 1996: 71).

Since strategies that fail to tackle the fundamental causes of unsustainability require a greater and greater proportion of the system's output to keep it from collapsing, they reduce its overall efficiency. Indeed, there is now firm evidence that the efficiency loss has been so great that the economies of some industrialized countries are running backwards. As they grow, rather than producing additional benefits, they consume more goods and services themselves than the new growth creates. Herman Daly writes:

> In fact, economic theory would lead us to expect [this] at some point. ... There is no *a priori* reason why at the margin the environmental and social costs of growth in GNP could not be greater than the production benefits. ... When rising marginal costs equal falling marginal benefits then we are at the optimal level of GNP and further growth would be uneconomic [as it] would increase costs more than it increased benefits. Why is this simple application of the basic logic of microeconomics treated as inconceivable in the domain of macroeconomics? (Daly 1998: 1).

Cost–benefit analysis indicates that the optimal level of national income has been exceeded in some countries. Until the 1970s the ratio of costs (the value of the things that were produced or the services provided simply to keep the system going satisfactorily) to benefits (the rest of consumable goods and services) was more or less constant. As a result, when the figures showed that a country's GDP per person had risen, one could be reasonably sure that the population was getting materially better off. Now, however, this is not necessarily the case. The Index of Sustainable Economic Welfare – a measure of the value of the output left for each citizen after the system has taken its share and corrections have been made for the irreplaceable natural resources producing that output used up – is now declining in several countries. In Britain (Jackson and Marks 1994), the USA (Cobb and Halstead 1994) and Australia (Lawn and Sanders 1997), for example, the decline began in 1973. It began in Germany (Diefenbacher n.d.) in 1980. In all cases, national incomes have been steadily rising.

These results are scarcely surprising as it is obviously more efficient, for example, to stop a pollutant getting into a drinking water supply in the first place than to take it out later. But wealth-destroying growth goes on because the firms that spill the pollutants make profits from polluting. They do not have to pay the full costs of mopping up and curing the sicknesses they cause. Moreover, as we have seen, investment might falter and depression might set in if too stringent safeguards were put into place.

In economics as in building construction, projects generally run more smoothly and are less wasteful if they are planned properly at the start. In both, if one erects a fundamentally unsafe structure one might well have to tear up the foundations and start again, exactly as the world is being forced to do in order to reduce its reliance on fossil fuels. In this case, the economic system is going to have to be totally transformed and a lot of the investments that have been made since the Second World War will turn out to be seriously mistaken.

The way ahead

If we reject the technocentrist position and accept that there are limits to the world output that can be achieved without exposing humanity to a high risk of catastrophe, we ought to redesign the economic system accordingly. What features would a sustainable world economy have?

First, it would not put all humanity's eggs in the one basket. Since a local unsustainability cannot cancel local sustainability elsewhere, a sustainable world would consist of a number of territories, each of which would be sustainable independently of the others. In other words, rather than a single global economy which would damage everyone if it crashed, a sustainable world would contain a plethora of regional (sub-national) economies producing all the essentials of life from the resources of their territories and therefore largely independent of each other. This is not to say that these regions would not trade. They would trade, but never out of necessity. Needing to trade rather than choosing to do so is often a sign that an economy is unsustainable, and could certainly lead to its becoming so. The only motive for trading in an economic system designed in accordance with the emerging ecological paradigm would be to increase a population's range of choice. Relatively trivial exchanges would take place like, perhaps, swapping apples for oranges. That way, if one economy got into serious trouble its neighbours would not automatically get hurt. Indeed, they would be well placed to help deal with the emergency.

The situation that these territories produced all their essentials of life for themselves would be more efficient than the present system under which a high proportion of the world's population eats the same foods, is housed in buildings constructed of the same materials, and lives and works in much the same way. Today's uniformity means that much of humankind competes in world markets for the same raw materials and thus puts sources under a high, perhaps unsustainable, degree of pressure. A greater diversity of diet, clothing, building materials and lifestyles would relieve these pressures just as it does in the natural world where species with their own ecological niches avoid competing directly with each other.

Regional economies would develop by finding good ways to use the resources of their immediate areas to meet the needs of local people rather than the demands of uniform markets far away. New cuisines and vernacular architectures would develop and new cultures would be born. With no absolute necessity to trade, there would be no great pressure within these economies to use their resources unsustainably, provided the local population did not exceed its carrying capacity. Moreover, the optional nature of trade would leave regional economies free to ban technologies suspected of having undesirable side effects regardless of whether other regions did so, thus speeding the rate at which the world could react to a sustainability crisis. In the present system, by contrast, the need to be competitive not only makes it impossible to take unilateral action to achieve sustainability, as we saw, but creates constant pressure to increase profits or employment by reducing environmental or social standards.

Of course, the fact that a regional economy was not compelled to trade would not make it problem-free. If it wished to maintain its sustainability it would have to be able to protect itself militarily and economically from territories that had destroyed their own resources by behaving unsustainably and wanted access to resources that had been managed well. The problem of providing military protection is outside the scope of this chapter. We should however note that if an arms race developed between a sustainable part of the world and an unsustainable one, the pressing need to use resources for the purchase or manufacture of weapons could destroy the sustainability of the former.

For economic protection, a sustainable territory would need its own independent currency and banking system. When a territory gets its own currency, its people no longer have to trade with the outside world to assemble the means of exchange to trade with each other. In other words, the volume of business they can do among themselves becomes independent of inflows and outflows of national or international currencies. It is difficult to become sustainable when one has to ensure that enough outside money is available for local trade to be carried on at the optimal level.

Similarly, if a territory has its own banking system it can ensure that interest rates are related to the rate of profit possible on projects within the territory rather than to the highest rate of return that can be found anywhere in the world. This means that there is very much less pressure for the territory's resources to be used unsustainably in order to generate the financial returns required for investment funds to be committed and projects to go ahead.

A sustainable region also needs to be able to prevent net capital flows across its borders either by enacting laws against them or by creating a social climate that makes investing elsewhere a matter for shame. Why? Consider what happens when a sustainable economy becomes mature – when its buildings are repaired and its capital equipment is replaced as it wears out, but no new buildings are erected or extra equipment is installed because the benefits from doing so are too small to make it worthwhile. In other words, all the sustainable projects that give a reasonable rate of return have been carried through and the territory's economy has ceased to grow significantly, although from time to time new technologies come along to make additional projects or production possible without upsetting the area's sustainability. The low rate of return in such an economy means that the owners of capital there will always be tempted to remove their funds to unsustainable or immature sustainable economies, where they get higher rates of return. If such capital movements happen, the mature economy runs down because funds for repairing buildings or replacing worn-out equipment get invested elsewhere. The resulting shortage of equipment causes unemployment to appear, increasing competition for jobs and pushing down wage levels. Fewer goods and services are produced, pushing prices up. Both these changes enable businesses to make additional profits and thus pay higher interest rates; when these rates match those available elsewhere, the capital outflow ceases.

Capital movements out of sustainable economies therefore reduce their output and shift a larger share of this smaller output to the owners of capital, who also benefit from the interest payments they receive from their outside investments. Allowing capital movements maximizes the return per unit of capital but not per citizen. Therefore, no territory can become sustainably mature until all others do too.

One might think that allowing outsiders to invest in sustainable projects in immature sustainable economies would help those economies reach maturity faster. This, however, is wrong. If the interest on this capital had to be paid in an external currency, which in turn had to be earned by selling goods and services on external markets in competition with output from places that subsidized their prices by using unsustainable systems, the need to trade would undermine the territory's sustainability.

Even if the interest was paid in a currency that could only be earned by trading in sustainably produced goods, capital transfers between territories or even parts of the same territory would be undesirable. First, capital creates work in the place where it is spent. In Ireland after independence, the banking system collected savings from rural areas to lend in urban ones, enabling factories, shopping parades, cinemas and houses to be built. This work attracted young men from the rural areas who needed housing, shops, pubs and recreational facilities in the towns, especially if they married a girl who came from the country herself. These needs created further demands for loans and more work for the building trade. Meanwhile, back at home, businesses went into decline because the young people left. It became very difficult to find new projects that would support the rate of interest being asked by the banks in view of the declining population. With fewer opportunities, emigration from the countryside proceeded and whole villages were completely abandoned. Capital transfers can therefore be destabilizing and undesirable *even within the same territory*.

A second reason for rejecting external investment is even more powerful. People investing outside the areas in which they live are only interested in the rate of return they get on their money. All other income streams from their investments, such as payments to workers and suppliers, are seen to reduce their profits, and every effort is made to minimize them. If someone invests in a project in their own community, however, they get a return on their money in many ways besides the interest they receive. Indeed, these non-interest returns could be so important that those financing the project would be prepared to charge no interest at all in order to be sure it went ahead. The project might, for example, provide employment for themselves or their children. Or it might increase incomes in the area and help their existing business do better. Or it might cut unemployment, thus reducing family breakdown and crime.

Community investment projects are therefore very different animals from projects run for the benefit of outside investors. They seek to maximize the total incomes the project generates in the community, not just the profit element. Far from seeing the wage bill as a cost to be minimized, they regard it as a major gain. Attitudes to work are different too. Whereas outside investors seek to de-skill factory work so that they can hire the cheapest possible labour, a community company,

particularly a workers' co-op, would want to organize the v
it is interesting and fulfilling.

Outside investors also have very short time-horizons, war
earn their capital back in three or four years. Communities, o . the
other hand, need long-term incomes for long-term projects such as
raising children. Community-owned factories would want to produce
for safe, stable markets, rather than for the market with the highest
immediate rate of return. Similarly, while outside investors merely
ensure that a plant's emission levels stay within the law because anything better would cost them money, a community company is likely
to work to much higher standards to avoid fouling its own nest.

A sustainable world economy would therefore be almost the opposite
of the present unsustainable one. It would be localized rather than
globalized. It would have no net capital flows. Its trade would be
confined to luxuries rather than essentials. Each self-reliant region would
develop to a certain point and then stop, rather than growing continuously. Investment decisions would be made close to home. And assets
would be owned by the people of the area in which they were located.

There is no space here to discuss how such a sustainable world
might be built, the steps that would have to be taken to establish a self-
reliant regional economy and how it would have to be organized so
that one section of its population did not take advantage of another.
This is a task I attempt in my book *Short Circuit* (Douthwaite 1996).
Here, I just summarize the essential features of a sustainable territory:

- It has a stable population.
- It provides the basic necessities of life for its population from renewable resources under its control and expects to be able to continue
  to do so without overusing or degrading those resources for at least
  the next thousand years. It is therefore able to trade with the outside
  world out of choice rather than necessity. This frees it from the
  need to do unpalatable or unsustainable things in order to compete,
  such as adopting potentially dangerous technologies or curtailing
  social protection provisions.
- It is able to protect its renewable resources and its population both
  militarily and economically. Its collection of economic protection
  weapons includes an independent currency and banking system. It
  has no debts to lenders outside and there are no net flows of capital
  across its borders, thus allowing its interest rate to fall to close to
  zero as it moves towards maturity.
- It does not depend on continual economic growth to stave off
  collapse. Its economy grows very slowly if at all.

Conclusion

The present world economic system is grotesquely unsustainable and for all practical purposes it is impossible for a sustainable world to emerge and be maintained via the workings of an unconfined, undirected market system. Accordingly, international efforts to achieve sustainability are likely to deliver too little too late, and the development of largely self-reliant regional economic systems is a better way to build a stable, sustainable world. Perpetual economic growth is totally incompatible with sustainability and in some industrial countries the growth process is now destroying more wealth than it creates. Growth continues to be the primary national objective in these countries, however, because unless it is generated, investors will withdraw and the economy will collapse.

The answer to the question with which we began this discussion – is it possible to build a sustainable world? – is clearly that it is. Unfortunately, however, since the unsustainabilities that threaten us have been created by the current dominant paradigm and it is virtually impossible to remove them while working within that paradigm, an entirely new way of thinking about the world has to be adopted first.

Notes

1. A wide-ranging and highly readable article reviewing past forecasts of 'scarcity and doom' appeared in the *Economist*, 20 December 1997, pp. 21–3.

2. For the price system to work properly it would have to allow for the rights of future generations to use resources. It would also have to charge enough so that full compensation or restoration could be made for the damage done to the environment and to human health as a result of the use of the resource.

3. A 3 per cent growth rate would lift the value of goods and services produced in the world to four times its present level at the end of fifty years. This estimate therefore assumes that the pollution from that output is halved.

4. Solow was later awarded a Nobel Prize for 'proving' that an exponentially growing population in a growing economic system could enjoy an increasing real wage (Peet 1992: 101).

References

Cobb, Clifford and Ted Halstead (1994) *The Genuine Progress Indicator: Summary of Data and Methodology*. San Francisco: Redefining Progress.

Daly, Herman (1992) *Steady-state Economics*. London: Earthscan.

— (1998) 'Uneconomic growth: conflicting paradigms', *The Social Crediter*, Vol. 77, No. 1, January.

Diefenbacher, Hans (n.d.) 'Towards a sustainable economy: six proposals to take a new look at statistical figures', Mimeo, FEST, Heidelberg, Germany.

Douthwaite, Richard (1996) *Short Circuit*. Totnes: Green Books.

European Workshop on the Impact of Endocrine Disrupters on Human Health and Wildlife (1996) *Report of Proceedings*, Weybridge, England, 2–4 December [EUR 17549]. Copenhagen, Denmark: European Commission.

Farman, Joseph, C. *et al.* (1985) 'Large losses of total ozone in Antarctica reveal seasonal $C10_x/No_x$ interaction', *Nature*, 16 May.

Fowler, Cary and Pat Mooney (1990) *Shattering: Food, Politics, and the Loss of Genetic Diversity*. Tucson: University of Arizona Press.

Jackson, Tim and Nic Marks (1994) *Measuring Sustainable Economic Welfare – A Pilot Index: 1950–1990*. London: New Economics Foundation.

Kelly, Kevin (1996) 'The Economics of Ideas', *Wired*, Vol. 4, No. 6, June.

Lawn, Phillip A. and Richard D. Sanders (1997) *A Sustainable Net Benefit Index For Australia, 1966–67 to 1994–95*. Griffith University Working Paper in Economics No. 16. Griffith University, Nathan, Queensland.

Maddox, John (1972) *The Doomsday Syndrome*. London: Macmillan.

Meadows, Donnella, Dennis Meadows, Jorgen Randers and William Behrens (1972) *The Limits to* Growth. London: Earth Island.

Mishan, E.J. (1977) *The Economic Growth Debate – An Assessment*. London: Allen and Unwin.

Myers, Norman and Julian Simon (1994) *Scarcity or Abundance: A Debate on the Environment*. New York: Norton.

O'Riordan, Tim (1981) *Environmentalism*. London: Pion.

Pearce, David, Anil Markandya and Edward Barbier (1989) *Blueprint for a Green Economy*. London: Earthscan.

Peet, John (1992) *Energy and the Ecological Economics of Sustainability*. Washington, DC: Island Press.

Pezzey, John (1989) *Economic Analysis of Sustainable Growth and Sustainable Development*. Washington, DC: World Bank.

Rachel's Environment and Health Weekly, No. 547, 22 May 1997. Maryland: Environmental Research Foundation.

Roe, David *et al.* (1997) *Toxic Ignorance: The Continuing Absence of Basic Health Testing for Top-selling Chemicals in the United States*. New York: Environmental Defense Fund.

Simon, Julian (1981) *The Ultimate Resource*. Oxford: Martin Robertson.

Solow, Robert M. (1974) 'The economics of resources and the resources of economics', *American Economic Review*, Vol. 64, No. 2 (May), pp. 1–14.

Swan, Shanna H. *et al.* (1997) 'Have sperm densities declined? A reanalysis of global trend data', *Environmental Health Perspectives*, Vol. 105, pp. 1,228–32.

Tainter, Joseph (1996) *Getting Down to Earth*. Washington, DC: Island Press.

UN (1997) *Global Environmental Outlook*. Oxford: Oxford University Press.

Wallich, Henry (1972) 'Zero Growth', *Newsweek*, 24 January, p. 62.

Worldwatch Institute (1996) *State of the World 1996*. New York: Norton.

. . . .

CHAPTER 9

Cultural Politics and (post) Development Paradigm(s)

G.H. Fagan

(On the opposite page of this discussion, I present a parallel cultural text of 'identities-in-culture' [McRobbie 1992: 731] which reflects a specific development location where cultural analysis meets development discourse meets everyday life. I have placed this 'conversation with a purpose' [Bhavnani 1991] alongside the more analytical text as a way of making sure that a voice of those agents of development is itself present, not trivial or irrelevant.)

Theoretical location

Development discourse in the late 1990s has met a theoretical challenge from the poststructuralist problematic with a cultural studies twist. Deconstructing the existing discourses (Gardner and Lewis 1996; Leys 1996) and embarking on theories for development through imagining alternatives (Escobar 1995; Santos 1995) have been the theoretical focus of 'postdevelopment' studies. The pressure for this shift in locus has come from interdisciplinary sources combined with a disciplinary malaise best described as an impasse (Schuurman 1993) in development studies itself. Any theoretical movement engenders tension, of course, but there appears to be a significant strain on this debate, which is enabling at one level but at another level disabling. In this chapter I wish to enter into the terrain of that debate and argue that a theoretical shift from cultural analysis to cultural politics would best serve post-development practice and strategizing. Second, I argue that this cultural politics would start from the location of material struggle as identified in 'development' contexts.

The tensions that arise in pursuing a poststructuralist trajectory are considerable. First, how do we deconstruct development without eradicating its more positive political moments? Does deconstruction entail a rejection of the entire political trajectory of development? The critique of development as a modernist discourse creates a concern that in the 'era of posts' a postdevelopment scenario might involve the conceptual

Reflexions: Development Conversation[1]

The political act is capable of contesting all of culture and placing all of its divisions into question. de Certeau, cited in Ahearne (1995: 136)

Honor: Tell me about yourself and why you have come here today.

Thembeli: I was born on a farm and I worked on a farm, but I left a long time ago, when I was young. I started to work when I was ten years old. I used to pick up the eggs from the coop. In my family there was no boy so I used to plough the fields, bring the milk from the cows, you know. They were the old days. When I was about fifteen or eighteen the other children came from Durban and they found me still on the farm. They told me, 'No, no, you must leave the farm – let us go together to Durban. We can have Christmas at home. You can work, you can be clean.' When you work on the farm you are always dirty, no matter how much you clean. So when I came here to Durban I was twenty-two years old.

H: Did you miss the farm?

T: I missed the farm because I didn't know the other [the city]. I was born in a farm. What can I say? It was nice to me, what I was doing it was nice. It is bad to work in farm, to be just working. No pay you know, just working for the parents, you know. So I started a new life here in Durban.

H: Did you get work?

T: Yes, I got work. I was a domestic servant. I was working for that Madam. Oh, that woman I used to work for! Mrs J ... She was very nice to me. I was working for her for seven years. Up M—— road. Corner of M—— road and she had four children. It was a hotel. She was the owner of that hotel.

H: What happened that you lost that work? Did she move or what happened?

T: No, she didn't move. The other man came there, he was working for someone in Durban. So he used to come to that hotel. So he proposed to me and I got in love with him so he took me to Zululand and he says he wants to marry me so he took me to his home. He was a married man and his wife was dead so he took me there and I was crying because I know that my mother doesn't know that I am not working there any more. She won't get money, because I'm not working any more. So I told him I'm worrying, I'm not happy. I love him, but I'm not happy with him because I knew that my mother does not know that I'm here now. I was in Zululand. Yes, I was living with his disarticulation of questions concerning inequalities and disadvantage. A second related tension is that the poststructuralist focus on language may lead to a replacement of the 'material' with 'representation' in explanations of politics (Crush 1995). In other words, there is a concern that a political economy of development will be sacrificed to 'scholarly representations of other scholarly representations of original representations – feasts of intellectual delights detached from the reality of poverty, racism, greed, theft, chicanery and exploitation' (Takaki 1995: 173, quoted in Mohan 1997: 312). A third tension arises where some theorists, working within a poststructuralist framework, turn from the language of critique (the hallmark of a social science and a political economy approach) to a language of possibility as a way of articulating new spaces for radical alternative visions and strategies. There is considerable discomfort with this shift on the part of those immersed in a social scientific research paradigm.

Throughout these debates a cultural analysis has proved the least contentious aspect. Unlike the politics of poststructuralism and postmodernism, it has not met with total rejection at any time within either the dominant paradigm or the radical paradigms of development studies. Cultural analysis has been seen as more or less acceptable to development theorists as a nonthreatening turn of events, which emphasizes the power of the local. It is not considered to have necessarily dire consequences for the essence of the politics of development – as might be entailed, for example, in deconstruction.

Cultural politics, as opposed to cultural analysis, can, for me, offer better purchase in the project of construction of a postdevelopment politics. This chapter thus seeks to examine what a cultural politics, as opposed to a cultural analysis, might offer to the construction of a postdevelopment scenario. I propose to map the transition from cultural analysis to cultural politics, with an emphasis on voice and situatedness, as a possible route through which to establish postdevelopment practice.

Why is postdevelopment my concern? The history of knowledge would lead us to be wary of simply discarding old knowledge just because it is subject to criticism, and development paradigms are sufficiently important to merit detailed consideration. However, to discuss the potential of a postdevelopment scenario is not necessarily antidevelopment. In this I differ with many of the views espoused in *The Development Dictionary: A Guide to Knowledge as Power* (Sachs 1992). Adopting the privilege of being antidevelopment is not, in my view, politically or morally viable when sitting in an 'overdeveloped' social and individual location. Rather, as argued by Knippenberg and Schuurman, those espousing the anti-development perspective are in children. So I told him he must write to my mother and tell her that I'm not working now because now I won't send money to my mother every month.

H: How much money would you send?

T: You won't believe me if I tell you I was earning twenty rand. No, it was ten rand. So sometimes I used to send my mother the whole amount and sometimes it was half. It was 1952, no 1954. Yes, 1954 I married that man. I married in 1954 and he died 1956.

H: Oh, he only lived two years?

T: Yes, then he died. Then I came down to Durban to Pinetown. When he died I wrote my elder sister. She was living in Pinetown. So I wrote to her. She said I must come down to Pinetown. So then I was living here in Clermont and I was looking for a job.

H: Did you go back to the woman you were working for before and ask her for a job?

T: I went to find Mrs Jones, but she was gone. She had a stroke. She had one daughter, she was overseas and she went to live with her. She sold the hotel to other people. So I came to stay here to Clermont.

H: And did you get work in Pinetown?

T: Yes, I was a domestic worker, I worked for Mrs H—— for a long time. I worked for her for seven years. When I worked for her I got sick. I got a bad hip – arthritis. So I went to hospital. I stayed in King George for three years, but I was crippled as you see me here. I looked for work but I didn't get work because I was crippled. So I started after the operation to do things by hand like I'm doing now. In 1970 my first child was twelve years old. She was here in Clermont, and when I was in hospital nobody helped me about my children, to go to school and this and that so.

H: Where were they?

T: They were here in Clermont.

H: Were they with a family? When you were in hospital who minded them?

T: The church. I gave them to the minister, and the church was minding my children until I came out of the hospital. They were going to school by the church – the church was helping them to go to school.

H: What do your children do now?

T: Oh, you know the children, today's children they are not nice. The eldest one she is not married, but the last one is married and they drink. That is what they do, they drink. I've got one boy, one boy is a driver, taxi driver. Yes he owns the taxi. He is better than the girls. My eldest daughter, she doesn't work. She crochets and does everything but she drinks, she drinks.

H: Do many women drink here?

T: Oh, the women drink here. Yes, they drink here, more than the men. Now as I'm old I'm living with my grandson of the youngest daughter. She had him before she got married and that boy looks after me nicely.

fact displaying a form of Eurocentrism (Knippenberg and Schuurman 1994). To shift to a postdevelopment scenario is to acknowledge fully the enormous difficulties associated with the dominant development discourse. It is a political acknowledgement of the injustices and un-equal power relations of the practice, a willingness to take that fully on board to such an extent that I wish to leave the problematic totally behind, if this is necessary to transform practices. There is a historical and conceptual appropriateness to contributing towards a postdevelop-ment framework in that the key theoretical and political limitation of a structuralist discourse, such as development, is that it cannot offer us sufficient tools for transformation. But that is not to lose sight of the fact that development theory, as a body of knowledge, is still useful in conveying the structural trends of disparities and inequalities on a global scale. Where it falls short is at the point where structural accounts argue that there is a prevailing logic that shows us 'how it is' and which gives us an understanding of why it is the way it is. There is little theorizing on how it should be or could be different, which would be essential to transformation. We have conclusions but no solutions. It is as if by describing, and describing again, how bad the situation is, that this will automatically lead to change. Absent from here is the pedagogical dimension to change, or the necessity of theorizing strategies for change. The belief in the power of domination binds the mind of the struc-turalist theorist in a way that a poststructuralist framework does not.

At this point, with regard to the parallel text on the opposite page, I wish to emphasize the need to engage the ambiguities of a local account. Its visibility serves to underscore from the outset how the political, economic and ideological materiality of culture shapes the rules by which everyday life is defined, lived and resisted at the individual level. It also places emphasis on the material reality of development 'needs' in particular sites and, arising from this, urges that postdevelop-ment theorizing should critically engage with, rather than seek to 'transcend', the development discourse.

What can easily be lost in a volume written by theorists who have an intellectual and political interest in a particular discourse is the specificity of the 'other-to-academic' voice and location. In the light of the poststructuralist insight that discourse describes, informs and con-stitutes practices, in my view to give parity of style and content to the conversational script between development worker and development agent and the academic script is a discursive ploy to ensure due intellectual modesty. It serves as a reminder to the reader and myself that we cannot substitute intellectual work for political work. Under-standing the politics of intellectual work is part of the academic text

H: What does he do?

T: He is doing standard six now. He is looking after me nicely. Yes, I live with him and he goes to school. In August there will be racing for the children. I heard that there will be racing for the children. And the trouble is this. I live by the shops and when I look out I was worrying about children. They love to stand by the shops not doing anything here in Clermont. There is no place to go, there is no place for children to play. Nobody to teach the children how to do the games, you know. So in August one day I took my pension and I asked how in Queenspark there is racing. So I said I must go and ask these children to not live by the shops, but to go and do something like games. Sometimes you hear them. They swear, they swear, they don't talk nice, these children, and sometimes my child used to go there because he has friends there. He can't just sit with me and that worries me because he is going to learn to do those things, but he does nothing. So I went there and that lady Helen, she asked me what I want. She was pleased to see me coming and ask how to teach those children games. So Helen she came here to Clermont one day and made an appointment. I went to the neighbours and asked if they can give me all these children to take to Helen. So they gave me thirteen children and we went to Helen. Oh, some of them they joined, and my grandson, and they are still doing that.

H: You've been around Clermont for a long time. Do you think it is changing in any way?

T: Changing a little, changing a little but not so much.

H: Is it getting better or worse?

T: Well, there is no fighting. No fighting and in the night there is no shooting, there are no people dying by chance. Someone shooting someone – that has stopped in our township. You can go to the other place in the township at night and you don't get hurt. Yes, that is better, but then for the children it is not good still because there is no place for the children for sport. Yes. That is the main thing, it is the main thing to avoid the children hanging around. If the children could get sport, that is the main thing, don't you think so?

H: I do think so.

T: That worries me a lot. That they can do nothing, because I'm living in a shack. You don't know what that is. You know these funny houses that are made by pieces of things. I'm living in that house. But it worries me. While I'm living there I don't like to say I'm living there in this shack. It worries me but I look to the children. It is especially what worries me about the children that they live in these places.

H: So you don't mind it, but you don't like it for the children, because they are young?

T: I think if they grow up playing sports they can see where they are going but this should never produce closure on political and practical work. Power and politics are not exclusively matters of textuality (Crush 1995; Escobar 1995), but texts can be used politically. The conversational, or practical, text is represented here as a way of ensuring a political presence of struggle. Thembeli historicizes her own past experiences and analyses her current and future prospects in a 'development' context. The voice of the 'development' agent is registered here where she names her 'development' needs and demands that they be met. The text records her material motivation in participating in the conversation, her understanding of the power relations of development projects, and the relational interactive quality of a 'development' site.

From cultural analysis to cultural politics

Vincent Tucker refers to the admittance of culture into the hegemonic structuralist development discourse as 'the cultural turn' (1997: 1). He traces how Unesco has assumed responsibility for the cultural dimension of development, and he describes the variety of approaches to culture taken by development theorists. Culture has been seen as the 'icing on the cake', a 'distraction from the economy', or the 'missing concept' (Tucker 1997: 2). Rather than promote an 'add culture and stir' approach, Tucker makes a bid to 'leave behind the epistemological illusion of concreteness' presented in sociological and economic data and move towards integrating political economy analysis and cultural analysis (Tucker 1997: 9). According to Tucker the political advantage of incorporating cultural analysis is that it presents us with a methodological tool for analysing the cultural production of resistance and 'if development is to be conceived of primarily in terms of struggle for the control of destinies' (Tucker 1997: 7) then we need just such an analysis.

To approach development from the perspective of cultural analysis is to ask questions about the meaning of development, about the production of knowledge, about who 'decides and who has the greater use of resources, coercive and persuasive, to make their version of reality stick' (Tucker 1997: 7). Tucker seeks to find ways to 'incorporate' those voices and points of view (the submerged and marginalized local forms of knowledge and the counterhegemonic movements) into development discourse (Tucker 1997: 11).

The problem with this is that 'incorporation' into a development discourse, and a focus on 'resistance' techniques may not be going far enough. Integrating political economy analysis and cultural analysis is a difficult task, since both approaches would have to be modified considerably. My argument is that cultural analysis would have to be replaced by to. But if they grow in that shade they won't have anything, they won't have anything.

H: Do you think all these changes in politics, Mandela being president, do you think that will make a difference?

T: I don't understand politics, and I don't know what politics is. People who know politics, like people who are educated, but I don't know what politics are. But I can really tell you that I don't see anything. Honest, I don't see anything, because before the vote they told us everything. They said you are going to vote, you are going to be leading a better life and you won't be living in this shack any more and your children will go to school. You don't pay. But this and that, they promised everything. Like heaven. Now I don't see that. [Laughing]

H: Do you see any changes? Does it make a difference that you have the vote?

T: No. Oh, to me I see nothing, honestly I don't see anything. I'm just living like always living before voting. I'm just living the same way.

H: Do you think your children will live the same as always then?

T: Yes, that is what I'm thinking, that is what I'm thinking, that is why I'm worried about the children. They must do something to make their life better. And the other thing: I'd be glad if the children go to school.

H: Do you think if they go to school that that will be better?

T: That is the only thing. That is the only thing will make the children go further. That is what I'm telling the children. The children say they have got everything for free, but I say no. Don't think you will get everything without paying. There are no free things. I'm telling that to my children. Not other people's children, but my children. I never, never, never believe you can get anything free, because by my mind I think that if the education is going to be free the people who make those papers and the factories who make those papers, who is going to pay them? Because all the papers, they must make the papers, so they must pay for it. When it comes to school, is there schooling for nothing? Do you think that is true? Do you think that is true? No it costs money. Even if the government is going to do something for the children, it still means we will pay a little, a little. But to say it is free is not true.

H: Does that make you angry, do you think they told a lie?

T: I think so. I think so sometimes. Sometimes I think so in my heart. I think so. Sometimes. In my insides I think they maybe were telling lies, because I don't see anything.

H: Where you live now, what is it called?

T: Here in C——— ... , in I——— ...

H: Have you water and things like that there?

cultural politics. Incorporation of cultural analysis into development discourse does not fully answer the critique of development discourse brought to light in postdevelopment theorizing. It neither thoroughly deconstructs the paradigm, nor does it explicitly focus on the production of alternative strategies; rather, it focuses on the cultural production of resistance at the expense of transformation strategies. The importance of culture to development discourse is seen to be that if development is to have a real value at the local level it requires a qualitative understanding of the complexities and dynamics of everyday lives. A second and related point made is that development must be an integral part of existing cultural and social relations.

Without negating this contribution I would like to turn to a debate in the dispersed field of cultural studies to explain why it would be appropriate to move towards a concept of cultural politics. There has been a growing concern since at least the late 1980s with the role of politics in cultural studies. The international conference 'Cultural Studies Now and in the Future' held in 1990, for example, saw a strong focus on difference, relativism and fluidity being openly contested by those of a more practical political persuasion.[2] The strongest critique of cultural analysis without the necessary element of critical, policy or politics came from Tony Bennett who at that time made a clear plea for the 'corrective' of policy to be reworked into cultural analysis:

> ... it is only by using the kinds of correctives that would come from putting 'policy' into cultural studies that cultural studies may be deflected from precisely those forms of banality, which, in some quarters, have already claimed it while also resisting the lure of those debates whose contrived appearance of ineffable complexity makes them a death trap for practical thinking. (quoted in Grossberg *et al.* 1992: 33)

Bennett argues the immediacy of this policy corrective on the basis that the road that beckons towards the 'phantom agents of much cultural theory', is littered with missed political opportunities. If cultural analysis is to produce a qualitative understanding of everyday lives, if it is really to engage the relationship between culture and power, the question of politics must, arguably, enter into the equation. The cultural analysis approach, which has too often celebrated difference, relativism and fluidity at the expense of cultural critique (Adam and Allan 1995: xiv), could greatly benefit from a focus on inequities or on how cultural production is implicated in relations of power. From a cultural studies perspective we can see that an engagement with 'underdevelopment' could afford the cultural theorist the space to engage with specific cultural problematics in a way that underscores

T: Yes, there is water, there is a tap where I'm living. Outside there is a tap [communal tap].

H: Is it dangerous to live there?

T: No, it is not dangerous. It's not dangerous. You know I don't want to move, because the transport bus stop is near, the shops and everything is here.

H: Do you pay rent?

T: Yes, I pay rent. I pay 28 rand every month.

H: Where do you get that 28 rand?

T: I get a pension, I'm a pensioner.

H: How much is your pension?

T: My pension is 390 rand.

H: Is it enough?

T: Not enough. You know that pension we got, that pension, it was Chief Buthelezi who gave us that pension. He gave us that pension. He went up and down asking government to give the African go-gos [In Zulu, grandmothers] the pension. And we got that up from 60 rand up to 370. This government put only 20 rand to increase that. To this government we have only 20 rand. That 370 we got that from that old government, you know.

H: What do you think about women? Do you think women can change things for themselves?

T: Yes.

H: You do?

T: How?

H: Like I think why did Mrs —— ask me to come here. I said to myself that is a place I'm going to change [myself]. It is a place to change the woman. As you came here you came to change the woman, so that proves that the woman is going to change. Because I came and I thought you were going to say no because I'm old. You'd say 'No, we don't change go-gos, old woman.' [Laughs] I thought you were going to say now we don't allow it. I do think that women are going to change because they will wake up and do for themselves. I think so.

H: Like what?

T: Like they are going to teach us how to sew, how to do the handwork and when we do the handwork you will support us to sell those and we must wake up. If you teach me how to do this and you tell me that I must go home and come back with this done, I must do that. Yes. And I think as you come from the other place you will help to support us about money because this country has no money. This country has no money. I think you will support us to do what we want to do.

H: What do you think people want to do?

T: Like I'm doing my handwork, but I have no place to stay to do my their relevance to the production of global and local divisions and hierarchies. Developing a critical approach in the cultural scenario would both supersede the 'add in and stir' solution (to culture and development) and act as a necessary prerequisite for combining political economy and cultural analysis.

Locating cultural politics in postdevelopment discourse

Cultural politics, as opposed to cultural analysis, has a dual focus. It would seek to break down the current material space allocated to, and produced for, agents and to build the will to overcome the absence of a discursive political formation that would best represent the interests of such agents in a specific site (Fagan 1995). Consequently, it is only through marrying the specific cultural politics to the external referent discourse (in this case postdevelopment discourse) that we can proceed. A cultural politics of postdevelopment would seek to forge links between specific or site-based discourses and a broader field of radically democratic discourse such as postdevelopment. Put another way, a cultural politics has the advantage that it deals with the specifics of the material and political space allocated to women such as Thembeli and it simultaneously draws on and contributes to the broader paradigmatic politics of postdevelopment transformation. This discourse is *post* development in the sense that it would involve a theoretical move beyond a structuralist framework to the language of reconstruction, transformation and possibility. A language of critique cannot, on its own, lead to a radical new imaginary.

The challenge then in a postdevelopment cultural politics would be to construct a discourse of social change, but without transcending the realities of the everyday lives and struggles of people like Thembeli. There is an ethical dimension as well in uncovering structural processes of victimization, of subordination, of localized, personalized poverty and of hunger. Cultural politics can help establish that practices of postdevelopment should be grounded in the material terrain that is occupied by the agents who identify themselves as in need of 'development'. It involves highlighting struggle in terms of acknowledging the specificity of demands, concrete resistances already in play and the effort being made towards a public sphere of influence. Blocking the creation of development 'victims' can be achieved through the theoretical articulation of these people as agents in a postdevelopment imaginary combined with a politics that builds on the cultural production of transformation at the local level.

Cultural creativity and the production of a cultural politics is a path

handwork. But I went another day to the Pinetown Centre and they said we
must make clubs. When we make clubs, groups, like working with fifty they are
able to give us what we need, like the huts to work. And when we sew they give
us machines, like to support our needs. But they don't support just one, one, one
[individuals]. We must make groups. That is why I came here because I want
to be one of this group to see how we can go. But I think that we will succeed.
I think you must help us to do what you are telling us to do, because we don't
know. You come and you say what work we must do. You know, when you've
been living in a poor place, because I've lived here for a long time, I don't know
where to start to tell you how we live here in this place. But you know how to
take the people out of darkness. I think you came to help us. [Laughs]

H: *Do you think L—— [the director of the centre]* came to do this?

T: *I've been friends with Mrs —— [a* different social worker] *for some*
years. She ran the club [ZANZE]. In 1981 I joined one of the clubs. It means
doing it for yourself. Mrs —— was a worker. She teaches me how to do
patchwork, as you see I've done this, and cooking. For example, if you have
one potato and one cup of flour, she teaches us how to do potato cakes.

H: *Are these things that your mother didn't teach you how to do?*

T: *No, She couldn't teach me that because she didn't know anything.*
[Laughs]

H: *But she knew how to work on a farm.*

T: *Oh, yes.*

H: *So you think Clermont isn't improving.*

T: *No, what is in Clermont? It's dirty. Clermont is dirty. They have their*
own stands but they don't know how to live clean, to clean their own place. I
think people must get taught how to live in their own place. Like making a
garden, plant plants, because it is their own place, but it is dirty.

H: *You have been involved in lots of things to make you improve yourself.*
You have tried to do a lot of things. You went to those meetings, to those 'do
it for yourself meetings'.

T: *Yes. I went to the meetings, but the thing is I haven't got my own place.*
I'm renting, but now you can't do what you like. You are just like a prisoner.

H: *Before this have you ever been with just a group of women working*
together?

T: *Yes. It was very nice because at that time we used to buy things like*
crockery together, one for one first then another, until we had one bought for
each six members. We used to work together.

H: *Was that good, did it work?*

T: *It was good, very good.*

H: *What happened then in the end?*

T: *They went on to do their own things.*

through which we can build a postdevelopment practice. Cultural production as a potentially powerful and potentially emancipatory force has to play a role in this process. A cultural politics of postdevelopment is based on the understanding that culture produces power, knowledge, subjectivities and identities so struggle at the cultural level is not only feasible but also necessary. Cultural politics sets as its agenda the deliberate influencing of forms of production, in other words what knowledges and identities are to be produced. Central to this is the understanding that social relations are as culturally as they are economically produced. Second, that rhetoric, ideology, and the articulations of a more egalitarian vision of society are as 'real', as 'material' and in certain instances as effective in emancipatory transformation as are the most material of economic changes (Ryan 1989).

This brings us back to the text on the opposite page. The individual experience of Thembeli in the development site can be a new point of departure for theorizing development theory and practice. In the first place, it establishes a material crisis. Thembeli lives in poverty but she wishes to transform her lot and she in conjunction with the development researcher would wish to bring about the meeting of some of the material needs she identifies. Here she outlines the specifics of her material location, the 'lived-in' relations of subordination. The text provides representations of her lived, negotiated and resisted everyday relations of subordination (financial, social and work relations). The dialogue tells what she experiences as the crucial and primary needs of her situation.

In the second place, Thembeli's text allows us to identify structural discourses of racism and development working hand in hand to establish relations of subordination in the interactional aspect of the development project dynamic. In so far as an ensemble of discourses – colonial, racist, sexist, development – have historically attempted to fix Thembeli in a subordinate position and the development worker as helper they have played a part in relations of subordination. In so far as this fixes her situation as an unavoidable social reality they are problematic. So, second, we have a discursive crisis of space (Harvey 1996) into which development work is invited. Postdevelopment strategizing must critically engage at this point, not dismiss the development scenario in anti-development rhetoric. At its best it can be inspired by a will to break through the current material and specific space allowed to particular people. Acting as a wider referent for broader democratic goals it can be used to contest the problematic aspects of the development rhetoric. But the forces that affect the everyday existence of people like Thembeli must constantly confront the postdevelopment trajectory.

H: Do you still meet those women?

T: Yes, like Mrs ——, she is very good, but she can't explain to the others.

H: You know this government Regional Development Plan, do you think anything is going to come through?

T: Here in Clermont there is no such thing.

H: What happens if you get sick and get to hospital?

T: You see before if a pensioner got sick you went to hospital. We didn't pay, but now we pay.

H: When you see the future here what do you think it will be? What do you think would be good for people here? Would you have a house?

T: I can tell you that what worries me is that this country has no money, the value of our money is going down.

H: You know a lot for someone who says you don't know anything about politics.

T: No, I hear when the people talk, but not to say I know what is right. I don't know anything. You know what happens when you live with white people. I stayed with white people when I was a domestic, that's why I'm not from here. You know on farming you grow up together with white people. When I was young I didn't know that you can't get in love with white people. I didn't know that when I was young. When I came to Durban I was twenty-two years. I came here in Durban and they said 'No.' They told me you mustn't talk to whites. They called them Europeans. It was too bad, because on farm we used to grow up together. I understand when they talk and I listen and I want to know what they are talking about. I want to know what is going on, but I don't say I know myself. [Laughing]

H: There is nothing wrong with saying you know.

T: No. One thing I don't know. It worries me, this name politics *I don't understand what is. That is why it's going on in my mind, that is why I don't like the name* politics. *Yes, that is what I feel about this government. This government is all right but this government has no money.*

H: Do you not think that before the government had money, but it kept it to itself. Only certain people got access to it?

T: Yes, that is what they did. Even now, even now, even now. The government it can give, it loves to give to everybody, but if the government gives away that money, spreads all its money to the plighty, you know, it goes down. Sometimes I can't agree not to give to the other people. But, you see, I think it is going like that. Even more the money's gone down, because I hear it on the radio. Always they say the money's going down, going down, going down, you know. Where we going to get the money, 'cause always they tell us it is going down, but the rand is going down every day, every day. So that worries me.

Cultural politics can help produce this confrontation by critically examining how ideologies and identities are articulated into concrete social practices. The cultural text on the opposite page gives some indication of the subjectivity, identities, struggles and articulations of women in a particular 'development' site in a specific time in a specific place. I read the text as underscoring a material crisis (Thembeli is barely surviving and in dire circumstances) and a discursive crisis ('development' discourse is problematic to the organization of an alternative). Thembeli presents herself as a serious actor, emotional, angry, thoughtful. She can reflect on her actions. She articulates that she is not satisfied with material conditions and that she wants and deserves something better for both herself and her community. She will work to this end. A cultural politics will look at this form of interaction, asking what are the power relations involved in the interaction recorded? All that is problematic in the development scenario is reflected in this conversational event. Unequal relations between different agents of development, worker/client, white/black, Northern/Southerner, rebound here, and are relived, at the cultural level. However, all that is positive is also present – working together to establish development needs with a view to achieving funding to set up projects that could meet some of the needs identified. Development discourses are not fixed, they are open to change. So too are those agents (project officers, researchers) working inside and outside the development industry. As Griesgraber and Gunter assert, this is a terribly important insight for those interested in effecting social change. Reconstituted development workers, researchers and activists are, and can become, active in social change and this is better than 'depoliticized irresponsibility'(Griesgraber and Gunter 1995: 157).

With Fredric Jameson, I argue that when it comes to reading narratives 'the primacy of the political interpretation' (1981: 18) is crucial. Thembeli occupies relations of subordination that warrant the articulation of her struggle as a political one. She lives under relations of oppression. Once we acknowledge this it is possible to develop strategies that move toward the challenging of, and transformation of, the material and discursive crisis of space she occupies. Any postdevelopment work must move forward in the belief that this is not only possible but also necessary. In conclusion, if policy is the corrective to cultural analysis, then a cultural politics may be the necessary corrective to postdevelopment. Development discourses and development projects operate in the material space of 'underdevelopment', and a critical cultural engagement of these must be accommodated in postdevelopment strategizing.

H: *Do you listen to the news every day?*

T: *Every day, every day on the radio. I read the paper.*

H: *Can I ask you a different question altogether? You know men and women, and between men and women, do you think things have changed for women with their partners or their husbands, or are they always staying the same? Do you think women now have a better life than they did before, or the same?*

T: *Yes, they have a better life.*

H: *Why?*

T: *Like, now they can buy flats, they are living in flats and buying and they do all the things for themselves, that they were not allowed to do before.*

H: *And they weren't allowed before?*

T: *No they couldn't do it before. Before a woman was a woman, but now they are free to do what they like.*

H: *And what do you think of that?*

T: *It is nice, it's nice.*

H: *Why?*

T: *It's nice when they have the right to do what they like. It is nice.*

H: *So it has become better, women are better off than they were? Because they can make more money or what?*

T: *They can make money themselves, you don't have to go to the husband. You see that it was bad before, when you were a woman you were supposed to ask your husband about everything, you see. Look, can you say to your husband that you want to ask for money to buy your pads, do you think? If you are a woman there are some private things you can't tell your husband. You must have money to do what you like. Before the men used to give them money and when you go to the shops the man would want change.*

H: *Do men take care of women?*

T: *What I see is that the men don't take care of the women. You know why? They drink too much. I'm living next to the place where they sell beer, you know. When the women pass by they just look at them and don't talk to them, to the ladies. What do you think of that? They are working so they are drinking the money from morning to night.*

H: *So they don't treat the women properly, because they are drinking?*

T: *I think so.*

H: *Have you anything else you want to ask me?*

T: *Yes. As I am living in this funny place in Clermont, that means that I don't get anything, like. I'm asking am I going to get two or three rooms to live nicely or am I just going to die like that?*

H: *I don't know.*

T: *What did you come here for?* [3]

Notes

1. This is an abridged and edited version of a conversation with Thembeli. She arrived at a centre where we (Fagan *et al.* 1996) were doing a pilot study for a Women and Empowerment Project. She had heard on the grapevine that something could be about to start there that would involve some kind of development project for women in the area. She had walked five miles in the blazing sun to get to the centre and wanted to be part of whatever 'development' or 'empowerment' was going to happen there. This particular empowerment project was blocked and the work was never finished because of political obstruction at the University of Durban-Westville from where the research project was launched.

2. The conference 'Cultural Studies Now and in the Future' was organized through the Unit for Criticism and Interpretive Theory at the University of Illinois at Urbana-Champaign by Lawrence Grossberg, Cary Nelson and Paula Treichler.

3. I do not mean this text to represent a straightforward rendering of the reality of an 'other', nor the production of the other as object, nor the unjustified seizing of the authority of authenticity. I, as the development worker, am placing myself in the knowledge process. The development context is speaking through Thembeli and me in this conversation. These identities are not just discursive or textual identities, they are real identities. At best I hope the text can be read to reflect the relational interactive quality of development work and the discourses that speak through us.

References

This list gives details of works cited in both texts of Chapter 9.

Adam, B. and S. Allan (eds) (1995) *Theorizing Culture: An Interdisciplinary Critique after Postmodernism*. London: UCL Press.

Ahearne, J. (1995) *Michel de Certeau: Interpretation and Its Other*. Oxford: Polity Press.

Bennett, T. (1992) 'Putting policy into cultural studies', in *Postscript in Cultural Studies*. New York: Routledge, pp. 23–38.

Bhavnani, K.K. (1991) *Talking Politics*. Cambridge: Cambridge University Press.

Canclini, N.G. (1995) *Hybrid Cultures: Strategies for Entering and Leaving Modernity*. Minneapolis: University of Minnesota Press.

Corbridge, S. (ed.) (1995) *Development Studies: A Reader*. London: Edward Arnold.

Cowen, M. and R. Shenton (1996) *Doctrines of Development*. London: Routledge.

Crush, J. (ed.) (1995) *Power of Development*. London: Routledge.

Escobar, A. (1995) *Encountering Development: The Making and Unmaking of the Third World*. New Jersey: Princeton University Press.

Fagan, G.H. (1995) *Cultural Politics, and Irish School Dropouts*. Westport, CT: Bergin and Garvey.

Fagan, G.H., R. Munck and K. Nadasen (1996) 'Gender, culture and development: a South African experience', in *European Journal of Development Research*, Vol. 8, No. 2, pp. 93–110.

Gardner K. and D. Lewis (1996) *Anthropology, Development and the Post-modern Challenge*. London: Pluto Press.

Griesgraber, J. and B. Gunter (eds) (1995) *Promoting Development: Effective Global Institutions for the Twenty-first Century*. London: Pluto Press.

Grossberg, L., C. Nelson and P. Treichler (eds) (1992) *Cultural Studies*. New York: Routledge.

Harvey, D. (1996) *Nature and the Geography of Difference*. Oxford: Blackwell.

Jameson, F. (1981) *The Political Unconscious: Narrative as a Socially Symbolic Act*. New York: Cornell University Press.

Knippenberg, L. and F. Schuurman (1994) 'Blinded by rainbows: anti-modernist and modernist deconstructions of development', in F. Schuurman (ed.), *Current Issues in Development Theory: Global Aspects for Agency and Structure*. Saarbrucken: Verlag für Entwicklungspolitik Breienbach Gmbh.

Laclau, E. (1996) *Emancipation(s)*. London: Verso.

Leys, C. (1996) *The Rise and Fall of Development Theory*. London: EAEP, Indiana University Press and James Currey.

McRobbie, A. (1992) 'Post-Marxism and cultural studies: a postscript', in L. Grossberg, C. Nelson and P. Treichler (eds), *Cultural Studies*. New York: Routledge, pp. 719–31.

Mohan, G. (1997) 'Developing differences: post-structuralism and political economy in contemporary development studies', *Review of African Political Economy*, No. 73, pp. 311–28.

Ryan, M. (1989) *Politics and Culture: Working Hypotheses for a Post-revolutionary Society*. Baltimore, MD: Johns Hopkins Press.

Sachs, W. (ed.) (1992) *The Development Dictionary: A Guide to Knowledge as Power*. London: Zed Books.

Santos, B. de S. (1995) *Toward a New Common Sense: Law, Science and Politics in the Paradigmatic Transition*. New York: Routledge.

Schuurman, F. (ed.) (1993) *Beyond the Impasse: New Directions in Development Theory*. London: Zed Books.

Takaki, R.(1995) 'Culture wars in the United States: closing reflections on the century of the colour line', in J. Nederveen Pieterse and B. Parekh (eds), *The Decolonization of the Imagination: Culture, Knowledge and Power*. London: Zed Books, pp. 166–76.

Tucker, V. (ed.) (1997) *Cultural Perspectives on Development*. London: Frank Cass.

Unger, R. (1987) *Politics, a Work in Constructive Social Theory*, Vol. 1: *False Necessity, Anti-necessitarian Social Theory in the Service of Radical Democracy*. Cambridge: Cambridge University Press.

. . . .

CHAPTER 10

Deconstructing Development Discourses: of Impasses, Alternatives and Politics

Ronaldo Munck

There have been many texts in recent years urging us to 'rethink' development and to move 'beyond' the perceived impasse in this area of knowledge and practice. The stakes in these debates are more than intellectual as the imbrication between knowledge and power is closer in them than usual. In this chapter I will reconsider the impasse story, which I see as limited by the modernist perspective shared by most sides of the debate. I then consider various alternatives to, or in, development that have been articulated forcefully in recent years. I see the overall tenor of these debates as a commitment to anti-modernism. Finally, I turn towards what a postmodernist development studies might look like. Contrary to critics who focus on the supposed apolitical nihilism of postmodernism, I argue that postmodernism is a way to 'bring politics back in' to the debates.

Beyond what impasse?

Nearly two decades ago, some authors (for example, Booth 1985) began to perceive an 'impasse' in development theory. That insight spawned several books (Schuurman 1993, Booth 1994) and became an established landmark in the teaching of development studies. But is there substance to this 'impasse' beneath the surface noise?

I would argue that at the root of this debate was a simple misunderstanding. The long-standing hegemony of the modernization approach since the 1950s had been challenged by the dependency approach in the 1970s. The dependency theorists stood on its head the vision of a world where all was for the best and development would be harmonious (see Kay 1989). Instead, they presented a bleak vision of the 'development of under-development'. The confusion was twofold. First, there was a slippage between the concepts 'radical' and 'Marxist' which led to the dependency approach being placed in a Marxist lineage. Second, and the main point here, there was an unwarranted belief that Marxism actually represented a radical break with the theoretical and political coordinates of the modernization paradigm.

It is now more widely recognized that Marxism is a legitimate heir to the Enlightenment tradition and, in its dominant strands, shares the evolutionist perspective so dear to the heart of the 1950s modernization theorists. By the early 1980s it was widely perceived that the dependency approach was providing diminishing returns both conceptually and politically. In that sense there was an impasse, because the modernization and dependency approaches appeared to checkmate each other. But the impasse was, of course, also the wider one of the 'crisis of Marxism', leading eventually to the collapse of socialism as we know it. From the present perspective, it would thus seem that the impasse was a political one. Basically, the vision of transformation in the developing/underdeveloped/non-European/Third World had faded. Burying their own impoverished version of Marxism was a prerequisite for the impasse theorists to embrace wholeheartedly the old modernization paradigm, suitably refurbished in 1990s garb to distract attention from its dirty 1950s clothes (see So 1990 on the 'new modernization studies').

As Björn Hettne writes, the impasse theorists engaged in 'two rather questionable retreats: back to the disciplines; and back to the conventional development paradigm' (Hettne 1995: 13). Some thirty years of debate around practical experience of and attempts to theorize development had, it seemed, come to naught. What passed as Marxism in the development debates became a scapegoat and justification for a return to conservative orthodoxy. Things were again for the best in the best of all possible worlds. One-time radical critics of the dominant development discourses were now back, or for the first time became ensconced, in the mainstream development journals, took on lucrative consultancies and became advisers to the great international pillars of the development industry.

Development studies was nearly always interdisciplinary, and this was one of its enduring strengths. It was a positive Enlightenment legacy to reject artificial disciplinary boundaries and seek a common approach to a common problem. The impasse theorists seem to want to put the clock back. David Booth, for example, argues that political economy 'needs to be scorned' not only because it acts as 'a cover for facile and irresponsible treatment of complex and technical issues' but also 'for tearing down barriers between some subject areas in a way that raises new barriers between others' (Booth 1994: 301). The language here is very strong ('scorned', 'facile', 'irresponsible') but the message is a simple conservative return to academic disciplines as self-sufficiently meaningful categories. For Booth, development theory (as with political economy placed in ironic distancing quotation marks) 'needs an even firmer and less qualified rebuttal' because it, apparently, became 'a vehicle for a package of neo-Marxist and other radical ideas' (Booth 1994: 301). There is nothing like the erstwhile radical for throwing out radical ideas.

While some writers sought to go 'beyond the impasse' (see Schuurman 1993) it was more common, as Hettne observes, to see a return to orthodoxy. Booth, again, can be used to illustrate this trend with his peculiar and revealing rejection of the gendering and greening of development theory, in spite of readily admitting that they have been 'major growth areas for research in recent years' and that he cannot think of much else which 'has done more to transform the agenda of social development studies' (Booth 1994: 299). Booth acknowledges that while this makes him 'an easy target for criticism' he has decided to stand firm against 'those who wave the banner of innovations in feminist research' and argues that 'the suggestion that there is a special magic associated with social research that concentrates on gender issues is naïve' (Booth 1994: 300). Again, the McCarthyite language and the subconscious guilt feelings overwhelm what might otherwise be a debatable point. The main issue is that feminist research methods have, arguably, caused a conceptual overhaul of the social sciences and led, for example, to a whole new area of feminist ecology. We can take feminism as a litmus test for those who wish to revel in their rejection of 'political correctness' and return to conservative orthodoxy and loyal support for the status quo.

This joint operation of back-to-the-disciplines and back-to-modernization also entails a return to Eurocentrism. As Ozay Mehmet writes, 'Euro Centricity, as a particular form of ethnocentricity, is closely linked to racist theories ... it is non-factual narrow mindedness, vain and misleading' (Mehmet 1995: 90). This deep-rooted Western tradition has always cast its dominant shadow over development studies. It counterposes its civilized to the barbarian of the Other, its rational to the Other's irrational, the West to the non-West. It is a worldview that pervades the very notion of development, which holds that the European model is the benchmark for all other types or modes of development.

Development, as Nederveen Pieterse reminds us, 'tends to be short for the western development model. The perspective remains linear, teleological, ethnocentric' (Nederveen Pieterse 1991: 14). There is an unshaken faith in the virtues of European civilization seen as a paragon of human endeavour. Progress is an article of faith which remains unshaken by all evidence to the contrary. There is a quasi-mystical connotation of development in this worldview and a near-messianic belief in a politics of redemption. The impasse theorists knowingly, or unknowingly, buy into this whole baggage when they turn their backs on radical alternatives. Furthermore, the very notion of an impasse becomes questionable when we realize the extent to which the broad field of development studies is actually unified in its fundamental tenets, whatever adjectives might be added in the various versions of development theory.

It is ironic that precisely when the erstwhile radicals were ending up in an 'impasse' of their own making, the 'development project' that had prevailed since the 1950s was itself entering into crisis. As Philip McMichael puts it: 'The development project had offered a *universal* blueprint for national economic development' (McMichael 1996: 147). The key words here are 'national' and 'economic'. McMichael and others associated with the emerging globalization paradigm argue that this project of national economic growth was in terminal decline by the early 1980s. The frame of reference began to shift from the national to the global arena. The development 'industry', or establishment, began to shift gears to emphasize the interrelatedness of national economies and the ultimate futility of national development strategies, once the *sine qua non* of their discourse. There was even a belated recognition of the gender aspects of development and the need for *sustainable* development, notwithstanding any sceptical interpretation we may wish to place on this turn.

The World Bank in its 1980 *World Development Report* 'officially' signalled the end of the long-running definition of development as nationally managed economic growth. Henceforth, 'development' would measure the extent of participation in and integration with the world market. The notion of 'reform' was also rewritten to erase any connotation of income redistribution or agrarian reform, to signify the extent to which market mechanisms should be given free rein. The internationalization of production and consumption had reached new heights. Concepts such as 'nation' and, particularly, the 'nation-state', began to fade in importance. McMichael goes so far as to detect a new 'globalization project' which has replaced the old 'development project'. This he defines as 'a world order in which states implement rules of *global* economic management' (McMichael 1996: 112). No doubt this process of globalization is uneven (as development was) but it makes little sense to cling to categories derived from the quite different immediate post-war and post-colonial world.

Taking a broader perspective on these debates about development we could argue that they are all centred around the belief that the project of (capitalist) modernity has not exhausted its positive transformative potential (see Passerin d'Entreves and Benhabib 1996). If we take the view that the Enlightenment ideals are still relevant and that modernity is still an unfinished project, then the modernization paradigm and the 'globalization project' are arenas for radical intervention. Modernist discourse unifies the whole field of development studies from the World Bank to the radical fringe. As Ulrick Beck writes:

> At the turn of the third millennium, civilization finds itself in a chaotic simultaneity of the non-synchronous: the transition into simple modernity now shaking the post-communist world and the countries of the south has its foundations and goals snatched away by self-transformations of industrial society. (Beck 1997: 16)

This analysis is used by Beck, and others in the Habermasian tradition, to resist what they see as the conservative or nihilistic tones of postmodernism.

Alternatives in/to development?

If modernism was an overarching problematic framing what questions were asked, which methods were used and which theories were employed in development studies, then counter-modernism might offer an alternative. Indeed, the late 1980s saw a flourishing of 'post-development' approaches (Sachs 1992; Rahnema and Bawtree 1997) which had more than a whiff of counter-modernism about them. On the whole, what was emerging was more an antidevelopment than a postdevelopment discourse. Gustavo Esteva is nothing if not forthright: 'You must be either very dumb or very rich if you fail to notice that development stinks' (Esteva 1987: 135). The critique of the dominant development paradigm(s) enjoined us to examine the 'other side of the story' of the development project: the view from below, the views of women, the view from the South. This section examines critically various varieties of this anti-postdevelopment discourse with a view to understanding it better.

The negative view of development is quite clear and, from a radical perspective, persuasive within certain limits. Attention is drawn to how labile the term is, its very plasticity lending itself to abuse. The pious 'motherhood and apple pie' image of development seeks to place it as an uncontested human good. Yet, for Esteva, 'the metaphor of development gave global hegemony to a purely Western genealogy of history, robbing peoples of different cultures of the opportunity to define the forms of their social life' (Esteva 1992: 9). The one true path to development/civilization/salvation became firmly established under the aegis of first British and then US imperialism. The West was best and the rest had to follow. Underdevelopment, from this perspective, is pure Western invention. Or, as Sachs puts it, 'Development has so persuasively spread [its] assumptions that people everywhere have been caught up in a western perception of reality' (Sachs 1992: 5). The mission of the development critics is thus to unmask these assumptions and reinsert the autonomous perspectives of the indigenous and the oppressed.

If the critics of development are dismissive of mainstream efforts to 'jazz up' their discourse by greening or engendering it they, for their part, wish to articulate 'anOther' development. This may take different forms but it always refuses to be sucked into the mainstream paradigm. Theorists of anOther development tend to prioritize the content of development over its form, which even the Marxist critics tended to emphasize. There is great stress on self-reliance, sustainability, cultural pluralism, and the need to prioritize human needs. This other development model seeks to transcend the limitations and constricting tendencies of the European model of development. Above all, it gives voice to the excluded, to the Other, to all the victims of 'development'. Or, as Björn Hettne puts it: 'Alternative development is a cry for visibility, participation and justice' (Hettne 1995: 161). This is a strong ethical perspective keen to develop a normative, rather than instrumental approach to development. Yet it rejects the hasty label of utopianism which it places on the mainstream approach because of its long-term lack of viability.

Though perhaps attractive at a superficial level, the theories of 'anOther' development leave a lot to be desired at the theoretical level. For all the talk about 'academic imperialism' in relation to mainstream development theory, its critics are not immune to the same criticism. Hettne himself admits that his search for an alternative development model takes him 'back where we started, in the "developed" world' (Hettne 1995: 207). More explicitly, he argues that 'Europe has a moral obligation not only to preach alternatives to others, but also to provide an example by practising them' (Hettne 1995: 207). Thus the gospel of alternative development will still be sung to a European tune. Third World states seeking good old-fashioned economic growth will not be taken in by this populist talk. Instead, Cowen and Shenton argue, 'trusteeship (though none dare speak its name) will have to be exercised by the knowing and the moral on behalf of the ignorant and corrupt'

(Cowen and Shenton 1995: 43). It would seem that the white man's burden still weighs heavy.

A somewhat less amorphous conception of alternative development is the orientation known as 'popular development'. Although, like its mainstream progenitor, it has many varied interpretations, it usually prioritizes such issues as gender, environment, participation, popular planning and a focus on needs. In a recent textbook dedicated entirely to explicating the concept of 'popular development', John Brohman argues that: 'The failure of contemporary development to meet popular interests underscores the need to devise more people-centred approaches which stress empowerment and participation' (Brohman 1996: 345). If neither Keynesianism nor neoliberalism can solve 'problems such as underdevelopment, inequalities and poverty' (Brohman 1996: 345) then everyone will see the advantages of a development approach based on popular empowerment. In a conclusion of breathtaking simplicity Brohman argues that: 'Popular development should be seen as a process which empowers people to take control of their destinies' (Brohman 1996: 352). Unfortunately, the world is not ready for such simple recipes.

In the first instance, the justification for the idea of 'popular development' in terms of the failure of the mainstream approach in terms of meeting human needs seems naïve. Whoever thought that the fifty years of the modern development discourse was actually meant to deliver prosperity for all? Certainly, the international development organizations have never had any problem in co-opting progressive-sounding adjectives to their conception of development. Endogenous, sustainable, integrated, human-centred and, now, popular development are still all forms of development. The new 'Holy Trinity' of engendered, sustainable and bottom-up development may be a laudable political goal, but we must not confuse rhetoric and reality. Another rather major omission in the concept of popular development is that it is basically describing something called socialism, the development record of which is far from unambiguous. There really is no magic fix that would make development both viable and politically liberating at the same time.

At this stage, it might be useful to return to the question of modernism and counter-modernism which permeates many of the accounts outlined above. Kate Manzo has taken Jacques Derrida's concept of 'logocentrism' and applied it usefully to development theory (Manzo 1991). She argues that logocentrism 'demonstrates how even the most radically critical discourse easily slips into the form, the logic, and the implicit postulations of precisely what it seeks to contest' (Manzo 1991: 8). The language of development is all-pervasive, as we have seen; consequently it is most difficult for alternative conceptions to break out of the prison of that language. If that was not bad enough, Manzo adds a corollary, namely that 'the pervasiveness of logocentric thinking in the field of development studies explains why subversive counter-discourses are not taken more seriously' (Manzo 1991: 8). Who, indeed, would reject the seemingly impeccable logic of economic growth and global interdependence to articulate stagnation and autarchy? Countermodernism is the mirror image of modernism and can never break its grip.

A good example of how logocentrism works in development theory relates to the dependency approach. Much as it wished to present itself as a radical alternative to the modernization paradigm it tended, in fact, to share the same discursive space. It operated on the national terrain and prioritized state intervention. When it did break totally with the diffusion model of progress it advocated instead a polar opposite – disengagement from the world economy – which was simply not viable. Modernization and dependency theorists operated very much as binary opposites, inextricably intertwined in one another's assumptions. To say 'black' when someone else says 'white' does not, necessarily, constitute a viable radical alternative. After all, the two theories shared the same aspiration towards development as a rational Western model of progress and they differed only on the means to achieve it. The 'impasse' in development theory that this represents is, ultimately, about the limitations of the Enlightenment model and the modernist project.

To sum up this section, I would argue that the whole alternative–development or antidevelopment cluster of theories has both negative points and positive potential. The publishers of Serge Latouche's *The Westernization of the World* argue in relation to the Western concept of development that 'oppressed people ... want nothing to do with this kind of development; they aspire simply to survive' (Latouche 1996: back cover). This may, indeed, be true but it is also symptomatic of the Eurocentrist paternalism that even the critics of Eurocentrism seem to share. Knippenberg and Schuurman go further, and argue that 'Models of alternative or "another" development which do not include solving the problem of material scarcity are theoretical exercises with no practical value' (Knippenberg and Schuurman 1994: 105). Indeed the critique of 'materialism' from the comfort of the West looks somewhat less than ethical from this point of view. The self-righteous tone of much of this literature says more about the authors than about the problems of underdevelopment (however defined) which cannot be simply wished away.

The main reason we may wish to inscribe some positive potential in the anti-development discourse is because it gives a voice to the excluded. It links up with the postcolonialism perspective in literature (Williams and Chrisman 1993; Ashcroft *et al.* 1995) in seeking to break with the cloying, all-embracing dominance of Western rationality. It operates a radical disjuncture with the essentialism of the mainstream development discourse. That the break may be incomplete, and that by setting up a binary opposition it still operates within the old framework, can only qualify these gains. Furthermore, as Ankie Hoogvelt points out: 'Postdevelopment theory and practice is different from antidevelopment sentiments in so far as it does not deny globalization or modernity but wants to find some ways of living with it and imaginatively transcend it' (Hoogvelt 1996: 16). It is along these lines that my inquiry in the next section will proceed in the spirit of critical realism and an engagement that does not presume to speak for others authoritatively.

Bringing politics back in?

From modernism to countermodernism, a somewhat too neat move takes us to postmodernism. Various views of postmodernism, on the whole critical, have begun to surface in recent development debates (for example, Marglin 1991; Crush 1995). My own view, not necessarily widely shared, is that postmodernism (or at least some of its themes) will allow us to bring politics back into the debate on development discourses.

Undermining the universalist pretensions of the Enlightenment is basic to the postmodern critique of modernist social theory. The notion that the whole world could be analysed according to objective universal criteria of truth, justice and reason looks particularly shallow from a Third World perspective. It is quite symptomatic, I believe, that when Habermas was asked whether his 'universal' model of discursive rationality could be of use in the Third World and whether Third World struggles could be of use in the West, he replied: 'I am tempted to say "no" in both cases. I am aware of the fact that this is a Eurocentric limited view. I would rather pass on the question' (Habermas 1985: 104).

The postmodern social theorists also tended to 'pass' on the question but they have since been taken up vigorously by Third World theorists themselves. A key postmodernist theme is Lyotard's proclamation that this movement/theory means essentially 'an incredulity towards meta-narratives' (Lyotard 1984: xxiv). And there is no clearer meta-narrative than the theory/discourse/ideology of development. It also follows that the Enlightenment notions of truth and objectivity mask underlying power relations. A claim to truth is also a claim to power. Nor does anyone have a legitimate right to speak for others. Methodo-logically, the main implication is that 'there is no single, privileged or single, unique paradigmatic way to think the unthought' (Hoy 1996: 13). So, the master key to the secrets of development and the 'expertise' of the development expert must be viewed with some scepticism.

The impact of Jaques Derrida in development studies can best be seen in the work of Kate Manzo (1991; 1995). Deploying Derrida's concept of 'logocentrism' (imposing a hierarchy on familiar dichot-omies), Manzo shows how 'even the most radically anti-ethnocentric discourse may evidence logocentric reason' (Manzo 1991: 8). The so-called impasse in development theory can thus be blamed not on the fragmentation of the field but on its very unity on essentials. For example, according to Manzo, 'the dependency school was unable to detach itself fully from the assumptions of the mainstream paradigm it sought to undermine because it was equally rooted in nineteenth-century social theory' (Manzo 1991: 30). Manzo pins her hopes on countermodernist or indigenous movements such as the Black Con-sciousness Movement in South Africa (Manzo 1995). What Derrida helps us understand is how the white European male has written the history of development, has sought to establish a foundation or source of truth and meaning valid for all, and has set up a standard ostensibly above politics.

Michel Foucault has had quite an influence on the development of Third World studies, to some extent compensating for his own lack of attention to the subject. Arturo Escobar, for example, has written an imaginative Foucaultian deconstruction of the development discourse (Escobar 1995). A fundamental insight pursuing Foucault's analysis of power, knowledge and discourse is around 'the extension to the Third World of Western disciplinary and normalizing mechanisms ... and the production of discourses by Western countries about the Third World as a means of effecting domination over it' (Escobar 1984–5: 377). Development discourse, from this perspective, is about disciplining difference – establishing what the norm is and what deviance is, indeed creating 'underdevelopment' as Other to the West's 'development'. Western forms of rationality and the imbrication of power and know-ledge in the development discourse/industry/practices have sought to normalize the Third World and its peoples.

Perhaps the most exciting, and far-reaching, interaction between theory and practice has been between feminism, postmodernism and development (see Marchand and Parpart 1995). Western feminism had for some time been coming to terms with the vexed question of differ-ence and the Third World 'Other'. Chandra Mohanty, among others, had firmly rejected the image of Third World women as uniformly poor and powerless in contrast to the modern ideal of Western woman (Mohanty 1991). The critique of essentialism in feminist theory represented a genuine methodological breakthrough in relation to both liberal and Marxist feminisms. When postmodern feminism began to engage with the issue of development, as Jane Parpart notes, it recognized 'the connection between knowledge, language and power, and [sought] to understand local knowledge(s) both as sites of resistance and power' (Parpart 1996: 264). We now accept much more readily that there are multiple, unstable and reconstructing identities involved in the development process.

I would argue at this stage that we are now clearly in a time of paradigmatic transition in relation to modernity in general and development in particular. Boaventura de Sousa Santos boldly takes it for granted that 'the paradigm of modernity has exhausted all its possibilities of renovation' (Santos 1995: ix). Thus, radical critique of the dominant paradigm will necessarily be from the stance of the postmodern although, it is to be hoped, without taking on all the excesses committed in the name of postmodernism. As Santos says: 'The goal of postmodern critical theory is, therefore, to turn into a new common sense, an emancipatory common sense' (Santos 1995: x). As with modernism and its stifling conservatism, some forms of postmodernism, in a pseudo-radical gesture, proclaim the 'end of politics'. On the contrary, following Santos, I would argue that 'postmodern emancipatory knowledge aims at the global repoliticization of collective life' (Santos 1995: 51). A radical reclaiming of the political is as necessary in the field of development as in the broader arena of societal transformation.

The new social movements are in many ways symptomatic of, and feed, the above moves towards a new societal and development paradigm. As Alberto Melucci has shown, social change is now widely perceived to have changed or evolved 'out of a linear, cumulative, global (if it ever was such in the first place) process into a discontinuous, fragmented, and differentiated one' (Melucci 1996: 112). The social movements are a sign of the fragmented postmodern society in which we now live. They are the visible signs of deep transformations and, arguably, portents of the future. The growing stress on identity politics and the increased recognition of the cultural domain are both symptoms of what amounts to a paradigmatic shift. Social movements have helped lay to rest the myth of totality and reinforced the notion that society has no centre, and that revolutions need not be the cataclysmic events so dear to traditional conservative and radical political theory.

In Latin America, since the mid-1980s there have been signs of a new postdevelopment glimmer, inspired in part by the new social movements. The very ideas of democracy, community and development are being reinvented before our eyes in a remarkable flourishing of grassroots activity. It is clear that the social movements across the continent, old and 'new', are a response to the failure of development to address the needs of the poor. These social movements seem to express a 'political' struggle for power or resources but also a 'cultural' struggle for identity. They also play a not inconsiderable role in de-mystifying development, a process that in recent decades in Latin America has spelt exclusion for most. The region's social movements, as Sonia Alvarez and Arturo Escobar argue, 'represent a tangible hope for imagining and bringing about different means of organizing societies in ways more conducive to genuine improvements in living conditions – both cultural and material' (Alvarez and Escobar 1992: 329). It is from such movements that a genuine alternative development strategy based on empowerment might materialize (Friedmann 1994: Chapter 3).

The specific Latin American postcolonial situation has thrown up particularly vibrant and novel challenges to development orthodoxy. The new 'utopian' postdevelopment scenarios have come out of the social movements and the reinvigorated post-dictatorship civil society more generally. As Fernando Calderón notes – in a broad synthesis of the literature on social movements, democracy and development – there is considerable 'evidence of a profound transformation of the social logic ... a new form of doing politics and a new form of sociality ... a new form of relating the political and the social, the public and the private' (Calderón 1986: 25). The social movements are symptoms of a crisis of development but they have also, at least in part, led to a new 'postdevelopment' mood in a radical postmodern tradition. A new social order and a new model of development will not emerge overnight but their seeds seem present in the complex reality of Latin America today.

In conclusion, if the limitations of modernism cannot be overcome by its binary opposite, countermodernism, perhaps postmodernism will offer a new horizon of possibilities. Of course, we are not talking about a naïve chronological conception of postmodernism which believes that it comes 'after' modernism, or implies that the agenda of modernism has been fulfilled in places such as Latin America. Certainly Latin American societies remained trapped in the failures of modern development and even some 'leftover' problems of pre-modernity. Yet the hybrid cultures of Latin America are also postmodern *avant la lettre*. In Latin America there has always been a creative rendering of theories and concepts developed in the West/North. This syncretism, as Fernando Calderón and co-authors explain, points to a process involving 'the creative metamorphosis of old forms into new ones, the transposition of universal theories and concepts into locally relevant forms of understanding and the rendering of ahistorical frameworks into concrete forms of explanation' (Calderón *et al.* 1992: 35). This is the type of task we need now to embark upon to imagine a postdevelopment era that avoids likewise the restrictions of modernism and the excesses of anti-modernism.

References

Alvarez, S. and A. Escobar (1992) 'Conclusion: theoretical and political horizons of change in contemporary Latin American social movement', in A. Escobar and S. Alvarez (eds), *The Making of Social Movements in Latin America: Identity, Strategy and Democracy*. Boulder: Westview Press.

Ashcroft, B., G. Griffiths and H. Tiffin (eds) (1995) *The Post-colonial Studies Reader*. London: Routledge.

Beck, U. (1997) *The Reinvention of Politics: Rethinking Modernity in the Global Social Order*. Cambridge: Polity Press.

Booth, D. (1985) 'Marxism and development sociology: interpreting the impasse', *World Development*, No. 13.

— (1994) 'How far beyond the impasse? A provisional summing up', in D. Booth (ed.), *Rethinking Social Development Theory, Research and Practice*, Harlow: Longman.

Brohman, J. (1996) *Popular Development: Rethinking the Theory and Practice of Development*. Oxford: Blackwell.

Calderón, F. (1986) *Los Movimientos Sociales ante la Crisis*. Buenos Aires: CLACSO.

Calderón, F., A. Piscitelli and J.L. Reyna (1992) 'Social movements: actors, theories, expectations', in A. Escobar and S. Alvarez (eds), *The Making of Social Movements in Latin America: Identity, Strategy and Democracy*. Boulder: Westview Press.

Cowen, M. and R. Shenton (1995) 'The invention of development', in J. Crush (ed.), *Power of Development*. London: Routledge.

Crush, J. (ed.) (1995) *Power of Development*. London: Routledge.

Escobar, A. (1984–5) 'Discourse and power in development: Michel Foucault and the relevance of his work for the Third World', *Alternatives* (Winter).

— (1995) *Encountering Development: The Making and Unmaking of the Third World*. Princeton: Princeton University Press.

Esteva, G. (1992) 'Development', in W. Sachs (ed.), *The Development Dictionary: A Guide to Knowledge and Power*. London: Zed Books.

— (1987) 'Regenerating people's space', *Alternatives*, Vol. 10, No. 3.

Friedmann, J. (1994) *Empowerment: The Politics of Alternative Development*. Oxford: Blackwell.

Habermas, J. (1985) 'Jurgen Habermas: a philosophical–political profiile', *New Left Review*, No. 151.

Hettne, B. (1995) *Development Theory and the Three Worlds: Towards an International Political Economy of Development*. Harlow: Longman.

Hoogvelt, A. (1996) *Globalisation and the Postcolonial World: The New Political Economy of Development*. London: Macmillan.

Hoy, D.C. (1996) 'Splitting the difference: Habermas's critique of Derrida', in M. Passerin d'Entreves and S. Benhabib (eds), *Habermas and the Unfinished Project of Modernity*. Cambridge: Polity Press.

Kay, C. (1989) *Latin American Theories of Development and Underdevelopment*. London: Routledge.

Knippenberg, L. and F. Schuurman (1994) 'Blinded by rainbows: anti-modernist and modernist deconstructions of development', in F. Schuurman (ed.), *Current Issues in Development Studies: Global Aspects of Agency and Structure*. Saarbrucken: Verlag für Entwicklungspolitik Breitenbach.

Latouche, S. (1996) *The Westernization of the World*. Oxford: Polity Press.

Lyotard, J.F. (1984) *The Post-modern Condition*. Manchester: Manchester University Press.

McMichael, P. (1996) *Development and Change: A Global Perspective*. California: Pine Forge Press.

Manzo, K. (1991) 'Modernist discourse and the crisis of development theory', *Studies of Comparative International Development*, Vol. 26, No. 2.

— (1995) 'Black consciousness and the quest for a counter-modernist development', in J. Crush (ed.), *Power of Development*. London: Routledge.

Marchant, M. and J. Parpart (eds) (1995) *Feminism, Postmodernism, Development*. London: Routledge.

Marglin, S. (ed.) (1991) *Dominating Knowledge: Development, Culture and Resistance*. Oxford: Clarendon.

Mehmet, O. (1995) *Westernizing the Third World: The Eurocentricity of Economic Development Theories*. London: Routledge.

Melucci, A. (1996) *Challenging Codes: Collective Action on the Information Age*. Cambridge: Cambridge University Press.

Mohanty, C. (1991) 'Under Western eyes', in C. Mohanty, A. Russo and L. Torres (eds), *Third World Women and the Politics of Feminism*. Bloomington: Indiana University Press.

Nederveen Pieterse, J. (1991) 'Dilemmas of development discourse: the crisis of developmentalism and the comparative method', *Development and Change*, Vol. 22, pp. 5–29.

Parpart, J. (1996) 'Post-modernism, gender and development', in J. Crush (ed.), *Power of Development*. London: Routledge.

Passerin d'Entreves, M. and S. Benhabib (eds) (1996) *Habermas and the Unfinished Project of Modernity*. Cambridge: Polity Press.

Rahnema, M. and V. Bawtree (eds) (1997) *The Post-development Reader*. London: Zed Books.

Sachs, W. (ed.) (1992) *The Development Dictionary: A Guide to Knowledge and Power*. London: Zed Books.

Santos, B. de Sousa (1995) *Toward a New Common Sense: Law, Science and Politics in the Paradigmatic Transition*. New York: Routledge.

Schuurman, F. (ed.) (1993) *Beyond the Impasse: New Directions in Development Theory*. London: Zed Books.

So, Alvin (1990) *Social Change and Development: Modernization, Dependency, and World-System Theories*. Newbury Park, CA: Sage.

Williams, P. and L. Chrisman (eds) (1993) *Colonial Discourse and Post-colonial Theory*. London: Harvester.

Index

Development and Environment Studies Titles from Zed

Zed has been a leading publisher of an exceptionally innovative and wide-ranging variety of books in Development Studies. Our specific lists in this area include:

- Globalization
- New Development Paradigms
- Experiences of Grassroots Development
- Studies in Structural Adjustment
- Sustainable Development in the North
- Environment and Development
- Gender and Development
- Urban Development
- International Health Policy and Practice
- Studies in Conflict and Violence in Society

In addition, Zed has published a number of *key student texts* in Development Studies. Recent titles include:

J. Martinussen, *Society, State and Market: A Guide to Competing Theories of Development*

Majid Rahnema with Victoria Bawtree (compilers), *The Post-Development Reader*

Gilbert Rist, *The History of Development: From Western Origins to Global Faith*

Wolfgang Sachs (ed.), *The Development Dictionary*

Frans Schuurman (ed.), *Beyond the Impasse: New Directions in Development Theory*

N. Visvanathan, L. Duggan, L. Nisonoff and N. Wiegersma (eds), *The Women, Gender and Development Reader*

For full details of these titles, our various Development Studies and Environment lists, as well as Zed's other subject and general catalogues, please write to:

The Marketing Department, Zed Books, 7 Cynthia Street, London N1 9JF, UK or email: sales@zedbooks.demon.co.uk

Visit our website at: http://www.zedbooks.demon.co.uk

Zed Titles on Multinational Corporations and Globalization

Globalization is the current term used to characterize what is happening in the world economy at the turn of the twentieth century. Integral to this process is the ever more dominant position of very large transnational corporations. Zed Books has published a distinguished list of titles examining these phenomena in all their variety and complexity.

Samir Amin, *Capitalism in the Age of Globalization: The management of con-temporary society*

Ricardo Carrere and Larry Lohmann, *Pulping the South: Industrial tree plantations and the world paper economy*

Michel Chossudovsky, *The Globalisation of Poverty: Impacts of IMF and World Bank reforms*

Jacques B. Gelinas, *Freedom from Debt: The reappropriation of development through financial self-reliance*

Terence Hopkins, Immanuel Wallerstein et al., *The Age of Transition: Trajectory of the world-system, 1945–2025*

Serge Latouche, *In the Wake of the Affluent Society: An exploration of post-development*

Hans-Peter Martin and Harald Schumann, *The Global Trap: Globalization and the assault on democracy and prosperity*

Stephen Riley, *Stealing from Capitalism: Corruption, development and poverty in the South*

Harry Shutt, *The Trouble with Capitalism: An enquiry into the causes of global economic failure*

Kavaljit Singh, *The Globalisation of Finance: A citizen's guide*

Henk Thomas (ed.), *Globalization and Third World Trade Unions*

For full details of this list and Zed's other subject and general catalogues, please write to:

The Marketing Department, Zed Books, 7 Cynthia Street, London N1 9JF, UK or email: sales@zedbooks.demon.co.uk

Visit our website at: http://www.zedbooks.demon.co.uk